JO MAY

A Barge at Large

Copyright © 2021 by Jo May

All rights reserved. No part of this publication may be reproduced, stored or transmitted in any form or by any means, electronic, mechanical, photocopying, recording, scanning, or otherwise without written permission from the publisher. It is illegal to copy this book, post it to a website, or distribute it by any other means without permission.

Jo May has no responsibility for the persistence or accuracy of URLs for external or third-party Internet Websites referred to in this publication and does not guarantee that any content on such Websites is, or will remain, accurate or appropriate.

First edition

This book was professionally typeset on Reedsy.
Find out more at reedsy.com

To Jan for her love and support

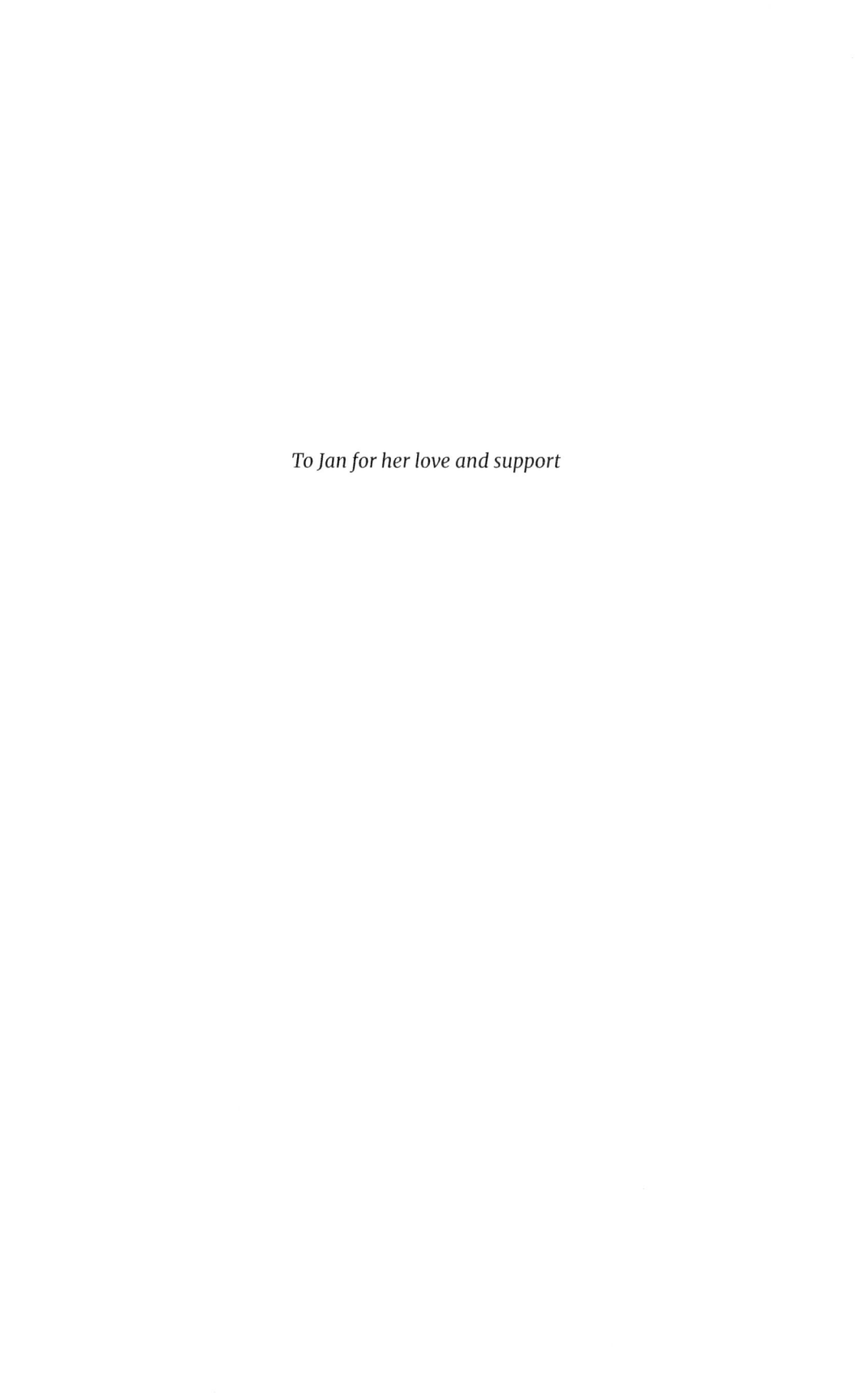

Contents

Vrouwe Johanna	1
James van Bond	11
Niggles and Dribbles	20
Learning Curve	25
Water, water everywhere	39
A Visit to Friends (!)	45
Blacking the Bottom	51
Snert	56
Trial Trip	62
Friesland	67
Lakes and Isles	73
Cease Fire	78
Payback Time	84
Lunch in the Engine Room	90
Northerly Limit	96
Bye bye Zwartsluis	103
BIG Rivers	115
La Belle France	125
The Magic of Nancy	136
New Friends	146
A snapshot of winter in Burgundy	157
The Grand Fete	164
Old Pals, New Pals	175
Fire in Bill's Hole	186
Winter in St. Jean de Losne. (Part 2)	200
Beaten by The Weather	210

Wonderful Canal du Nivernais	221
Stuck in The Loo	233
Canal du Bourgogne	245
About the Author	254
Also by Jo May	256

Vrouwe Johanna

Part One

Holland

'START WRECK,' yelled my mate, Dave, from across the boatyard – rather unkindly.

He was encouraging me to fire up our old Ford engine. It was also a warning to both fellow boaters and natives. Our dear old motor smokes a bit you see and if anyone was either cooking outdoors or had clothes on the line, now was a good time to take evasive measures – to prevent things getting covered in a shower of soot. It was time to set off for on our first proper trip. Time to treat our trusty, rusty barge to an adventure.

But, hang on, we're getting ahead of ourselves. We've had a few trial runs. Little trips and learning experiences that I really need to tell you about. Some of them were a moderate success, one was a total shambles. Plus, there had been lots of hacking about with the boat's insides to transform a smelly, badly constructed living space into something vaguely habitable, at least for a couple with low expectations.

Yes, I must share our growing pains with you.

What follows is a gentle, occasionally coherent, account of what happens when you make the life-changing decision to live part-time in a country whose language you don't speak and on whose waterways you are afforded the opportunity to cause bedlam. Our vague plan is to stay in Holland a while before setting off south for Belgium then France. It begins a decade into the latest millennium and sort of dribbles on from there. Hopefully there is something for boaters and non-boaters alike - also for those who like to travel and for anyone considering trying something different. We have no idea how long it will last but I can say that there have been times when we wish we'd never started. There are however more encouraging moments. I will recount both just in case you are wondering as to whether to have a go yourself.

So, going back a few months..........

My first question to Klaas (the boatyard owner) is whether I can trim his bush. He greeted my request with arched eyebrows. I hurriedly explained that I was the owner of the scabby hunk of old iron across the waterway and that we couldn't get on our boat because of the rampant foliage. I borrowed a saw and left before he got cheesed off.

The boat was delivered to the boatyard last week by the vendor and it appears he'd just abandoned it. There's no way I can expect my wife or elderly dog to scrabble through the undergrowth, you never know what you might come across in there, so I really need to hack one or two limbs off.

Our barge is called Vrouwe Johanna. She was built in Groningen, Holland in 1905. The hull is iron, the top-sides, added later, are steel and the interior is a right old mish-mash of wood, plastic and fag ash. She's come to us via a succession of owners, the latest of whom obviously didn't know a great deal about joinery or plumbing – which is probably why he's a prison officer.

Jan and I have just arrived from the Motherland and we're gazing (with some trepidation) at what will be our new home. Not immediately, because there are minor renovations to carry out, like creating new bedroom, kitchen and lounge, but eventually. Our barge in all fairness is a bit moth-eaten and will need a bit of fettling, but we'll get there. In the meantime we've booked into a nearby B & B for a month. Hopefully that should be enough time to turn the boat around. Mmmm.

So, where are we?

Holland. A town called Zwartsluis in the province of Overijssel. It is located in the municipality of Zwartewaterland, at the mouth of the Zwartewater River. No, we're not much wiser either. What I can tell you is that it's about an hour and a half (in the car) north of Europort (Rotterdam). What is clear immediately is that, with all randomly placed consonants, we may encounter some difficulty with the language. The boatyard we are in is called De Watergeus, run by a Dutch couple called Klaas and Metsje. They will become allies and friends, in addition to supplying knowledge, equipment, raw materials and counselling.

So, with their help and plenty of Dutch courage, we begin our new adventure.

We settle in the B & B with a clunky fold-down bed. Had I been born in 1905 like our barge, I may have had to endure this level of discomfort had I been unfortunate enough to have a spell in hospital. It creaks like mad and has a corrugated iron mattress. Conditions are a bit cramped. Before long we have clothes on the floor, dog on the clothes, even clothes on the dog. The latter because I can't figure out the ancient heating 'implement'. Believe it or not it's a step up from our previous three months in our flat in Shropshire.

Getting here has been a test.

We'd been nervous and slightly daunted as we'd cast off in Shrewsbury - but excited and keen. For the big move we'd made two trips to Holland, both Hull to Rotterdam. The first with the skipper, dog and as many necessities that we could cram in, the second just me with the car packed to the gunwales. Chasing a dream, nothing comes easy but our immediate concern boarding the ferry was our fifteen-year-old dog. They'd forecast force eight winds in German Bight and when we'd seen the dog's quarters we doubted she would see the night out. She was billeted off the car deck, through a thick steel door, down a short steel corridor in a room the size of a downstairs loo in a steel cage as big as a double kitchen unit with steel bars to the front. No blanket, no water, no exit.

We had boarded at six in the evening and would disembark at eight the following morning. We could visit the dog before departure at 9.00 pm but after that only when accompanied by a security guard, and then the only place to go is the car deck. I went down at about 11 and gave her a look around but she was distressed and not impressed by a green-painted steel floor. After that I left her alone till morning with the ship creaking and rolling and seriously feared that she would expire during the night. Luckily she's made of stern stuff. She was obviously upset but hadn't even mucked up her cell and waited till we got through customs to have a pee on a patch of grass. Then she'd jumped back in the car and slept.

The dog's passage had cost £15, so on an hourly rate that's not bad, but if there's a next time she'll be pumped up with tranquilizers.

Cruising into Europort is an experience in itself. It is a huge complex of wharfs, freight and passenger terminals with boats of every shape and size lumbering about. Watching a tug gently nudging a big freighter into its berth is fascinating. The whole is watched over by numerous wind turbines spotted randomly like the survivors of a forest fire.

'Only about an hour to run,' announced the skipper on the drive north, 'we're making great progress.' Then my windscreen wiper fell off. We were on a busy motorway near Amersfoort and it was lashing down. We crept to the next service station and I bought a €6 tool thing from the café and managed to improvise a repair. I respectfully requested that she keep her progress reports to herself for the remainder of the trip.

The only 'testing' situation of note on the 2nd journey occurs on the ferry when a 20-stone lass from Germany queue-barged and nicked the last treacle sponge from the running buffet. With a clatter of hooves she rushed back to her friends with a grin on her face. This is the nearest you'll get to a one-woman stampede. We were crossing the German Bight which is rather appropriate.

My wife, the dog and I are staying at a B & B, run by Richard and Jenny who are delightful people. We share one small room but it is only a 60-yard walk to our barge. (Metres actually, and probably nearer 55 - a yard on the continent is where you put knackered agricultural machinery). The location is ideal because our first project is to re-hash the bedroom before we move on to the boat.

In the B & B, in the room above us is a German man, a man who should never be out of work. He sings constantly in a muffled and totally tuneless manner and could make a living with a travelling 'troupe' imitating a vacuum cleaner. It's a bit unsettling really because he appeared for breakfast the following morning wearing a wig that, on anything but the closest inspection, looked exactly like a bobble hat. He is a businessman, a cheerful man and, thankfully, soon to be a travelling man once again.

I'd had to leave the skipper and the dog alone for five days while I went back to England to pick up the rest of our stuff. She was very uncertain about being on her own in a new country, not speaking a word of the language. The only real problem came from the two occupants who followed bobble-hat man in the room above who conducted a burping competition till the early hours - until receiving a red card from Jenny, the owner.

Water-borne access to our mooring bush is via a narrow entrance off a large commercial canal called the Meppelerdiep (after the town of Meppel to where it runs). The port area is about 600 metres long and opens up to a width of about eighty metres before narrowing again. – the approximate shape of a lemon. Where the port narrows it splits into two fingers separated by a peninsula. We are at the bottom of the left hand one, the right being the main town moorings. Altogether there is mooring for perhaps one hundred boats and the whole area is surrounded by houses and water-related businesses.

Jan had been cleaning the boat while I was away but now I go and have a look at our new home. It's not huge but it's certainly chunkier than our narrowboat and the prospect of cruising it gives us the collywobbles. To get out of the mooring we'd have to move sideways and perform a reverse. No matter which analysis of the Netherlands pleasure boat market you look at there are a great many boats about, hundreds of thousands, and it appeared that a fair proportion were between us and open water. So, we forget about that for now.

Moored immediately behind us is an 'imitation' policeman called Rob. He is a Dutchman who owns a decommissioned police launch and who claims he is single-handedly controls crime in the boatyard. He even has what looks like a police uniform hanging in full view when his door is open - although he tells me it is his Dutch Navy uniform. He says rather wistfully that he used to be in Naval Intelligence and even more wistfully that he hasn't got many friends (which I find hard to believe as he's a decent guy).

Rob's boat has a big engine and he measures his trips carefully. (His boat used 60 litres per hour at full whack). After all the water police, like their land-based colleagues, need to charge around making lots of noise to feel important – or rather, to be a visual deterrent. Most importantly though he speaks to us, and in good English. The fact that he's immediately prepared to open lines of communication with a couple of foreigners who've bought an old tin can is a relief. We have someone with whom we can share our angst and we chuckle at the thought of sharing a mooring with an ersatz policeman called 'Rob'.

Zwartsluis (zwart - black, sluis - lock) is a fairly quiet place and skipper said as much in the post-cards she wrote to the mother land. Two hours after posting them the town was shaken to its foundations. Three stages were erected and the mother of all one-night pop festivals boomed out till four am. People obviously came from miles around as the place was packed. They dashed around buying tokens from a shed before going to the beer stall to swap them for a glass of ale. Quite why they couldn't dash straight to the ale stall and pay cash remains a mystery - keeping the person in the token shed in full employ perhaps. Makeshift stalls sell food in a variety of mysterious shapes with unfamiliar odours. We decide to research the origin of these delicacies before actually eating anything. Besides we'd just had corned-beef hash.

I'm not sure whether we are shrinking but the Dutch do seem a tall race because we spend the time peering through people's armpits. One thing that is noticeable is that, although we are outsiders and shorter in stature than 99% of the throng (over four years old), we don't feel threatened. The atmosphere is one of celebration not intoxication (how's that for a political sound bite?). This festival was rock / pop orientated but as we would discover, many different forms of music thrive here and music festivals seem to be just one of the traditions that the Dutch preserve so well.

The wind is a factor; when blowing from the north / north-west over the

Ijsselmeer (which used to be called the Zuider Zee when attached to the North Sea before the construction of a huge dyke), a surge of water is forced, from this now freshwater inland 'sea', into the canal and river system, raising the level anything up to two feet above normal. When blowing from the east the water level is not affected but there's a nagging pong from the nearby biscuit factory.

We begin poking around our boat with little understanding about what we are poking so call the vendor and ask him to come and explain what everything does - or as we would discover, doesn't do. In the meantime, I make a start on the bedroom.

The hull is over 100-years-old but to reach it I have to strip away about forty years-worth of other peoples 'improvements'. Layer-upon-layer of wood, plastic and insulation are removed and by the time we've taken 3 car loads to the nearby tip, the front of the boat has come up 2 inches. Getting rid of the rubbish is an eye-opener. You drive to the tip where they weigh your car on arrival and departure and investigate what type of waste you are getting rid of. You are charged therefore not only by weight but also recyclability. Wood, cardboard, glass etc. is cheap but old insulation or plastic is costly.

There is dry rust on the bottom plates so I have to scrape all this out then oil the exposed hull. I'm told that a centimetre of rust is equal to a millimetre of steel so according to the survey, we should be OK. While under here I discover the depth-measuring bit of the depth-finder with a wire coiled up next to it that isn't attached to anything - which is one reason why that particular piece if equipment doesn't work. At least now I've reached a stage where I can be constructive and begin to build our bedroom.

The town normally appears short of people, the exception being Sunday when there is a service on in every one of the numerous churches. The skipper was invited by Jenny (B & B) to a service and she reckoned there were between five and six hundred people crammed in. It's not a big town so a high percentage must be God-fearing folk. About half-way through the hour and a half service, just as the vicar was psyching himself up, people started delving into pockets and handbags for what the skipper presumed was money for a collection. It was however for a custom that she had a job getting her head around, namely the 'passing round of the mints'. She surmised it was either to help the worshippers through the sermon without coughing or the precursor to a bout of communal snogging. Well, snogging is frowned upon in this God-fearing town and the sermon was in Dutch so she put her money away and sucked on her mint. Church bells ring throughout the week telling us the time every half hour but on Sunday its bedlam, it sounds like a campanologist's convention where ever more complicated rhythms are clattered out by fiercely competitive purveyors of the bell-ringers art.

The boat vendor, Mr van Woerden, arrives and assumes we know plenty about barges because he rattled through the systems with some fervour, luckily in passable English. I understood some of what he said and took notes. After he left we began to learn about our boat. Knobs were pushed and switches flicked with a mixture of expectation and trepidation as a series of strange noises echoed throughout the vessel. Many were labelled, but in Dutch, some obviously incorrect and some gave no indication as to their purpose whatsoever. Sometimes when a knob was pushed or turned sometimes nothing happened at all which was alarming because it was possible that in some dark corner, unheard, some piece of equipment had lumbered into life. We've tried most things but not the hot water / central heating boiler yet. This is partly because I've removed and replaced a radiator and am unsure of my plumbing skills. We really don't need a flood in our new part-finished bedroom - after all the basic principle of a boat is to keep the water on the outside – the longer I delay re-filling the heating system, the longer this principle will hold true.

The original idea was to live in the B & B for a month in order to complete the bedroom thus ensuring a trouble-free transition from land to water. Due to the problem deregistering our boat prior to purchase that plan has gone belly up and we have had to move on to the boat two weeks early as the B & B is booked up. Hence we have a decent size lounge with a blow-up bed, dining table with benches and our two big armchairs which we'd lugged over from England, sharing space with assorted building materials - but we're doing OK. There is a small and basic kitchen, a shower and loo room and the wheelhouse. It's big enough but the more space you have the more you fill.

Narrowboat living has been good training.

Some things are unfamiliar like the 'sea-loo' - it looks rather basic but you tread on a pedal which initiates a pump (which makes a filthy racket) and poof, as if by magic, everything disappears – hopefully outside. There's even a washing machine in the wheelhouse which looks like it was first used by Neolithic man but it works. We are hooked up to the mains at present but when (and if) we're on the move it will run via the generator. Now this generator is a beast, in stature it is bigger than the engine (Beta 38) we had on the narrowboat and of similar horsepower. It squirts water out of the back in a raging torrent but it does need to be substantial because it powers the 15Hp bow-thruster which runs off 380-volt electricity through a complicated series of boxes, fuses and about 300 miles of wiring. Understand all that? No, me neither.

One thing that we love is the way that the waterway community is thriving – real part of life here. Zwartsluis is built around the water and although only we English people seem to live aboard, there are boats galore. Pleasure boats cruise and moor among huge working barges. We are pretty in awe of it all, especially the big ships, but the Dutch seem just to accept it for what it is. Perhaps their excitement is bubbling away below the surface. We're having to learn a new culture and it's a good job the majority of the locals speak English. I have to say that most are really helpful in a no-nonsense way that seems to be the Dutch manner.

We have become friendly with our B & B hosts. I recall an evening sharing coffees and according to our host, 'a liquor that boat people drink', called Beerenburg. Now Richard is a bit of a joker so whether this truly is the preferred tipple of the boat people or whether he was trying to foist off something he'd had on his shelf for fifteen years, I couldn't say. Whichever, he tucked into it with gusto, as did I. It's a kind of medicinal compound that is not only 30% proof but doesn't leave you with a hangover the following morning – because you invariably don't wake up till the following afternoon.

Our Landlord, proprietor of De Watergeus boatyard, is called Klass. He is fluent in English and German (where many of his customers come from - the German border is less than 2 hours away) in addition to his native Dutch.

He is an electrical genius, able to fathom out and fix the most complicated system – a skill I hope he will put to good use with us. Not that there is too much that doesn't work, I just need to know a little about how it works. His wife, Metsje, is a lovely lady who seems to look after much of the office work. She also appears to be a trained counsellor. This is useful when their clients are presented with invoices. They rent out boats, a couple of which are in the €250,000 – €300,000 price bracket, but on his moorings are boats of all shape and size. Mostly Dutch, a few German and two English couples in addition to us. We English are temporary, waiting to move on when various parts get fixed or when enough courage is summoned.

Compared to our narrowboats we have reasonably large tanks, 1600 litres red diesel in two tanks, 250L white diesel and 2000L water. Red diesel is no longer allowed here for propulsion although it is for heating and running the generator so I may have to convert one of the red tanks to white. We need some red diesel and the cheapest place to get it from is from a bunker barge moored on the outskirts of the neighbouring town of Meppel. Filling these tanks will be no laughing matter either with red diesel at 76 cents (55p ish) per litre and white at about €1.20. This will be our first cruise and to say we are nervous is an understatement of the first order. But if we knew how the trip would turn out, we would never have set off at all.

James van Bond

As we prepare for our first solo voyage; we are anxious. Our uncertainty may strike a chord with anyone who has agonised over severing the umbilical to terra firma for the first time, or for non-boaties, doing anything new. All manner of pathetic excuses surface. The material of a nearby flag actually twitches indicative of an imminent cyclone and we certainly don't need an audience. Suddenly there is a busload of gawping Saga-trippers gumming ice-cream waiting for a disaster. We decide to give it a go, just quietly slip out, confidently with graceful nonchalance. Unfortunately, our dear old boat has other ideas.

Any hope of anonymity is blown out of the water due to the fact that the engine is a bit smoky – in fact it's a lot smoky. Despite our main audience being forty metres away across the harbour, their cornets get a coating of black dust when we fire up the main engine. Fortunately, oxygen masks 'appear from overhead panels' and there are no fatalities. The applause at this point is muted. Someone later gave us a photograph of the moment of our first departure - but we couldn't see anything. It looked like he had just pointed his camera at a cloudy sky. The smoky engine is booked in for a fettling in a couple of days but we want to have a cruise, besides we need diesel.

So, we set off under our own smoke for the first time. We managed to turn it round, thanks largely to the bow-thruster, and when we got going forward the boat handles OK, particularly when we didn't have to turn a corner. It's flat bottomed and someone with a similar boat describes the handling of such craft as like pushing a supermarket trolley with one finger. Slowly we get the hang of it. Actually, as the engine warms up the smoke lessens considerably – so no wildlife suffocated on our outbound trip. We head for the town of Meppel, 11 kilometres distant, and moor up alongside the diesel barge - rather heavily, with a bit of a thump. It was when we set off again that things went awry. Almost immediately I noticed a juddering, so in a state of some panic we moored up not 200 metres from the fuel barge. Looking at the engine it was obvious there was something wrong with the main coupling (which basically connects the engine to the propeller shaft) so all we could do was stay put and call Klass (our boatyard owner) who promised to come out and have a look - but not until Monday morning. It is now Friday, late afternoon.

As you can imagine, it was all rather disappointing. But if we had to be marooned we couldn't have chosen a better spot. The problem was that there was a sign (in Dutch naturally) that we were pretty sure said, 'absolutely no stopping or mooring under any circumstances whatsoever'. We were outside a very exclusive-looking boatyard called Holtermann Yachting, home to about twenty exclusive-looking cruisers, all immaculately clean, dark blue below, white uppers, with gleaming stainless steel accessories – including anchors. The grass was neatly trimmed, the wooden pontoons were pristine and the stainless steel bollards gleamed. I thought it prudent therefore to go and explain the owner of said boatyard why a knackered old barge was lashed to his finery.

It turns out that it is Meppel's busiest weekend of the year. It's their classic boat festival, and being about 4.30 on a Friday afternoon, activity was frenzied as people prepared to pop into town on their boats for a weekend of frivolity. Among this frenzy was Mr Holtermann himself. He was a little nonplussed when a short, ill-dressed Englishman tried to explain that he'd 'granny-knotted' himself to his posh piling for the weekend. He was mid-thirties, tanned, bare-chested and had sunglasses perched on his full head of black hair - in short he looked rather like James van Bond. With furrowed brow he accepted my mumblings and with a look that said, 'if you give your boat a bit of a wash and put some decent clothes on I suppose I'll have to put up with you', he swanned off to tend his fleet.

Anyone seeing us from the canal would have envied our position. It was thirty degrees so we'd got the picnic table on the freshly cut grass and made the most of it. We were opposite a container terminal where 100m barges were being loaded but it was all part of the adventure and a fascinating insight into the real workings of the waterway. Despite their size, they do not cause us much trouble, there is negligible wash and they are only creeping along at this point. There is a bit of 'suck' and we strain to and fro on our lines but all in all no problem. Much worse was the little blighters in speedboats who chuck us about no end.

We decided to scout the area and found that the single restaurant within walking distance, a steakhouse, didn't accept credit cards. We'd spent virtually all our Euros on diesel so only had 18 left. The staff, realising our boating and fiscal predicament were fabulous, and worked out that we could have two beers, two diet cokes, one 'starter-size' rack of ribs and a strawberry ice-cream!

Two days later we are helped back to base lashed alongside another barge. Rob the imitation policeman cruised with us to prevent piracy. A refuelling trip that should have taken three hours actually took three days. Breakdown apart, the only thing that really annoyed us was a parrot in Van Bond's marina. It had been taught to wolf-whistle – and did so constantly. What made it even weirder was the owner of this damn bird was sitting in the stultifying heat, under a tree wearing an anorak, apparently oblivious to his bird's sexist outpourings.

Before we'd left on our ill-fated trip we'd been invited by David and Jane (English / Swedish combo) to come and sample meatballs from her native land – a celebration of our inaugural voyage. As she'd not made them for a while she'd had a trial run on the Wednesday so she and David had a meatball dinner. As we failed to turn up on the Friday, they had a double helping to wade through. We didn't have their phone number so couldn't alert them to our predicament. We finally made it round to their place the following Tuesday, when she again made meatballs for our benefit. David was getting proper fed up with them by now and ploughed through half-a-dozen with a pained expression. We enjoyed 'em though!

Shopping has been another challenge. Some things are obvious by the pictures on the packaging, but other things less so. We enjoy a curry so shopped accordingly, minced beef, a curry mix and a number of random herbs and spices. We were slightly disappointed later that evening to tuck into 'minced beef sweet and sour' – and no, it won't catch on! We drove to Meppel to 'do a shop' and, from a hot-dog type stand, had what the vendor translated as baked fish in spicy batter. We thoroughly enjoyed it and when the skipper returned to ask what type of fish we had eaten she was told, 'nearly one-o-clock'! Not everything is straightforward. On another occasion we went to the B & Q-type suppliers because I had cocked up some woodwork and we needed a second batch. Now, the skipper religiously checks the till receipts to ensure that we are not overcharged. We returned home to discover that we'd left half the stuff on the conveyor belt which rather defeated the object.

Another thing the Dutch don't seem to do is ovens. Whether in house or boat they appear to cook primarily on the cooker top or in multi-purpose microwaves. Whereas in the UK, the supermarket shelves are groaning under the weight of oven-ready chickens, joints of beef, pork, lamb etc. here in provincial Holland the joint (of meat) is a beast of myth. We are missing our roasts but it doesn't seem to hinder the physical development of the locals as the majority turn into substantial, meaty individuals. Perhaps it's just because we are in rural Holland that we English are not catered for. No doubt we'll find out as we travel. Not everything is to our taste however. Now remember I said that wood is cheap to dispose of, being recyclable, as it is either burnt for power or shredded to sawdust. Well, I suspect it was used to pad out the Hungarian Goulash Croquette I bought the other day.

Apart from the mechanical hitch, our boat interior is now nearly habitable. The previous owners were heavy smokers so we've had a good scrub and we've now got hot water. The central heating boiler wouldn't light initially but when I summoned Klass, to his great credit he said that if he was to do it, it would cost us, so suggested I have a go myself. He explained what I had to do and hey presto! I've learned to dismantle, clean and re-assemble our Kabola boiler.

Desperate to show off our renovated bedroom to our Dutch friends, Richard and Jenny, we invite them round for dinner. His enthusiasm was tempered a bit because he couldn't stand upright in our boudoir. Whereas we are both (some way) under six feet, he is about six-six so he crabbed about like a discontented vulture. But he muttered positively and politely. We served them Irish stew at his request, a thank you for their help and friendship. It was actually nothing like an Irish stew but either he didn't know or was too polite to say. Subsequently we find out that his mother is English so I hope she doesn't discuss the matter with her son or we might be rumbled. The evening was rounded off standing in the wheelhouse, drinking Beerenburg and being devoured by mosquitoes. Our first guests had come, survived and gone and for the first time our boat really felt like home.

We are trying to learn a few words of Dutch (which I find very difficult) so out with the phrase book and off to the bakers. I asked for two croissants but walked out with three, unwilling to return one and show my ignorance - but at least I got the right shop and the right product. Two is twee (pronounced tvay) and three is Drie (pronounced dree) so I can only presume that the shopkeeper had a hearing impediment. When you say to a local that you're sorry you don't speak Dutch and ask them if they speak English, they reply, almost without exception, 'a leetal beet' - which denotes virtual fluency on their part and shame on mine.

We go to a classic boat festival in neighbouring Hasselt, a small town about 6 kilometres away and it is a wonderful experience. There are in the region of 200 classic boats, both sail and motor which are privately owned and present strictly by invitation only. Most boats are moored four or five deep on the main waterway, the Zwarte Water (black water), but they also fill the single channel canals that run through the little town. The boats within the town are just for show and the owners have a weekend of being pointed at and the opportunity to discuss their particular craft with anyone who wants to stop and chat – which many do. The canals, just wide enough for two four-metre-beam barges, are set well below narrow cobbled streets that run down each side. Neat trees set every eight or ten yards leave just enough room for car-parking for the small stone terrace of houses that line the canal and have a terrific aspect.

On the main waterway scenes from the turn of the twentieth century onward are re-enacted. Cargoes are off-loaded from 'working' barges via rickety cranes or shovel and wheelbarrow into ancient trucks or tractors with trailers. All the work is done by folk dressed to the period – clogs, flat caps and neckerchiefs. It's a fascinating insight into the history of the waterways. Judging by the throng of people at the event, and despite the fact that these ancient ships are a common sight, it is wonderful to see the continued enthusiasm for their heritage. Many of these old barges have been converted exclusively for live-aboards, their holds covered to create (in some cases) luxurious interiors, but thankfully plenty of originals are cherished. The working folk of yesteryear inhabited a very different world. Families lived in cramped, low accommodation with few facilities, much the same I suppose as the boatman's cabins on early working narrowboats. On the quay we saw the working boats supported by rope and sailmakers, wool spinners and eel smokers, people in simple, traditional dress - and clogs. When the noise died for a moment you could hear the creak of the old wooden ships. The occasional flap of sails sounded like a muted round of applause. All the people working the boats solemnly played their parts and you could almost feel their struggles. The whole combined to create a wonderful atmosphere.

One boat carried shells, tonnes of them, which were taken by wheelbarrow down ramps, tipped into a truck and transported a few hundred metres to kilns where they would have been piled on smouldering peat and left for about five days to create lime from which they would make lime mortar for use as a construction material. The kilns are now just for show. Due to stringent pollution regulations no one is allowed to set fire to anything. There were also old steam and diesel engines clacking and hissing away, also some ancient out-board motors dating back to the early 1900's. All working and very similar in design to the seagull out-board my father used to putt-putt around with in the early seventies. To satisfy the modern-day shopper, there were market stalls lining the main street with a mix of boaty stuff, books and food stands in addition (sadly) to a little tat from the Far East. But overall it was fabulous day out, not without a touch of humour. We decided to take a little boat trip up the waterway to see the spectacle from another perspective. We boarded, but were a little surprised when the little wooden craft shot the 60 yards straight across the river where everyone else got off! The trip took about twenty seconds and the boatman politely tried to ignore us as we sat tight to a rusty pontoon awaiting the return trip. Two Euros each, 120 yards, no sight-seeing and we ended up back where we started. It was also on this day I was to hear a phrase that I have never heard before - nor am I likely to hear again. We were accompanied by Jane, one half of the Anglo / Swede couple, (Dave had been left on the boat to clear up an overflowed toilet). Jane had bought a pair of smoked eels from one of the smokers on the key and when she came to visit our boat (for a glass of wine) later in the day told us that she had eaten one and really enjoyed it. Time was getting on (and we'd run out of wine) and by now Dave should have finished mending their loo so Jane said, 'I really must be going to get some tea ready, all I've had today is an eel!'

My wife has commenced art classes. She was in the local art gallery and learned (over the period of about 3 hours due to language difficulties) that the proprietress ran an art class. I have to admire Jan, it's brave of her to plunge into a hoard of foreign painters, speaking barely a word of their language. There were between six and eight 'students' at any one class, all of whom were known to each other. Fortunately, one of them, a lady called Desiree, glamorous by name and nature, spoke pretty good English and became Jan's verbal go-between and good friend. She is a lovely person and genuinely generous of spirit. She translates the constant bickering between two sisters who attend the class – an extraordinary pair, one of whom exclusively paints the front end of cows, the other the rear. They have become well-known locally for their bovine interpretations and actually sell a few I gather. The head OK, to a point, but quite who buys the rump end remains a mystery.

Jan left for her first class at 7.00 pm on a Wednesday evening. She went on her own, wishing to prove that she 'could manage by herself in a foreign land'. By 10.00 pm there was no sign of her and I was a bit concerned. I set off with the dog to look for her. At 11.15 pm I finally found her wandering home. She'd only just finished – that's over 4 hours! She explained that after two hours (during which there had been a mid-session coffee break) everyone stood up and shuffled around. She presumed this was the end of things and started packing up. No, no they told her, we're not finished yet, it's Vine Time (wine time – time for a glass of something unpleasant with an assortment of hams and cheeses). They had another Vine Time at 10.00 pm before a final flourish just before end of play at 11. Poor Jan wasn't used to all this and was so exhausted I had to carry her brush home.

Desiree's partner is a chap called Erik whose obsession with the diminutive MR2 Toyota sports car is legendary - in MR2-obsessive circles. They live in a small house on the edge of town with a garage that is conservatively twice the square footage of the house. In there he not only keeps his special weekend MR2 but also his 'go to work' one. In addition to tonnes of spare parts there is also a mysterious, tarpaulin-clad, car-shaped lump in the corner. This turns out to be a Ford Capri from the 1970s in which Erik wishes to be buried! His plan is to be cremated, have his ashes thrown in the Capri which will then be crushed and interred in a hole. I kid you not!

From the Hound of Vrouwe Johanna

Well, here we are. Goodness knows where that is, but we're here nevertheless.

Our hosts are nice people; he looks a bit like a Pink Floyd groupie but he's very chatty, likes a roll-up and enjoys a glass. She's very neat and proper - religious you know. Not sure how well Dad will manage with her. He'll have to mind his p's and q's – or z's and w's that they have here.

I know we've travelled some distance, in some discomfort I might add, and even though it all seems a bit new, Dad is hacking about enthusiastically. It was difficult to imagine how he could make things look worse, but he's managing it.

I'm a bit nonplussed frankly. After all the trauma of getting here and hours spent bashing about with the boat (which frankly doesn't look a great deal different), they go and spend three days parked opposite a container terminal. What ARE they thinking?

I'd have thought they'd have had enough of old boats, but no, they drag me round a veritable graveyard of dented metal. Nor sure what the point of it all is really. What's the attraction of watching old folk shod in clogs shovelling shells into a wheelbarrow?

Actually, it's not been a good few weeks at all.

Mum was out at art and Dad took me for a late-evening walk. It was a combination of factors that turned the episode into a disaster. We're moored on a rickety pontoon for a start. There's a bit of a drop from the boat to the slippery planking and a gap between the boat and the pontoon. And it's dark – and my eyes are not what they were. Dad's torch just wasn't up to the task and, well, I fell in. I know, I know, you're not supposed to jump in in the winter, but I assure you it was an accident. Went with quite a splash too I can tell you - it's about four feet drop. Then I got a bit disorientated. He was flashing is torch and shouting (my ears aren't what they once were either). I got a bit mixed up and started swimming out towards open water rather than the bank. He'd got little choice really - either leave me to swim off towards the biscuit factory or come and help. Well, in he jumps and drags me into shore.

I think we were both quite lucky, it really was very cold. Anyhow, when Mum gets home Dad's kneeling in front of the fire in his underpants blowing a hairdryer up my rear end. Undignified doesn't begin to cover it. What she thought, goodness only knows.

I'm sure things will improve.

Anyhow, I'm just getting used to this lap-top so allow me to go and practice and I'll report back soon.

Love Bonny

Niggles and Dribbles

I've begun to tackle a job that has every indication of being testing and protracted – wiring. Not installing new necessarily but trying to untangle a forest of multi-coloured mangrove roots. Most major pieces of equipment (engine, genny, inverter, charger etc.) can be switched on from either wheelhouse or engine room. Interconnecting wires have no colour coordination, some change colour mid-stream and others just peter out. I'm worried about bringing the whole system to a grinding halt but feel I must at least begin to grasp their workings. I'm also doing all this from a position of some weakness – lack of electrical savvy and partial colour-blindness (red / green; which is not ideal for electrics!). So far I have removed about a quarter of a mile of redundant cable with no ill-effect; it seems that whenever the ownership of the boat changed hands previously, a new owner would hack off wires that didn't appeal, and simply add a new loom. This, I feel, will be an ongoing source of irritation.

One thing with which Holland is synonymous is bicycles. Not only is the country's geography ideally suited to the activity but there are dedicated well-maintained cycle paths everywhere. While marooned in Meppel after our breakdown I'd cadged a lift to retrieve our car and, now back in Zwartsluis, had to return to collect it so I borrowed a bike from an English friend. I maintained a punishing pace on the modern 21-gear machine. With clothing plastered to my torso and wind whistling through my helmet I was in that dream-like state achieved by the super-athlete, coasting down the Champs Elysée acknowledging the cheers of the crowd as I cruised to my first Tour-de-France triumph. You can imagine my disappointment when I was overtaken with some ease by a 12-year-old schoolgirl on a 'bone-shaker' who wasn't even dressed for competitive cycling. The majority of Dutch bikes are the sit-up-and-beg type, which are obviously more hi-tech than their 'John Mills film era' appearance. As the girl's jeans, anorak and satchel disappeared up the road I was left to reflect on my advancing years and the inadequacy of fancy-shaped, modern machinery.

Listening to the BBC World Service (the only English-speaking channel I can pick up on our old wheelhouse radio) the weather-lady predicted slow-moving showers, a description apt for some boatyards I have visited, but not De Watergeus here in Zwartsluis. They repaired our broken coupling efficiently, quickly and at very reasonable cost, so we are ready for another trial run. We wonder how many trial runs we will have before we can call them something else. Our engine, old smoky, has been attended to and is infinitely less pollutive so with the boatyard engineer at the helm we go out to test the new coupling. He pilots our boat at a speed far greater than I would dare to go and declares himself satisfied so we return to our new temporary mooring which is bow-on to a rotting pontoon. Boat access is now achieved via a hastily cobbled-together boarding ramp constructed from an old bedhead and some short lengths of roof-lath. Neither the skipper nor the dog are impressed with these arrangements – it's even worse than the mooring where the dog jumped in. In fact, when the wind is from the west and the water level has risen you have to be a bit of a goat to get aboard. I'm even deeper in the mire when the skipper discovers grease on her little vanity mirror. I'd had to have a look under the engine. It was a confined space and the only way to diagnose a small oil leak was….., well, you get the picture. Save to say I am not covered in reflective glory at the moment.

Moored nearby is the most beautiful sailing tjalk owned by a very friendly German guy called Rolf. It has historical importance because it's in near original condition (built in 1863) down to mast, rigging and structure. It is 24 metres and the interior is fitted out in a manner that would grace any 'executive living' magazine, but all done blending original ironwork with aged pitch pine, indirect lighting and modern appliances. However, he has just found rot in the top of his mast so an unscheduled trip to a repairer is on the cards. I suspect that surprises are one thing we are going to have to expect! My friend calls Rolf 'Tiller the Hun', which is a bit unkind.

In a way I'm glad we've had a week's torrential rain interspersed with the odd thunderstorm because we can determine where any leaks are. We have a nagging dribble through a kitchen light but apart from that we remain pretty dry. I know how hard it's raining because of the intensity of drip falling from the wheelhouse roof with a clang onto the metal gas locker. Today sounds like an American level-crossing so I know it's a real humdinger. Actually, it's been a 'wet moments' sort of month. The pressure relief valve on the hot water tank leaked. OK, it wasn't new, but it has probably had years of trouble-free pressure-releasing and the confounded thing chooses now to have a spurt. The man from the plumbers merchant looked in some bemusement at the pitted, furry object I wished to replace and obviously took this 'thinking time' into account when raising his invoice. The other leak was the pressure switch on the main water pump-accumulator thingy. It simply gave way, thankfully as I was prodding it at the time, and it showered the engine room in a heavy drizzle. I've replaced both at some expense and we're fine – till the next time – and there WILL be one.

Our current niggles are shaded by the difficulty Klaas (boatyard owner) has had with one of his hire boats. A German holidaymaker tried to fill the water tanks by inserting the hose into the toilet breather-pipe. The holding tank exploded so the inside of the boat filled with a one week supply of second-hand knockwurst. All left the €250k cruiser a tad unsavoury.

Today we have witnessed another traditional Dutch occasion. It was a 'flower festival' with a difference. Instead of erecting a hamlet of marquees in a park (where the largest and most prestigious is the temporary home to the R.H.S., presided over by a battalion of blue blazers and blue hair do's) wild, imaginative frameworks are built on flat-bed articulated lorries and decorated with thousand upon thousand of multi-coloured dahlias. They really were stunning A pirate ship, a Dickensian street and an underwater coral scene were among a dozen amazing creations. But this was in no major town or city, the event took place in a small country village accessed via 'C' roads and the floats parading through the narrow streets were higher than the two-storey houses. The floats then parked up for the afternoon to be photographed and gawked at.

Talking to one local, he said that the frameworks, which took weeks to construct, are all ready by Wednesday evening so each float had two days in which to attach the fresh flowers in time for Saturday's parade. It's competitive too, by the time we arrived in early afternoon, the judging had been completed and rosettes from first to twelfth had been awarded. Local and regional businesses sponsor the floats which are brought to life by enthusiastic locals acting out scenes reflective of their particular theme, and with real passion. For example, the girls on the coral float were painted and dressed in aquamarine and were precariously perched on their coral 'drifting' in the current, some fifteen feet off the ground. Locals had opened up their gardens to friends and family to party and not for the first time (nor last no doubt) we felt very much the outsiders – which we were. I was dressed in black shorts and black shirt, perfect choice for someone wishing to maintain a degree of anonymity among this colour-fest!

Our temporary mooring is on the periphery of things and although we are grateful for an electricity hook-up, filling up with water for the first time was a bit of an adventure. Our 'water-point' turned out to be a hose that needed hauling up from the canal bed where it had been anchored with a house brick in black mud (in case someone stole it we presume). Actually, it's down there to prevent freezing in winter. I ask Klass if the water from the slimy nozzle is actually safe to drink and he replies, 'we always boil our drinking water in Holland'. Anyhow no lumps came out when I turned it on so, via 60m of hose back to the boat, we take 2 hours to fill up with 2000 litres.

When you're engaged in a renovation project its head down and keep going – show scant regard for the outside world and battle on. You lose track of time a bit, so that when I asked the skipper what day it was, to make sure that the shops were open, she replied, 'it's about Thursday'. The same day in fact that I saw an extraordinary sight. Three-hundred metres away by the side of the waterway there is a house re-roof nearing completion. A three-storey property the top two of which are within a huge, steeply-sloping roof. Getting tiles from the garden to the ridge is being performed in relay up a series of ladders, three people clambering up and down to meet each other. It is lashing down and blowing at about 25 mph and the middle roofer is around 60 years old - and wearing a tweed skirt! She's at it for around 8 hours – they're made of stern stuff here. As one local told me, there's no bad weather, just bad clothing.

Our English friends, Dave and Jane, invite us round to their boat as there is the potential for a 'music night'. A converted fishing boat from Friesland (north-west Holland) has moored alongside them and the owner, his wife and four friends have been boating since childhood so know a thing or two about how to pass an autumn evening. At about 10.00 pm Dave (an accomplished musician) gets his guitar out and strums a few chords. Within minutes heads perk up on the adjacent boat and the crew drift over with an assortment of instruments including a guitar, mouth organ and a rattle. No-one appears to know both tune and words but it's not important as the international currency of music has created new friendships and is instrumental in creating a few next-morning headaches.

Mosquitoes are a nuisance and as Dave and Jane's 'ultra-violet' plug-in flycatcher is unequal to the task, Jane wants to try those extendable sticky fly catchers. Dave hates them. 'Ugly damn things that keep getting stuck in my hair and don't work anyway', he mutters. While he's away for a few days Jane sets out to prove him wrong. It doesn't go too well because after a couple of days she has only attracted one midge. Unwilling to admit defeat, she goes out and buys a battery-powered electric fly-zapping squash racquet and spends the next evening with a bottle of wine electrocuting mozzies - which she then transfers to the sticky paper by way of a pair of eyebrow tweezers. Thus, Dave arrives home and, by foul means, has lost the battle. He was last spotted cruising towards Maastricht with his head swathed in sticky brown fly papers full of electrocuted mosquitoes, and a midge.

Learning Curve

This dear old boat is the third one I've worked on. The first two, narrowboats in the UK, I kitted out from scratch. In other words bought the hulls and started from there. The first was 'serviceable', the second rather better. Not cabinet-maker standard but generally fine both aesthetically and practically. Creating the inside of a boat is known as a 'fit-out'. If you have a go you need to be either a competent all-rounder or a quick learner with some knowledgeable friends. Working on our present boat is something else altogether because I'm working with someone else's previous efforts – not all of them to be frank, that accomplished. Whether it's a new job or a refurbishment you need to be prepared for setbacks and frustration before you breathe a sigh of relief at the end of the job.

The following may be either warning or advice for those contemplating a fit-out for the first time. For those who have already had a go themselves, you may recognize part of it........

The self-fit out.
   Items required:

1. Time
2. Patience
3. Money
4. Skill
5. Equipment
6. Imagination

7. Planning and Organisation
8. Adaptability
9. Sense of humour
10. Liquid refreshment
11. A medical team

We'll take these in turn with a brief explanation of each.

Time

The Gregorian calendar, Greenwich Mean Time, Eastern Standard Time and Tea Time all have something in common. They are (or were) all recognised, trusted and quantifiable standards by which we live.

'Canal Time' is something else altogether. Invented for the waterways by the folk of the waterways it is a unique and largely mythic medium used to frustrate, amuse and confuse anyone unfamiliar with waterways and boats.

Time is infinite, it has been going for ever and it will never end - the human mind cannot comprehend something that does not have a convenient start or finish. Because Canal Time is based on the principal that time is irrelevant, its wily creators have found a way to circumnavigate one of mankind's great conundrums.

When starting a fit-out you may as well sling your timepiece in the cut and invest in an artificial daylight machine because things rarely happen when you want or expect them to. You have to take advantage of opportunities when they present themselves, whatever time of day or night, and be prepared to work around 'flexible' delivery times.

BUT, we as outsiders are entering an alien world and there is no reason why anyone already working to Canal Time should change to suit us.

The sooner we understand this basic principle the better.

Patience

Because 'in the kingdom of the novice 'fitter' Canal Time is King', patience is something you need in spades. Most of us have to learn a new language - swim, skeg, calorifier, tumblehome etc. etc. Old hands are delighted to spend a couple of weeks explaining the workings of a classic engine (a single cylinder Bolinder engine for example) but try and get someone to connect your gas regulator in a hurry and it's a different ball game. The difficulty is that you can't complete chosen task A before you complete tasks B, C, D, E and F. If you can't get assistance with task F, the whole lot becomes a part-finished muddle that lies in a tangled heap alongside last month's part finished muddle.

Money

Whether you buy a bare shell or a sail-away completed to whatever stage, you are purchasing a long, gaping tube into which you pour money. Nothing costs as little as you imagine unless it doesn't work. Usually any boat-related purchase is 'specialist', 'miniature' or both; and you have to pay for it. A rough guide when comparing your original (wildly optimistic) estimate with actual cost is roughly equivalent to the Celsius / Fahrenheit conversion - double it and add thirty.

And never forget all those costly little items that make boating such a joy on an ongoing basis, such as insurance, mooring fees and licence.

Skill

Some of the skills required are as follows: plumbing, electricity, woodwork, metalwork, painting, mechanics and design. If you have them, great, if you don't, any work you can't do yourself is going to cost you. In fact, some of the costliest bits are where you have cocked-up and are forced to engage the services of a professional.

During diagnosis each professional head shake is charged at a fiver and each 'tut' a tenner. Following which there is disassembly, re-build and system test, all at £x per hour, plus parts, plus VAT – net result: for you, a badly bruised budget - for the professional, a fortnight in Florida.

You CAN do what we did; buy a 'build-it-yourself' book and just have a go. Our first weeks cruise was followed by a fortnight in dock screwing back all the bits that had dropped off, but the self-satisfaction is huge.

Any B.I.Y. book should contain a chapter on amateur problem solving such as how to stop that annoying dribble under the sink without having to take the lavatory out.

Equipment

You will need access to a full set of tools. I say 'access' because most households have a basic set of equipment, some of which works and some of which we know how to use, but there are some expensive items that you require just for the occasional job. A copper pipe-bender for example. You're not going to go and spend fifty quid on a new one just to bend a couple of bits of pipe. Another example is metal hole-cutters – that is circular cutters that cut holes in steel up to 10mm thick. You'll need a number of different sizes to make holes for where fresh water comes in and waste water goes out, plus an arbor to attach them to the drill, plus a drill with adequate power, plus some hole-cutting oil. All this lot for half a dozen holes after which they will never be used again. So, you either borrow the items (preferable) or get a professional to do the job (probably in about 3 months) knowing that the following morning they will be down the travel agent booking for Orlando again.

The two most crucial items are a hard hat and knee pads. Much of the time fitting out is spent working at low level with your head clacking around in a cupboard making electrical / plumbing connections or mending something.

One other item worth purchasing at the outset is a big hammer for use when all else fails.

Imagination

Whether in a house or a boat, if you're like us, you have probably spent hours looking at other people's efforts trying to get an idea on a lay-out and design. Then, on a boat from a practical point of view, how on earth do you shoehorn everything into such a small space?

Compared to a land-based property you have a fraction of the space within which to build a mini-house and somehow you have to avoid getting your tackle entangled with the fan belt while watching Bargain Hunt. You really have to imagine everything working with some semblance of functionality from a starting point of a big ugly steel tube and a perplexing pile of raw materials.

Optimism and positive thought can be a powerful tool for the Fitter – even better than a hammer. The one thing that keeps you going through all the lows and lows is the thought of sitting proudly on the front deck in the evening sun supping your beverage of preference swapping tales with a fellow boaters.

What you must avoid at all costs is the negative. Never, for example, imagine sitting on the loo in full view of Canary Wharf because you've sited the loo near the largest window and you've forgotten to put up a curtain rail. Think positive or you'll never start – or worse, you'll get 6 years into the project and give up.

Planning and organisation

We spent endless hours and a dozen cases of Australian Red deciding on a lay-out – and we still made a mess of it. At the 'empty steel tube with a floor' stage we'd stuck miles of blue masking tape all over the floor to mark out rooms and appliances. The sheer quantity of tape were testament to the number of rejected ideas. In fact, by the time we'd finished, there was so much of the stuff on the floor we left it in place and saved money on a carpet (which by the conclusion of the project was a welcome saving).

You can't plan enough because adding or altering something after you think you've finished, can be a nightmare.

For example, you've installed everything down one side of the boat and when you remove all your tools and ton and a half of off-cuts, the vessel develops a serious list, unnoticed as your equipment was acting as a counterbalance. All your stuff is now in the back of the car (for the last time, thank goodness!) awaiting despatch to a car boot sale or the tip, when you realize you have a tilt. The only way to alter the ballast and rectify the lean is to unpack the tools from the car, dismantle the TV cabinet and hack a hole in the floor to create access to the bilge. You move / remove as much ballast as you can, leaving some finger ends trapped under concrete slabs, but invariably end up with a few 56lb weights hidden in subtle locations such as the kitchen cupboards or under the bath to try and correct the list. All this is avoidable through a bit of careful thought (if you're like me though, a stubborn, 'intelligent', smarty-pants man, you'd rather get stuck into something male like screwing wood to the walls and ignoring that o-so-boring planning stage).

Likewise, being organised and tidy in a confined space is imperative. I was forced to borrow a jigsaw on one occasion as mine had disappeared. It was unearthed more than a week later when my wife decided to have a clear-up and discovered it under a mountain of dust and wood-shavings. From that moment on we had a good clear-up once a month, every month, without fail.

Adaptability

I very much doubt if any original plan is adhered to without one or a dozen subtle alterations during 'works in progress'. Usually this is down to poor planning. Everything looks fine on paper (or computer screen) but when you come to the build it becomes obvious that you may have overlooked the odd practicality issue - such as having to remove the fridge and lavatory every time you want to use the washing machine. This has the potential to become somewhat irritating in the long term.

So, you adapt, problem solve, make things easy for yourself. Answer - simply do away with the loo, fridge and washing machine. Because you can't store fresh food or wash clothes it means your journeys will have to be planned around mooring alternate days outside pubs and launderettes. Where these facilities are unavailable you'll be forced to eat roadkill and wear disposable nappies.

Through this one typical example we've adapted both fit-out and lifestyle.

Sense of humour

This is undoubtedly the single most important weapon in our armoury. The ability to chuckle at a squashed thumb or chortle at a throbbing cranium will diffuse many a tense situation and is a skill born of painful experience. Don't take things too seriously, important though they may be.

While fitting out our first narrowboat - at the 'blue tape on the floor stage' - we were planning one of the most important bits - the position of the loo.

The shell was completely empty except for an upturned Dandelion & Burdock crate which, for planning purposes, doubled as the bog. I was sitting on said crate waggling my arms about 'Birdie Song' style to ascertain if there would be enough elbow room between the bath and the cooker. By the time I got to ask my wife which side she would like the toilet paper holder she was in such apoplexy she was rolling about on the floor clutching her tummy. She looked in some discomfort so when I asked her if she would like to use the toilet it only made matters worse.

We amateurs try very hard and, especially the males of the species, attempt to retain a modicum of pride throughout our endeavours. We do make cock-ups, the trick is to keep the doors shut and the windows masked up so no-one else can share your misery. The odd consoling word from an understanding wife certainly helps too, such as the tender moment I shared with my wife when she said, 'never mind love, I'm sure the next cupboard you build will have the door opening outwards.'

Liquid refreshment

During the early stages of a fit-out the water tank, diesel tank, calorifier and bath were all redundant so we filled them with Australian Red. As the build progressed from aft to fore the antipodean nerve-agent was consumed. The first couple of glasses, immediately after breakfast, were merely relaxants allowing us to tackle any task, no matter how difficult, with casual professionalism. At the end of a day a considerably larger quantity was required so we were unable to focus on the days balls-ups. An unexpected bonus was that by the time we'd completed the back cabin, the weight of installed materials countered the weight lost from the now empty diesel tank – hence the integrity of the ballast was maintained. Not that we could see it at the time but one of the seven in-focus photographs (out of roughly eleven thousand) happened to catch the boat from the right angle and proved this hypothesis.

Medical team

We retained a full medical team on permanent standby. Members included a triage nurse, a chiropractor, a psychiatrist and a substance abuse counsellor. As the months passed and the build progressed, all were called on with increasing regularity and arrived with looks of bewilderment at the astonishing variety of injury we suffered in such a small space.

The triage nurse used acres of bandages and plasters and two dozen tubes of Savlon before we had to admit defeat and call in a mechanic to fix the leaky exhaust.

On one occasion the chiropractor was called on to extricate me from the cupboard under the sink when I'd developed a full body cramp while trying to connect the shower. Neither of us could work out why the shower had to connect under the sink but we're back to the planning issue.

Six months on my psychiatrist and I are working through a recurring nightmare about a short, achy-jointed bloke trapped in a biscuit tin with an assortment of power tools.

Actually, to be perfectly honest, we had to let the substance abuse counsellor go. Not because she wasn't good at her job, quite the opposite, she was excellent. The problem was that most of the time I was so pissed I couldn't remember what we'd been talking about.

Any time spent doing something I couldn't recall was time I could employ better elsewhere.

Footnote:

We've done two fit-outs. The second is an improvement on the first, though considering we should have known what we were doing second time around, there is still the odd 'anomaly'. I will mention one - for some reason (stupidity?) I have plumbed the cassette lavatory to the wrong pipe resulting in the unusual phenomenon of a hot flushing loo.

One chap did try and help on one occasion but inadvertently mixed up a small jar of milk with the setting agent from my two-part epoxy putty. He was summarily dismissed when a cupboard fell off a wall and my tea set solid. I was within two weeks of completing the job when it was pointed out by the same bloke (in an effort at spiteful revenge for his sacking) that I had been wearing my knee-pads upside down for the previous seven and a half months. He hadn't thought to mention it earlier and, to my considerable irritation, he laughed till he wept.

While I was in the local hospital having my pencil removed from behind my right ear under local anaesthetic, he was undergoing more drastic surgery to remove an electric drill from his back passage. Finally, you are forced to unleash your finished project for appraisal by outside world. However successful your fit-out, expect no more than guarded enthusiasm from a fellow amateur or a 'humph' from a 'professional'. Never was a truer word spoken in humph………

To continue..

A German gentleman taking great care over the safe return of a hire-boat spent twenty minutes mooring up. Bow thrusters, stern thrusters and main engine were all glowing red hot as he nudged perfectly alongside the quay kissing the jetty with the feather-light touch of an alighting moth. Waving casually to his crew in the bow, he exited the wheelhouse to receive due plaudits. Then disaster, he tripped over the guard rail and by means of a very unpleasant cartwheel-type affair, landed in a heap on the concrete three feet below. 'He'd have been better diving off the other side', whispered the bloke who'd just arrived to inform me my batteries were knackered.

You need to be careful who you snigger at as opportunities to make an ass of oneself are almost boundless. Two days later it was my turn. As the crow flies we had to travel 50 metres to replace said batteries. The journey was extended by a further fifty metres as we had to reverse out of our mooring then go forward again through quite a narrow gap between moored boats then reverse at right angles to the same spot where our hire-boat friend had fallen off his boat. There was quite a wind blowing and as we traversed the gap I touched one of the boats on our starboard side. Our forty-tonne iron hulk brushed gently against a few kilos of ornate wooden rudder attached to a small motor yacht. The tortured squeaking noise, far out of proportion to the actual collision, cut through the wind like a sick siren. Not much escapes the attention of 'Rob the imitation policeman' and sure enough; 'DAMAGE!' he yelled with extreme excitement, just in case I wasn't awake. Then, not to appear too enthusiastic and because we are friends of his, added, 'Oh dear'.

Our friend Dave, not renowned for his turn of speed, in a moment of unprecedented action, leapt off his boat and shot round on his bicycle to inspect the carnage. To everyone's disappointment (except ours) there wasn't much to see. The tiller arm was at a peculiar angle despite my hope that it was meant to look like that. But I knew that this piddly broom-stick size piece of wood was going to cost me. The skipper wisely judged this a good moment to go shopping in case I blamed her. I was highly embarrassed and fearful of a hefty repair bill. However, Klass told me not to worry as the owner of the previously undamaged boat was away for a couple of weeks. By the time he got back it would be as good as new - the guy would never even know that an idiot Englishman had driven over his steering apparatus.

However, our travails paled compared to those suffered by the owner of a boat that had sunk at its moorings. When we first came to Zwartsluis, about twelve months ago, looking for a barge and moorings this same boat was sitting on the bottom with just its wheelhouse poking out of the water. Klass had managed to re-float it and effect a temporary repair ('it's making my yard look untidy', he'd understated). Then he'd towed it round to the public moorings in the centre of town a few hundred yards away. You'd have thought that the boat owner would have learned his lesson and had the thing repaired, but no, he continued to neglect it and it sunk again. It settled in the mud, bits of detritus floated free and it began leaking oil. The Dutch authorities take a very dim view of pollution and ordered the poor boat's immediate removal to a knackers yard. You've never seen so much equipment. A floating crane, a huge flat transportation barge, two tugs, a police vessel and ancillary land-based support vehicles all rumbled into town. Because the boat had settled in the mud they were unable to get straps underneath to lift it and despite a couple of hours effort from the tugs, the boat remained stuck fast. Divers went down to try and attach lines, a tractor shoved from the shore, chiefs yelled at Indians, Indians yelled back, the watching crowd went home to download photos and returned with picnics and Tilley lamps. Finally, after eight hours, the boat came free, was lifted onto the transportation barge and was duly carted away. It was so sad to see a once proud vessel in such a state.

No boat deserves to be neglected like that. But the dear old girl had the last word - the bill for removal, around thirty thousand Euros.

Right, it's time to start on stage two of our renovations. Stage one was the re-vamped bedroom now we're going to build a second bedroom and new bathroom (the electrical re-hash was mandatory and was just slipped in so doesn't count as a stage in its own right). We'll call the bedroom Coventry because it's where I'll disappear to when the skipper has had enough of me. This is quite a major project and Alan, a boating friend from the UK, is coming to give us a kick start. Before he arrives however, I encounter the first difficulty. The timber I've ordered is dropped off 200 metres from the boat as the lorry driver refuses to brush past a conifer and risk scratching his vehicle. I tell him I'll get a saw and hack off the offending limbs but by the time I return he's dropped the lot beside a busy road and scarpered. Included are fourteen full-size sheets of 12mm plywood and suddenly the place is like a ghost town so I'm on my own. Having lumped three or four down to the jetty I'm having dizzy spells and by the time the whole lot is within striking distance of the boat I've just about had it. They still have to be carried down 30 metres of rickety wooden jetty and we find that they won't go through the wheelhouse door so we have to remove the big hatch in our bedroom roof and manoeuvre them all in through there. Then it starts raining which adds to the jolly atmosphere. Apart from a minor plumbing disaster on our second narrowboat this is the first time I've wet the bed in quite a while so now the skipper is not best pleased either. By the time all the wood is stacked neatly in the lounge we're both ready for a fortnight in Corfu. But that's out of the question - the plywood at £60 per sheet has seen to that.

Actually, we had quite a result on that. Our friends Richard and Jenny from the B & B have an account at a local builder's merchant and we were able to book the supplies to their account and get a decent discount. It was very strange walking in, ordering nearly a thousand pounds worth of stuff and booking it to someone else - trusting lot, no?

While recovering from this trial of endurance we have occasion to witness a rowing race with a difference. A dozen or so chunky boats, each seating 8 oarsmen (or women) and a cox wallow round the local area in search of an unworthy cash prize. We have seen the odd boat crewed by chunky ladies battle up and down the local waterways for the past month and presumed it was merely a masochistic way to battle the bulge. It transpires that this is all taken rather seriously and crews (some extremely competitive, others more 'social') travel round the country to various venues in a sort of tortuous rowing roadshow. Crews are sponsored by local businesses and, as with other Dutch traditions we have witnessed, the crowds turn out in some number to cheer on the unfortunate incumbents of these craft which, in design, look more suited to lifeboat duties than speed. We have no idea who actually won but it is obvious that some crews are near manic in their desire for victory and when two boats tangle, both with each other and a lock gate, one doesn't have to be fluent in Dutch to comprehend the mutual ill-feeling.

Thankfully we still have the car which very useful for collecting supplies. Zwartsluis is only a small town and the nearest big B&Q type shop is in Zwolle about ten miles away. On our first trip there we got hopelessly lost around their one-way system. We passed the same petrol station three times and on the third occasion actually had need of its services. We have actually only seen one single English registered car locally in a year, and that was being escorted somewhere by the police after parking illegally in a bus stop, so people tend to stare at us. It means that because the vehicle stands out any little indiscretion is amplified. For example, when I was on my own and drove into an auto-pay car park and had to collect a ticket on entry, the machine was selfishly positioned for left-hand-drive cars. By the time I (as a small person) had tried to reach across to the passenger window (in a big car), knocked the car onto gear (which thankfully stalled against the handbrake) and my top half had slipped into the passenger foot well, I was getting some rather bemused looks from the locals.

Sometimes the dreamy notion of a life (or part of one) on the water is in complete antitheses to the actual living of it. This morning for example we have woken up to an inch of water in the bilge. I've stated before that the general idea is to keep the wet stuff on the outside of the hull so when I see a scummy mess sloshing around under the water and diesel tanks I get very alarmed. First thought, 'gad, we've sprung a leak'. I haven't spent much time in the 'tank room' below the wheelhouse floor, not that we've neglecting it, more that there have been other matters which have required our attention. I scrabble around with a torch and mirror praying that I don't see water bubbling-up from below and am quite well acquainted with this 'nether region' by the time I discover that the shower pump has packed up and that part of the frothy mess is in fact shampoo. A relief in some ways but a messy clear-up follows (including a pump and a packet of nappies) and a new float switch on the shower. This of course is the original shower. By the time we've completed stage two we'll have a brand new one, no chance of that leaking ...... mmm.

To paraphrase Craig Medred (outdoor columnist with an Anchorage newspaper who writes of the dangers of the vast Alaskan wilderness to tourists and visitors), "Living on a barge is a good place to test yourself. It's (sometimes) a bad place to find yourself".

From the hound of Vrouwe Johanna

Not sure whether it was the dunking I got in the harbour but I've not been in the rudest of health. Had a touch of the runs – or in my aged state, the ambles. I'm sure it's nothing to do with this foreign food, although even they don't know exactly what they're buying half the time.

I enjoy music, particularly partial to a bit of Bach, but the evening we went to was in a whole different league – lower. No-one knew any words, which was probably incidental anyway because it sounded like everybody was playing different tunes. And what on earth possessed the ginger-haired monster from Friesland to bring a rattle along goodness knows. He'd have been better off bludgeoning an oil drum with a mooring stake.

And the more red stuff they drink, the louder and more out of tune they get – while believing it actually sounds better. Actually, Dave could play a bit but even his skills couldn't make up for the others' inadequacies.

You've never seen anyone so red in the face. All he did was carry a few bits of wood down the drive. He's just taken a perfectly good load of stuff to the tip only to be replaced by another lot. The only difference is that the original smelt of history, while the new stuff smells of preservative.

Now he's commandeered the services of his mate, Alan. He's six foot four and built like a tank. Dad gets in enough of a tangle with Mum in a relatively small space, how on earth he'll manage with Al will be anyone's guess. I have to admit though, anything that will speed the completion of this dirty, dusty project will be a blessing. It doesn't get much worse than finding splinters in your porridge.

His steering record has taken a battering too. He only went 100 yards and trashed something. Poor old Dad, I'm sure he felt a bit of a chump. What he needs is a confidence booster. I'm going to suggest he finds an abandoned lake to have a practice – although I'd better pick my moment, he's a bit prickly just at present.

I've perked up anyway!

Love Bonny

Water, water everywhere

Our next-door neighbour, Rob, likes to give me a daily weather forecast. He waits for my appearance at first light and exits his boat suitably attired. Unfortunately, recent reports have been largely unintelligible due to wildly fluctuating weather. During wet and windy periods he's blown horizontal as he hangs on to a cabin rail and his words are plucked away into an adjacent hedge. During cold snaps he's so well wrapped up that his forecast is lost inside his muffler. Sadly, neither of these scenarios is conducive to cruising and the only boats moving are the commercial carriers that have to work to earn a living. The boats are huge so less affected by bad weather. They also have powerful bow and stern thrusters and the skippers are highly trained.

Water and the weather of extreme importance to the Dutch. Around a quarter of the country is below sea level (in the case of the eastern Rotterdam community of Prins Alexander Polder approaching 7 metres) and they have fought a battle with the elements for over 2000 years. They have to constantly balance the North Sea trying to get in against rivers trying to get out.

Water levels throughout Holland are measured against a fixed point, namely the Normal Amsterdam Water Level or Normal Amsterdam Peil (abbreviated to N.A.P.) There is a special bolt in Amsterdam's Muziektheatre (Music Theatre), and the top of this bolt is the standard level by which water levels in the Netherlands are compared. Thus, when a place lies two metres below the top of the bolt the Dutch say that it lies two metres below N.A.P. The waters are muddied somewhat because Amsterdam is settling by 2cm per century though it is likely that they will continue to use the N.A.P. as their gauge – until it disappears.

Even where we are, many miles inland, the water levels are constantly monitored. We don't need an expert to tell us that the levels fluctuate. One day we have to climb up a couple of feet to get off the boat and a few days later we step down and here it has nothing to do with tides, it is dictated by wind direction and rainfall. Out on the coast however it is a different story.

I go and speak with one of a team of guys who manage the local sluice and pumping station - although while speaking to one of his colleagues later it appears that divulging trade secrets is taboo but it's too late, my informer, Cerrit van Dam, has already spilled the beans. The first letter of his Christian name is pronounced with a sort of guttural, throat-clearing noise and when I try and repeat it the rest of his name is lost in a soggy mess. He offers a sympathetic grin when I tell him I'll go away and practice. Now I've got a sore throat and a damp jumper so to avoid personal trauma and spitting at him I have decided to call him Mr van Dam to the relief of us both. In fact, it's only now that I wonder whether he was taking the mickey – the bloke in charge sluices and water levels - Mr van Dam!! Surely not.

The sluice he monitors is basically a large pair of lock gates. On the day that I see him there is a skein of Geese pointing east but travelling west, blown by a 'significant air movement'. As I've said, when the wind blows from the North West, a surge of water is literally blown from the Ijsselmeer back up the canal system and when the water level at Meppel, 11 kilometres inland from Mr Van Dam's sluice, reaches between around 56 / 58 cm above N.A.P. the outer gates are closed. This is fine except after periods of heavy rain when water flows down the system from the north and east. Because the gates are now closed, water builds up on the 'inland' side so now the pumps are used. The adjacent pumping station has three pumps and each one can move 33 cubic metres of water a second. The night before I spoke to Mr van Dam, all three pumps had run for six hours.

Tides are not an issue because of enormous sea defence projects undertaken in the last century. Although Holland has been affected by serious flooding for centuries, it was a severe storm and accompanying flood in 1916 that finally prompted the Government to begin work to reclaim the Zuiderzee, a shallow inlet of the North Sea. The Zuiderzeewerken (South Sea Works) are a man-made system of dams, land reclamation and water drainage works. The biggest structure within the project is a 32km dam linking the provinces of North Holland and Friesland, literally blocking out the North Sea. The Afsluidijk ('closure dyke') was completed on May 28th 1932 a new inland lake was created and the Zuiderzee became the Ijsselmeer.

Included in the project were shipping locks and discharge sluices at each end of the dyke. Periodically the lake is discharged because it is fed by fresh water from rivers (including the Ijssel after which the lake was named) and drainage from the polders (reclaimed land).

Thanks to all this effort we are not affected by tides but rather more importantly Central Holland is protected from the effects of the North Sea, they have potential for increased food supply from reclaimed land and improved water management. I am astonished when I speak with a young guy working in a café part way along the Afsluitdijk. He tells me that even though he has lived in the town of Dan Helder, close to the southern end of the dyke all his life it was only when he started working in the café, where there are many historic photographs of the barriers' construction, that he realised the true scale of the project and its vital importance. Another 'pit stop' along the Dyke is called Breezeanddijk, which about sums up standing on a man-made barrier between two large bodies of water. It is the middle of winter and I encounter, perhaps not entirely unexpectedly, a mini-bus full of Japanese camera-snappers.

There was another disastrous flood in 1953 in which nearly 2000 people died (the same storm also severely affected the UK where over 300 people died). Within the tragedy there was an astonishing tale. At 5:30 AM in the morning of February 1st one dyke called 'the Groenendijk' broke under the immense pressure of the water. With the gap widening the mayor of Nieuwerkerk commandeered a ship called "de Twee Gebroeders" (Two Brothers) and he asked the captain, Aire Evegroen, to sail his ship into the hole and plug it. He did so successfully, firmly lodging his barge into the dyke. Despite warnings from experts that the dykes were insufficient, it took these calamitous floods to make people realize that something drastic need to be done and quickly. The plan was to build dams, storm-surge barriers and sluices on all river mouths in addition to smaller 'compartment dams' further inland. 1958 saw the opening of the first stage of a massive project called the Delta Plan - a storm barrier on the river Hollandse Ijssel which protected the highly populated Western part of the Netherlands (the Randstad) against flooding. The following fifty years has seen numerous astonishing feats of engineering and by some, Deltaworks has been termed the eighth wonder of the world. Safety has been the first priority but it all this had to be accomplished taking into account environmental factors, including maintaining tidal movements in various places while keeping vital shipping routes open. With sea levels rising and the land of Western Holland slowly subsiding, battles have been won but the war is not over.

On the home front barely a day goes by when I don't go in the engine room and kick something, but I learned a trick recently when confronted by a floating 'berg' of bubbles floating past our boat. The cause it transpires is the periodic addition of washing-up liquid to the raw water cooling system. The resultant frothy cloud from the exhaust is not only great fun for any children watching it is also supposed to clean out your exhaust (according to Klaas).

Anyhow while the locals have been constructing dams we've been building a second bedroom and bathroom and if they thought that damming the Rhine was a problem they should have tried connecting our shower drain. The second bedroom has bunk beds (the top one folds down to make a sofa) and will double as a 'den'. During the build the skipper requested a collapsible top bunk, and unkindly pointed out that with my joinery skills there should be no difficulty there. While we struggle, we've been taking solace from wine that tastes like it's previously flushed someone's exhaust and cooking on our new Remoska, an electric Czechoslovakian pan which is taking some getting used to. As opposed to the appetizing three-word ditty associated with a breakfast cereal, our first attempts at Yorkshire Pudding went slap, sizzle and sag and looked like something that would appear out of the wrong end of an anaemic cow. But it has opened up a whole new world of culinary delight, even if the majority is unrecognisable. You gather we are still without a proper cooker – that will arrive with stage 5 of the masterplan when I build a new kitchen.

The ancient city of Groningen (from where our barge originated in 1905) is not only twinned with Newcastle, it is also a lovely city. However, the purpose of our visit was not to sample the fine restaurants or experience the romance of the canals, home to a wide variety of fascinating boats, no, we went to investigate composting toilets which is about as unromantic as you can get. The loo we'd gone to view was a bit of a wash-out being expensive, inefficient and bulky – rather like the author, except it used more energy. The upshot is that we've still got a gap in the shower-room for a lavatory - if we ever find something suitable. If we don't, we already have a rather nice red bucket, which at the moment is upturned in the lounge with a lamp on it.

The skipper continues to do her bit for Anglo-Dutch relations as the following brief encounter demonstrates. While 90% of population of Zwartsluis is in Church on a Sunday morning, she goes for a gentle cycle ride to ward off the effects of a nasty weekly tablet. As she is sitting on a bench an elderly motorcyclist pulls up nearby and waves his arms to attract her attention. The temperature is barely above zero as the motorcyclist stops his machine. He heaves it up onto it's stand, steps off the bike and begins to remove all his cold-weather gear: gloves, silk scarf, helmet and finally balaclava. He asks the skipper a question to which she replies, 'sorry, do you speak English?' The man glares at her for a moment and with the Dutch equivalent of 'oh, for goodness sake', puts back on balaclava, helmet, scarf ……..and she's made another life-long friend.

It is rather frustrating being immobile, I've even tried cadging a ride on a couple of big commercial boats just to get out on the water but they were either too busy or not insured - allegedly. The only private boat I've seen motoring recently was skippered by a Dutchman who was not only experienced enough to battle the elements but was also trying winter cruising for the first time. Judging by his blue-tinged extremities and general damp demeanour he would rather have saved his diesel. 'It's quiet on the water though', he told me on a positive note, as he battled to unravel his frozen hosepipe.

Around here when its sunny and warm they go boating, when its sunny and cold they cycle or walk, when it's raining they go to Church and when its frozen solid they go skating. When the Zwarte Water River floods (as it did recently) the run-off floods adjacent fields – when these freeze you have a huge ice-rink. The locals dust off their skates, wrap up warm and off they go. Experienced skaters, hands clasped behind their lower back, glide with a slow, effortless rhythm. A technique that allows them to travel substantial distances from town to town along the canals during a prolonged freeze. The last big freeze was about eleven years ago and we are in the minority hoping the next one will delay its appearance for another year. I'm a bit mystified as to why there are a couple of wooden dining chairs in the middle of a field, but skating behind these is how the youngsters learn. As I watch the skaters, a large working barge ploughs along the river in the distance through the freezing mist – it's quite a sight.

In fact, this turns out to be quite a big freeze. So much so that the ice is about twelve centimetres thick. We're stuck fast in the ice and the locals mark out a four hundred metre track on the inlet behind our boat. Adults, kids and even dogs slither around and one family brings a couple of benches and a brazier onto the ice and has an impromptu picnic. Not sure a brazier on the ice is a great idea but they seem happy enough.

A Visit to Friends (!)

There was a slight delay before work commenced this morning while I rounded up our neighbour's chickens. I rarely get too intimate with other people's livestock but there was an element of self-interest on this occasion as these rambling roosters produce splendid free-range eggs. Animals and boats form a tetchy alliance and apart from the guy we met on the Kennet and Avon a couple of years ago who kept chickens in a pen on his roof, it is usually limited to cats and dogs. Our American friend, Joe, was seething recently after his cat knocked 'a large malt whiskey' all over his charts. It was patently obvious that the cat had got to the whiskey before Joe because his beautifully structured tirade was the product of a strictly sober mind.

I have been offered a boat trip with our friend Rob. After a couple of months tied to a collection of rickety wooden planks it will be great to get back out on the water. His boat is ex-police, it can cope with all conditions and he's been boating for many years. It is the time of year for the hardy and the experienced, he's both so we are in safe hands.

Preparations are complete and the big engine roars into life. His two VHF radios are switched on and the coffee is brewed, stewing in a rather smart Thermos flask - he's even got out two clean cups. Rob usually boats solo so everything he needs for a trip has to be pre-prepared - like his wide-necked plastic bottle next to his captain's seat. Because I'm thick he has to explain what this is for but mercifully he stows it before we leave. There is a child-like excitement about us as we set off in anticipation of a cruise through the countryside. However, 130 yards into our voyage the channel is completely blocked by a huge barge coming off a slipway after repairs. When fully laden this beast will weigh over 1000 tonnes but even empty it is not something to argue with and because it is floating high in the water it is somehow more imposing. All we can do is sit and wait, but even idling in neutral Rob's engine is using about eight litres of fuel an hour so he rather hopes that the delay won't be protracted - especially as the point of his trip is to go and buy diesel. His boat is extremely manoeuvrable. Because his propulsion system is a Schottel which enables the propeller to turn through 360 degrees, there is no rudder, so to reverse he merely points the propeller backwards. There are two dials on the dashboard, one below the other. The top one points 'north' and swings right and left through a 180-degree arc to the horizontal indicating forward direction while the bottom one points 'south' and shows movement astern. Well Rob seems to have got the hang of it anyway.

Finally, we're out on open water heading for the diesel barge eleven kilometres away. While he goes to use the more conventional alternative to his plastic bottle I take the helm, and I love it. The day is overcast and the misty, grey light deadens perspective in an already flat landscape but there are indications of spring, ducks squabble and huge flocks of geese take to the air then settle again as we pass like a huge ripple on a shaken blanket. We can hear their grumbles even over the noise of the engine. Skeletal trees are no hiding place for the buzzards and misty breathed cows stoically await warmer times. Round a distant bend we spot a large dark shape and despite the use of binoculars we are unable to tell which direction it is moving. We have a small wager. I say it is coming our way and Rob insists it is moving away from us. It is actually a stack of plastic-wrapped silage spookily arranged in the shape of a boat.

Rob's coffee is black, evil stuff strong enough the give an elephant dizzy spells. He reckons it keeps him alert but there is a better than even chance that neither of us will sleep for 3 days. Our trip was only short but my, was it good to get out. We only met one other boat in the couple of hours we were cruising and that was a research vessel testing the canal bed for pollutants. Good job we didn't chuck the coffee over the side.

Our hull is due for blacking. It has been arranged at a nearby slipway on our behalf by Klass. 'Expect a call any time within the next week', he told us. That was two weeks ago. Surprised? No. We have boated long enough to know that we are now living within 'canal time'. So, we wait. (see 'Fit out' above)

We have plenty to do mind you. I have just completed a job designed by the Prince of Darkness to madden and frustrate - tiling. Oh horrid, dirty, unfathomable enterprise, but necessary if you don't want your walls getting soggy. And.... it's one more room habitable. Next we will titivate the lounge, revamp the kitchen, re-do the loo......oh well, there's time for all that.

There is a cultural gulf between the UK and our near-cousins as indeed there may be between a boat-dweller and a 'normal' person. Consequently, when a 'boaty' visits a landlubber from another culture it can have disturbing results. It here that I précis a visit to our friend's home.

Saturday evening

8.30 - Arrive at Dutch friends' house with bottle of wine & a bunch of flowers in the company of another couple (Richard and Jenny) for a 'Music Evening'.

Temperature in the house is around 80 degrees which is about 20 higher than our boat. Jan removes coat and first layer of 'indoor' clothing. All doors and windows are hermetically sealed to prevent the ingress of any unnecessary fresh air. Polite conversation for half an hour with no sign of sustenance whatsoever

9.00 - Industrial strength, freshly-ground coffee arrives in washing-up-size bowl

9.05 - Huge wedge of cake arrives; 85% buttercream, 10% fruit and 5% cake

9.07 - Uncorking sound from kitchen. (Wife removes second layer of clothing).

9.10 - Coffee re-fill

9.12 - Large cream-filled brandy snaps, in shape of a hunting horns, arrives

9.20 - Politely refuse more coffee, ask for directions to 'heads'

9.25 - Worried wine is evaporating in over-hot kitchen.

9.35 - Jan and self go and stand outside in rain to cool off.

9.45 - Glass of wine! (Jan removes third layer).

9.55 - Large serving platter arrives upon which:

Smoked eel

Smoked Mackerel

Smoked Salmon

Salted cod

Smoked Herring on rye bread

10.00 - Wine refill

10.05 - Second serving platter with:

Assorted spicy sausage

Scrambled egg and Palma Ham 'trumpets'

10.10 - Wife removes yet another layer to surprise of hosts

10.15 - Third platter arrives:

Assortment of cheeses

Smoked eel 'pate'

Something unrecognised and unpronounceable with chopped onions

Crackers

10.20 - Politely refuse offer of coffee. Wine refill

10.50 - Still nibbling smoked things

11.20 - Feeling queasy. Lady of the house invites me to play Yamaha electric keyboard.

Render appalling version of Candle in the Wind in 'Grand Piano mode' to muted reception

11.27 - Visit heads again

11.30 - Lady of the house sits at keyboard.

Initiates rhythm section, backing vocals, auto-chord and echo functions and plays very acceptable version of Bridge over Troubled Water with left nostril to rapturous acclaim

12.40 – 3.00 am - More wine, light snooze and a little smoked herring

Sunday

09.30 - Intestinal chaos

10.00 - Politely request that good lady makes no mention of anything smoked.

Make tentative plans to invite Dutch friends round for a few cans of John Smiths Bitter, a meat pie or two and some faggots.

10.45 - Restore order - bacon (unsmoked) and eggs while watching Driving Miss Daisy.

11.30 - Commence lengthy nap.

Being middle aged it is a constant struggle not to lose ground to the physical elite, so I cycle - to the chandlers, the shops, the pub, wherever. I was recently described as 'an assortment of flabby bits draped over a steel frame' which is wholly unjust as the bike is aluminium. I'm still passed by 3-year-olds with stabilizers, but I just pretend I'm sightseeing. Staphorst though is a nearby town too far for me to ride to so we go in the car. It appears to be a town peeking nervously into the twenty-first century from under the skirts of its traditional dress but restrained by the fundamentalist Christian beliefs of a (decreasing) portion of the population. Some still shun television and due to their unwillingness to have vaccinations on religious grounds the town became known for an outbreak of Polio in the early 1970's. Swearing is also strictly forbidden which tested me to the limit during a visit to an independent local butcher. 27 Euros for a small saddle of lamb!

'We don't eat much lamb around here,' he tells me.

'Really?' I replied.

He'd spent five minutes upending his freezer in search of the near-mythical beast so out of politeness as much as anything I felt I couldn't refuse it. Perhaps they don't breed sheep because they are not tall enough in times of flood. Cattle are what you see mostly, partly because the soil is too damp and peaty to support much in the way of arable crops. Many of the farms in Staphorst are thatched, Low Saxon type and border the main street arranged in a herringbone pattern at an oblique angle away from the road. Although the town has now spread from the original ribbon settlement, many roadside farms have green doors and window shutters under a thatched roof and the land stretches away behind in a long, slim sliver. I daren't suggest that they are perfect for breeding long, thin livestock, like snakes, I just get the feeling that they wouldn't find it amusing. As a new generation takes over the running of the farm, they live at the front so, to keep the family together, the buildings are extended at the rear to accommodate the retiring family members. Consequently, some of the farms are quite a size.

The moment we cast off is approaching and the skipper was asked recently where we intended to cruise the boat to which she replied, 'Well, first we want to travel round Holland but eventually we hope to cruise in France.'

'Oh really, where?'

'All through'.

'Where's that then?'

From the hound of Vrouwe Johanna

Pity I'm not a bit younger, I could have a field day with the wildlife. The long-eared owls are the most frustrating, swooping down out of the trees just out of reach – little blighters. They are silent so I can't hear them, my eyes are out of date so I can't see them and when they do get near I can't jump more than a few inches. Getting old is no fun.

What is fun is listening to Mum and Dad. When she does a job she just gets on with it, quietly going about her business. When he does something, everybody has to know about it. Who the heck is interested in the gory details of changing an oil filter? Now he's wandered off towards the back end with a lump hammer........it's best not to ask!

Love, Bonny

Blacking the Bottom

Well, no-one said it would be easy. The total distance we travelled to have our boat blacked was no more than a kilometre each way but boy, did it present a challenge. The boatyard has been trying to fit us in for some time and the 'expect a call any day now' turned into a month. The waiting was not exactly in the hip-replacement category but it was long enough. Consequently, when you get the call to go, you go – or go to the back of the queue. The yard is one that services commercial vessels and so we work around their schedules. The phone call comes in brilliant early-morning sunshine, by the time we've got the engine and genny fired up it is misty and when we untie it's a genuine grade one pea souper. To get away from our mooring we have to shuffle sideways, reverse in a gentle parabola through an avenue of moored boats and spin through 180 degrees - a bit like the Jolly Green Giant on Come Dancing. I can't forget that the last time we traversed a similar avenue I trashed someone's tiller - and that was going forward in perfect light - so my apprehension is matched only by a wish that I'd had less of Shiraz the previous evening. The fact that I'd left my distance glasses in the bedroom was irrelevant as we could barely see two boat lengths.

When we got to the end of the 'arm' (down which the town of Zwartsluis, our boatyard and numerous moorings are located) we had to join a large commercial canal for a short distance. At the 'T' junction the skipper was standing point and the fog was so thick that I, steering, couldn't even see the opposite bank. It didn't help that we weren't exactly sure where the entrance to the boatyard was and we were mighty glad that there were no

1000-tonners passing at that moment. The off-shoot leading to the yard is the width of three and two-thirds commercial barges – and there were 3 moored abreast. This meant we had about 2 feet either side while inching down what we hoped was the right hole. Then because there was a barge moored bow-on facing us we had to negotiate a chicane to enter a basin with a large slipway to starboard that was full of boats. There was no sign of human life whatsoever. We moored against an old working barge and within the office block I found 20 employees in a smoke-filled room 'at coffee'. Very important to the Dutch are coffee-breaks, everything stops officially at least twice a day. Of course, just after we moored up the sun came out.

Later in the day they had taken the boat up on the slip and we were called for an inspection. I was worried about this because around the waterline and tiller the paint looked had looked very tatty for some time. Our boat was at the bottom of the slipway down the slope from a number of giants and the only way to get to it was to stoop and crab beneath these other boats – a bit creepy really as the upper ones were sitting on an assortment of steel frames and lumps of old timber. There was a native prodding the hull and jabbering to a colleague but gratifyingly he switched language and told us our paint was in excellent nick and a good coat of primer and 'industrial' topcoat would be plenty – much later we were to find they were wrong.

While our boat was up in the air we stayed on our friends Broom (boat). They'd brought it over from England the previous year and our friend Pat was not best pleased when I'd suggested that she'd travelled over the North Sea on her broom. The boat has not been lived on throughout the winter so 'needed an airing' as the central heating had been drained. Heat was supplied by an oil-filed radiator supplemented by the hot exhaust blasted against the hull from next door's central heating boiler. Truly grateful as we were for their generosity we were glad when, three days later, we got a call that our boat was ready. Thankfully the fog had long gone - thanklessly it had been replaced by squally showers with 30 mph gusts which, for an amateur skipper, was rather worrying! They had taken it off the slip and moored it in a cul-de-sac full of sparking, hissing welders who were attaching small rusty steel bits to much larger rusty steel bits. The wind was whistling, pinning us to the same barge we'd moored next to a few days earlier – consequently getting out was a bit of an ordeal. The whining wind and whitecaps reminded me of Blackpool in November and it was my first taste of handling the barge in a strong wind. Had we not had to shift it I would have left it where it was till things calmed down. With a lot of revving and some appalling language we extricated ourselves from our hole and got her back home without hitting anything much to the disappointment of the hordes of repairmen, carpenters and painters lining our route waiting for a lucrative disaster.

Whoever had programmed us two such tricky days had a cruel sense of humour, not unlike the person who thought to put an 'S' in the word lisp, but despite the challenge we made it back thafe and thound.

There is a well-known saying in the Netherlands, 'God created the world but The Dutch created Holland', and we saw this first-hand on a visit to the fishing port of Urk. The town used to be an island in the salt-water Zuider Zee (South Sea) until the Afsluitdijk was completed in 1932 creating the fresh-water Ijsselmeer – so Urk became an island on a fresh-water lake. But still they weren't finished mucking around with it as, in 1939, another dyke was built in effect running through Urk north / south. Gradually the water was drained inland of the dyke creating a polder (reclaimed land). Currently therefore Urk is a town on the shores of the Ijsselmeer. It has every right to have an identity crisis but, though not a large port, it is frequented by big commercial vessels plying their trade within the Ijsselmeer and beyond. Also, a fishing fleet, inland waterway boats of all shapes and size, yachts and a variety tugs and service vessels needed to look after all the moorers and visitors. Because all the shops were shut for lunch we took to a second-floor restaurant overlooking the port. We ate a fish soup made with a healthy variety of the local marine-life and watched a large barge setting off into the mist of the blustery Ijsselmeer.

The canal running through the new inland polder is about four metres below the level of the Ijsselmeer. The land is criss-crossed with drainage channels and is as flat as it gets – except that is for Schokland which used to be a small island in the sea but is now a small island in the middle of a field. It comes complete with wharf and mooring bollards which although useless for the purpose intended, give a fascinating glimpse of yesteryear.

I hitched a ride with American Joe and wife Emmy on what may well be their last boat trip ever before returning home to start farming goats. Joe has been boating all his life and on this frosty but bright sunny morning I find it hard to imagine him just giving it all up. I'm amazed he's got this far actually because his deck is gloss painted and like a convex ice rink. They are really finishing in style - boat in a paint shed and them in a caravan in a car park for a week. If they'd have thought to position the caravan anywhere except behind the toilet block at least they'd have had a view. He told me that, by tradition, when he returns to the west coast of America he will walk inland with an oar over his shoulder. When he gets to the point where people no longer recognize what an oar is, he will set up home. I never did find out what prompted him to want to farm goats.

I bid them farewell and start walking back with an ever-developing headache so I call in at the petrol station for water and Paracetamol. Each tablet is individually packed in a bomb-proof plastic wrapper so I have walked a full kilometre before I've got one open; but it looks a little unusual so I check the box - 'FOR AGE 1 – 3 YEARS. RECTAL APPLICATION ONLY'. Even if I'd been closer to the age range, dropping one's trousers on top of a dyke close to a bus route is asking for trouble. With furrowed brow I returned the unsuitable item to the garage where I received a snorting chortle from the lady in the shop – a tale she will no doubt relate at her clog renovating class.

So, the bottom of the boat looks half decent - good job it's not visible because it would put the rest of it to shame, at least till we have chance to get to work with our orbital hacker and a paint brush. There's about six acres of paintwork to have a go at, including some unpleasant rust-coloured patches, but the weather is not suitable so it's time to have a go at servicing the smelly, oily bits - after I've replaced yet another an air-release valve on the central-heating boiler that's just started leaking. I have to say that the valve was past its best and a little crusty looking but I was still surprised when the man in the plumbers merchant asked me where I'd dug it up. Perhaps if I'd laughed at his little witty he wouldn't have charged me over thirty Euros for a few bent bits of copper and a new valve with a red plastic bit on top. I've postponed the engine service for a day or two – I've just got clean for the first time in weeks.

We have had house guests, namely Jan's daughter and boyfriend - hair dryer, hair straighteners, high heels et al. – and she's just as bad. They are the first people to test out our new bunk beds and even if they did get back on the train looking like they'd been laying concrete for three days, I'm sure they'll soon be back to normal. Mind you, it's a definite improvement on the narrowboat for Carly where she slept on the floor in the lounge on a leaky inflatable mattress next to a snoring dog.

When you are renovating a boat most of the work is done behind the scenes where you never see it - plumbing, wiring, insulation etc. etc. I'm used to people coming on board and admiring Jan's paintings and even she now has the grace to look sheepish because, without the wall to hang it on, there wouldn't be any artwork. It's true though that without finishing touches the whole is dragged down - a room without a carpet is like a bridegroom wearing wellies. So, to get round this conundrum I've decided to leave the wheelhouse a mess. After all, its unique, there are not many places where you have to wipe your feet before you leave – and it's a talking point, and a future project. We all need a project.

Snert

We took a cruise to Bird Island. Sounds romantic doesn't it – conjuring up images of a tropical Pacific atoll or stormy crags off Western Scotland. Well, it's not. This one was a low-lying blob of land in the middle of a lake over-run by stunted trees and nettles. As we passed there was a group of environmental hob-knobs, most of whom looked to have overdone the facial hair-restorer, crowded under a scruffy awning releasing balloons – guaranteed to deter even the most self-respecting avian. In high summer it is (allegedly) a haven for twitcher tourists and their quarry. Perhaps we'll return – perhaps not.

However, it was good to be out on the water. There's not too much traffic about yet because the weather is still chilly and many boats have only recently been craned back into the water from their winter hard-standings, but there are stirrings. Intermittent clouds of diesel smoke from dormant engines waft over the region like isolated thunderheads and the boat yards are busy repairing bits that have not wintered well. The large charter barges known as the 'Brown Fleet' are over-painting winter's ravages and making their first forays out to the lakes with groups of muffled up adventurers.

Prior to our big 'off', we have been making final preparations. Well, when I say final, nothing really ever is final when dealing with a temperamental old boat; it's really a case of trying to avoid having to call out the AA (in fact either AA!), but when we leave I want to be sure we've done all we can. We have been waiting for a couple of major jobs to be done, shuffling about the diesel tanks and installing an alternator upgrade, but unfortunately there's been 'trubble ut mill'. The head mechanic has gone off in a huff after a barney with the boat-yard owner and number two mechanic has taken another job which is well-paid including business class flights to his various places of work. Sounds fabulous, except his first assignment was repairing a huge diesel engine in Siberia. Last I heard he was reviewing the situation. Mind you even Siberia is probably a step up from scrabbling around with my old generator. Anyhow, as a consequence the yard is now very short-handed because the hire fleet needs regular nurturing and the only way for us to get the jobs done is to do them ourselves under instruction from Klass. He has been very fair by showing me how to do things then monitoring my stuttering progress. Of course, we save a fair amount of money in labour and I have tackled things I would never previously dreamt of doing but most importantly I am discovering much more about the workings of the boat. I've also learned how much filth you can be covered in and still be recognisable as human and how much skin you can scrape from various parts of your body falling out. But we've just about done it - with some assistance.

The English fraternity here (now four couples after a recent arrival) help each other and Peter Dresser has been a huge help. He's a slim man and amazingly fit for his sixty-eight years and he spent over five hours crunched up at the front of our engine helping me fit the alternator. According to a Dutch friend this helping-your-neighbour concept is alien to them. If you point out your problem to a Dutchman hoping for assistance he'll just agree that yes, indeed you do have a problem, then disappears for a cup of coffee.

The boater's psyche is often geared to social opportunity and so it was with the arrival of the aforementioned English crew. A welcoming get-together was organised at which a healthy quantity of nondescript local ale was consumed. There was another cause for celebration because one person, who for obvious reason shall remain anonymous, reached nirvana when for the first time since procuring his new teeth they actually worked in perfect syncopation with his jaw. It took an unseemly quantity of alcohol but proved beyond doubt that the new gnashers were indeed a beneficial investment. As we are setting off imminently no doubt another 'meeting of the committee' will be convened to 'bid us farewell' (or some such words).

One piece of kit we have invested in is a GPS Chart Plotter. It will show us precisely where we are, where we are going and the exact position where we ran into something. Due to its amazing technology, it can show you an overview of the whole of Europe or focus right down to an individual pontoon. A flashing symbol marks our position on the map and when I zoom in it shows our barge moored in the car park exactly where we used to park our car before we sold it.

If we actually needed one, we had a reminder yesterday of the potential dangers of boating. A 57-year-old London man was reportedly washing off his boat while moored on a pontoon adjacent to a barely moving river. His wife, who was inside the boat at the time, heard a splash but thought nothing of it until she went outside and noticed her husband's shoes in the water. He had fallen between the boat and the pontoon it appears that he had been dragged beneath the boat, presumably by the current. He was in very cold water for about 12 minutes, much of it actually trapped underwater, before someone hauled him out and he was given emergency first aid by an ambulance crew. They got a pulse and he was rushed to Hospital in nearby Zwolle but sadly he later died while in intensive care. A truly terrible episode and one that has made all boaters here pause.

Even the experts get it wrong sometimes. After recent heavy rain there was quite a flow through a nearby sluice-lock. A 100m barge judged passage to be possible despite three red triangulated lights which serve as an advisory warning of strong current. As he progressed through the sluice he struggled more and more until eventually coming to a complete stop. His huge engines were at full revs, so much so that the stern of the boat was dragged down and you could hear it bouncing on the cill about three metres below the surface. I suspect the majority of us have gone through a bridge hole on a narrow canal and have witnessed the water rushing by as it is sucked below and around the boat. Well, this barge was fully laden with gravel and over 1000 tonnes so the torrent of water was enormous. He had struggled for over half-an-hour and would have already used about 100 litres of diesel to go nowhere when he eventually gave up. He reduced power and allowed the boat to be 'washed' back through the sluice to a point where he could moor and wait for the flow of water to subside.

But we also have constant reminders of why we love the waterways so much and recently we had another. I was leaning out of the wheelhouse door enjoying a glass of red. It was well after sunset and a crisp, clear night with a bright moon. A small skein of geese flew close and low and the moonlight, reflecting off the still water, under-lit the birds making their reflections look like ghostly, silver shadows. It was so still that we could hear the gentle whoosh of their wings as they passed. This in contrast to the family of long-eared owls who live nearby and silently patrol the area each evening.

We visited the small town of Guithorn known as the Venice of Holland. This was partly my attempt to re-build my points tally with the skipper after a slight how-do-you-do. The special birthday trip I'd promised her the day before the car was sold was a jaunt to the local rubbish tip. To compound the felony all the shops were shut for some local festival so I was in the doghouse. I'm not sure it worked but I tried to convince her that had I not messed up her birthday so disastrously we wouldn't have visited Guithorn, a beautiful little town criss-crossed by tiny canals over which lovely little wooden bridges served thatched houses, some of which are inaccessible by any other route. Many of the small boats are owned by cafés and restaurants and used to ferry punters from outlying carparks. Outside one of these establishments was an A-board advertising something with the unappealing name of Snert. Snert in this context was not referring to the internet acronym Sexually Nerdish Expressively Recidivistic Troll nor Hagar the Horrible's dog, no, here it is pea soup - an industrial winter brew in which you can stand your boat pole, often filled with sausage and lumps of pork – very tasty too.

Another creation of mine is a raised steering platform in the wheelhouse. We could barely see over the dashboard nor see the bow which was hidden below the bedroom roof so I had to raise the floor somewhat - after all we like to see what we're running into. During testing the first platform spun round on the uneven floor so I found myself facing backwards - ideal to view the trail of devastation in our wake but worrying for anyone approaching from the front. The skipper suggested that I re-position the rear-view mirror at the back of the wheelhouse so we could see forward while looking backwards. Perch-prototype two is better, even if we do keep tripping over it.

During our re-hash we've put in a lot of work and learned a huge amount about the boat works. We hope she'll be good to us on our journey when we set off to explore new waterways and new countries. We're not sure if we'll come back here to Zwartsluis next winter. We know there is space if we want it and we know that the good friends we've made will give us a warm welcome, but the world is a big place. Despite the obvious shortcoming of being a little flat, we have come to consider the town and area home and never once have we felt threatened. We've had culture differences, like when the skipper asked for a pot of tea and got a teapot the size of a mop bucket with one teabag in it - but we have overcome the hitches, generally with a degree of humour.

When we started messing about with narrowboats a number of years ago we knew next to nothing. A calorifier might well have been a device to measure how fat you are and a tumblehome was something you did after a night out but now we're wiser, much wiser - just a pity we can't remember most of it.

From the hound of Vrouwe Johanna

I'm even more perplexed than usual. They got all excited preparing for a trip. Ropes off, electricity cut, lights on, water in – then went about 300 yards in the fog to a filthy boatyard. What the……

Then we have to go and live in a plastic box for three days – with no proper heating. I just wish they'd explain things. Why didn't they book me into the B & B for a couple of nights?

I like the natives but they do surprise me sometimes. Like why they would build a boat dock, with bollards and everything, in the middle of a field – I mean it's all very pretty, but for such a practical bunch they don't half make some daft mistakes. The owners must have been mighty disappointed when no boats turned up.

And then, just when I was about to abscond – folk from the real world turn up! What a joy to see Carly and Richard – but I'm sure they were a mystified as me regarding our 'primitive' living conditions. More importantly it was a great relief to find out that, in a land far away, there still exists a race with at least a shred of common sense.

Another peculiar habit they have is drinking expensive red water. Dad and his mates think that the more they drink the funnier they get. Seems to me that they tell the same stories at least three times a night and find it more hilarious each time. If I hear one more Monty Python sketch.....

I mean, for goodness sake, what's so funny about a dead pirate????

I'm retiring early.

Love, Bonny

Trial Trip

When our friends Peter and Pam (twenty-year veterans of the Dutch waterways) asked if they could come for a ride on the boat we jumped at the chance. They suggested a four-hour return trip to nearby Hasselt, I suggested a four-day trip that took in the odd lock and bridge – and a little local V.H.F. procedure and where to root out free moorings and...... well, you get the picture. Any morsel of knowledge gleaned from this pair would be invaluable so off we set for our first multi-day trip.

We left in a general hail of indifference except for a few good friends and the boat-yard staff who clapped and cheered and waited for a cock-up. More by luck than judgement we extricated ourselves from our rickety pontoon and set off a little unsteadily. I felt a bit like a learner driver whose clutch-control is minimal as the car hops along. The biggest problem was that it was blowing a force five, gusting six, and although the harbour was sheltered, it was as we got onto open water that the tussle began. It's a little like driving a car over a frozen lake. When the boat is blown sideways you have to correct it by steering into the slide and wait an eternity for anything to happen. As soon as you begin heading for something like the right track you have to anticipate where the boat will end up after it has finished slipping and re-adjust accordingly. Going in a straight line with a strong wind directly from the side requires steering into the wind and crabbing along at an angle to keep on track. Now this is OK when you're on wide water with nothing else around but when you come upon a 1000-tonne opponent crabbing towards you in the same manner maximum concentration is required – believing in some deity also helps. There are at least three ways to counteract the effects of a crosswind, a keel, leeboards or stay at home - none of these were possible so we battled on.

The wind is so gusty in Meppel, where we stop for diesel, that when I cycle into town I have to get off and walk. Mooring up next to the bunker barge was a right old palaver. We had to swing through 180 degrees turning across the wind but as we approached there were two big commercial barges jockeying for position against a loading dock immediately opposite the barge. In addition, there were two cruisers right behind us and one coming the other way. There was some juggling of rudder and engine, a lot of language and a bumpy landing all for the pleasure of paying for enough diesel to one-third fill the tanks – cash equivalent of a respectable second-hand car.

Soon we approach our first lock. To be frank there aren't that many because the country is so flat. Even though we did up to a thousand in a season in the UK, the first new anything can make you a bit nervous. But we remind ourselves, if we're nervous, we're alive. We have to cope with the traffic-light sequence that we'd learned from a book but it's rather disconcerting for real when the wind is rattling you about. The road barriers come down to temporarily halt progress in 'the real world' before a bunch of foreigners, mishandling part of the frustrated motorist's heritage, trundle through and into the lock. I'm sure there will be sterner tests - we were the only boat in the lock and it fell all of about eight inches.

Next job was to find a mooring then coast into it without trashing anything. Peter knew of a spot an hour further on and it turned out to be perfect for novices with a dog. It was in a small lake just off the main waterway. There were three wooden jetties running parallel to a short peninsula that ran out into the lake – and only one other boat - surely we couldn't run into that! Deciding to celebrate with a cuppa, we hadn't even got the kettle warm when we ran out of gas. Great planning - no spare, so it was time to test the electrical upgrades. We had microwave, kettle, slow cooker and Remoska running through the inverter (two items at a time so as not to blow the roof off the batteries) - just the problem now of replacing the juice in the batteries, which hopefully we'd do through our new alternator while cruising the following day.

We're now off the commercial canals and its mid-April so this year's hire-boats are starting to hatch. Because we potter along at a stately 6 kph. we are passed by just about everything that's not moored up. The wind has eased to a 4 but it is still gusty and even though the cruisers that go past are smaller than us we are pushed towards the bank as they approach and sucked back as they pass meaning we weave a drunken course. As seems to be the case in the UK, the hire boats pass anything of interest at the greatest possible speed in order to get back to base on schedule.

Another first is an automatic lift-bridge activated by the breaking of an electronic beam on approach. The beam is roughly fifty metres short of the bridge and when broken a dot-matrix display next to the bridge tells us (presumably.... it's in Dutch) that the system has been set in motion. Of course, we are now going really slowly (our boat takes a distance to stop) so we have to hover, which in a cross wind is not so easy, then wait for the road barriers to drop, then wait for the lights to go from red (stop) to red / green (prepare to move) to green (go). Usually between midday and 1.00 pm everything stops for lunch so the lights are on double red – yes, even a fully automated bridge has a lunch break! Presumably there is someone in a shed somewhere watching remotely on telly.

Our second night is spent adjacent to a National Park called Weerribben which is a system of waterways and woodlands fashioned from former peat diggings. It is so peaceful and I see my first curlews and a pair of deer come out of the trees for supper. The fisherman I approach obviously likes his privacy too as I was greeted with a grunt as he focussed on his float. I was only going to tell him that his coat was trailing in his maggot bucket and his bait was crawling up into his pocket, but he would find out soon enough. This is also reed-cutting territory. It is cut for thatch roofs, of which there are many throughout Holland. It is harvested towards the end of the winter into early spring and stored in sheaves to dry. The night we stay they are burning off stubble and palls of smoke drift over the woodland in the evening sun and we can see isolated fires in the distance as night falls. The wind has dropped away now (as it often does in the late evening), there is a faint smell of smoke, the nightlife is chattering and we have a wonderful snapshot of this part of rural Holland.

Our barge is reasonably well equipped and we have most mod cons. Peter and Pam regale us of stories of their boating over the years. Particularly the early days when the kids were young and money was so tight as to be nearly non-existent. They used to wash dishes and clothes in canal water and light the fire only when wood was available – which was only sometimes. Pam tells me that one freezing morning they woke to the desperate screams. Chris, their son, was trapped because his hair had frozen to the window.

I cycled a couple of kilometres into the village of Ossenzijl for supplies which included a large bag of potatoes. I had to cross automatic bridge and, as there was a boat approaching, I put a spurt on. A local lady, alerted by my wheezing and my bicycle's rattling, turned to investigate just as my potato bag burst. Much to her obvious amusement I chased my bobbling spuds down the road and by the time I'd retrieved them the barriers were down. The lady alerted her neighbours and they muttered and smirked as an idiotic Englishman wobbled away with potatoes stuffed in every pocket and down his shirt-front.

We motored through a delightful little town called Kalenberg, delightful to look at but not to steer through as it was rather narrow with a series of right-angled bends. Boats, not built to withstand the attention of something large and heavy, lined the waterway and we met too many others coming the other way for comfort. Progress was sedentary at best. And half-way through, another first – a clog bridge. At various locations you have to pay for passage through a bridge. As you pass, the operator passes down a clog on a string on a pole into which you must place your fare. Presumably if you refuse or miss you get clonked round the ear with a wooden shoe.

The final town on this trip was Blokzijl (pronounced 'block-sile') and here we negotiate a town-centre lock watched by an assortment of locals and sightseers. We shared the lock with another boat, unusual because it was a little rowing boat and the single-handed owner asked us if he was going the right way for Amsterdam. Now that is a trip that we, in a decent sized boat, would plan for and worry about but in a twelve-foot wooden boat with only a pac-a-mac and a box of cheese sandwiches for company....well, he was intrepid if nothing else. He did have a small mast and sail for when the wind was favourable but he was certainly doing it on a budget.

A couple of hours down the way we moored, again for free, in the middle of nowhere. For company we had two boats - a lovely cruiser housing a smashing Dutch couple and something that looked like a shed. The proprietor of the shed had taken on board about three dozen too many lagers and when he came to join us for a mutter he spilt more down his front than he swallowed, probably a good job. He realised he was pickled and later came to apologise. He knocked on the door and presented Jan with a rather withered collection of weeds he'd picked specially to offer in supplication. Three hours after we had moored our intrepid rower powered past in the gloom.

So ended our first real excursion which gave us a real buzz. I have one or two jobs to tackle (servicing the injectors on the generator and installing a battery monitor) then we're off on our own. Tally eau!

Friesland

Jobs done, we're off. A friend, Baz, has hitched a lift to the first lock from where he'll cycle back. He wants to see how his new rattling, squeaking bike handles. Quite why he can't start from his own boat is a puzzle – just curious about how our boat handles probably. He bids us bon voyage at the lock and sets off homeward sounding like a load of badly oiled nuts and bolts bobbling about in a tin can. Our last tie with the old homestead is severed and away we go. One of the things we are wary of is not being able to find a mooring so we stop on the first public one we come across. It is 200 yards from the lock where Baz got off, next to a busy main road and almost within shouting distance of our home port but we bring the beast to a halt and tie up successfully employing a bewildering assortment of knots. We've done OK today and don't want to spoil a perfect score so this will do nicely.

Our initial destination is Friesland, one of the Netherlands twelve provinces, situated in the north-west corner. The Romans were apparently the first 'tourists' here over 2000 years ago and according to the tourist atlas we picked up 'they were impressed; I am sure you will be too!' To get there we initially travel the same route as our trial run with Peter and Pam and the familiar ground is reassuring in fact for our second night we moor up with a few yards of the previous occasion at Weerribben. There are roughly a kilometre of moorings and ours is the solitary boat – perhaps they knew we were coming.

To gain access to Friesland from this angle you have to go through a lock that one of our friends termed 'ferocious' so it is with apprehension we break new ground and approach our nemesis. The lock rises all of twelve inches and it's virtually impossible to detect any movement. Either someone's winding us up or they've got the wrong location. This lock is 'the gateway to Friesland' and it does begin to get noticeably busier. Without knowing much about the rest of Holland, I'd liken Friesland to our Lake District – without hills. All the lakes are interconnected by a myriad of waterways, though some are not suitable for us due to bridge height restrictions. Hire-boating is big business and there are many firms all over the province renting out motorboats, sailing boats and sloops. Add to this sailing schools (they sail the canals as well as lakes), the vast variety of private boats and the odd magnificent sailing charter ship from the 'brown fleet' and I can imagine that the place is chaos in high summer. Germany is only a couple of hours by road so the overwhelming majority of visiting boaters are German and many boats fly the black, red and yellow flag.

Weekends are particularly busy when flotillas of sailing dinghies can be seen at most points of the compass over the flat landscape. We are under 20 metres long so are classed as a 'small ship' and as such have priority over absolutely nobody. If we 'matchstick' a dinghy basically we're responsible – we have to give way. Naturally they don't want to be trashed and we watch each other keenly but if it came to the crunch we wouldn't have a deck to stand on – much like cars with cyclists. So, if you want to live long and prosper in Holland ride a bike and sail a dinghy at weekends.

There are plenty of free moorings, many with neatly mown grass with bollards, stakes or rings to tie to. They do vary though, some are isolated wooden pontoons anchored a few yards from the bank adjacent to reed beds (so no good for dog access), others are pontoons with a walkway to the bank and some are actually on the bank itself. These are plentiful but if you're going to moor for a day or two you need to stock-up with everything as there is rarely access to the outside world. There are no services (electricity and water) but many have rubbish disposal bins available. Many of the free moorings are provided by an organisation called Marrekrite (unique to Friesland) and their moorings are distinguished by a small blue sign set on a pole. They produce a basic map with hundreds of red dots depicting their sites with detailed regulations about how to behave – ours sadly was in German which is one of the vast majority of languages not in our repertoire. To join the 'Marrekrite club' we buy a small rectangular flag costing eight Euros (although this is entirely discretionary, it's just the done thing) which flaps proudly below our courtesy Dutch flag on our mast. The Marrekrite flags are a different colour each year to thwart the 'thrifty'.

The other two mooring options are either to drop anchor in a lake (which we've not tried to date because the anchor winch seized up in about 1940) or go into one of the many towns and villages. These you generally have to pay for at an average rate of about one Euro per metre per night (although many seem to have a sixteen Euro maximum). At the best one's electricity, showers, launderette, water and rubbish disposal are included. Occasionally you have to pay for the extras on top. These urban off-shoots can be rather narrow and twisty so you have to be careful, especially as there are invariably boats moored on either side and be doubly cautious when it's windy. Because you can't see what's ahead round the twists and turns you might not even find a mooring and some of the turning opportunities are a bit tight.

Because weekends are busy we have got into the habit of mooring up on Friday afternoon and staying put for a couple of days. Thus, one Friday we found a perfect freebie a few kilometres from the town of Lemmer. It was hot, flora spring juices were flowing and thousands of friendly, flying beasties came to pay a visit. On the first evening we had the company of a couple of German boats. Conversation over the twenty-four-hour period was a bit limited but I did glean that the two gentlemen were called Goot Morgan and Alf Viedersen. They were replaced on the second evening by a large cruiser whose inmates set up a large BBQ and yelled cheers at one another as they popped beers. Although I recognised the drinking toast, any chat was again limited as it transpired that they were Russian. They were all male, topless, lean and heavily muscled; they looked like a Special Forces unit out on a jaunt but they were friendly enough in a waving, bottle-raising kind of way.

The dog nipped over and did a major whoopsy uncomfortably close to their BBQ so it was left to Jan to dash over with a shovel and prevent an international incident.

We have four different types of map including the 'sat-nav' so when we travel we formulate a daily route-plan. To date not one single plan has been completed for one reason or another – here is one example. We decided to visit the town of Sloten (spelt Sleat in the unique Friesian language) to have a look round and do some shopping, before continuing a few kilometres to another mooring. But this was 'pinksterdag' (whit Monday) when the whole of Holland takes a day off and apparently comes to Sloten. The place is absolute bedlam - hundreds of boats, thousands of visitors and because it's Monday, the shops are shut! The canal route through the town is through a lifting bridge that carries the main (and only) road across the waterway. Not only is there a bottleneck of boats waiting for the bridge in either direction, the bridge itself is being used for an event known as the Elfstedentocht (officially the eleven cities skating race where competitors skate almost 200 kilometres on frozen canals between eleven 'cities'). Climate change means that the canals are freezing less frequently but there are alternative ways to complete this challenge and it was two of these that we became entangled with. We arrived in the morning and moored a few hundred metres short of the town. I cycled in to assess the situation and nearly drowned in a sea of people all trying to catch sight of some four-thousand five-hundred motorcycles taking part in their version of the Elfstedentocht, all squeezing their way over the single bridge. The cacophony from bikes of all size and vintage was extraordinary - as was the racket from natives of all shape and size who cheered them on while drinking beer or slurping ice-cream. It looked like it was some people's first exposure to the sunshine this year so puce was a popular skin colour – perhaps that's why they call it pinksterdag. The bikes eventually passed through en route to shatter the peace of their next 'city', Stavoren, out on the coast.

   Periodically the bridge was raised to let through a flotilla of boats from each side as the motorcycles piled up waiting for passage over the canal like a swarm of angry hornets – we judged it prudent to stay well out of the way till things had calmed down after lunch. Between noon and one-o-clock everything grinds to a halt on the waterways allowing the bridge operators chance to regain their patience so we aimed to set off a little after one when the post-lunch rush had subsided – mmm! Early afternoon saw the arrival of the second string of 'eleven city challengers' - the cyclists – all twelve-and-a-half thousand of them! I cycle back into town again to see what all the fuss is about. Twelve-stone (plus) of fairly unfit, indifferently attired, portly Englishman sat on his ancient 'bone-shaker' watching some of the throng pass through before it all got a bit tiring and I retired to a café for a restorative. Talking to the lady who ran the establishment, she told me that people come from all over the Netherlands (in addition to Germany and Belgium) to take part and a few have competed between fifty-five and sixty times and yes, 'it's always a bit busy round here when the weather is good' – which today it is. I speak to a competitor, a perspiring, wobbly-legged chap standing under a tree having a much needed drink, who tells me he has sixty-one kilometres to go. He looks pretty healthy considering he's already cycled about one hundred and forty. Sloten is a lovely old town and the support for this age-old marathon merely re-confirms the Dutch love of their traditional events. The only thing that reminds me of home is the smell of chips wafting from a mobile chippy which has set up in the main car park to tempt those less inclined to physical exertion.

Competitors are still piling through towards the checkpoint where they have their card stamped (as they do at each of the eleven cities as proof that they have completed the course) as I return to the boat – exhausted. The route I must take means that I have to cycle alongside the 'real cyclists' for a couple of hundred metres receiving some odd looks from the crowds lining the route as I rattle past. I was very fortunate to avoid total embarrassment because a hundred metres after I had left the crowds behind the chain came off my bicycle creating a fearful racket as the chain rattled around inside the plastic chain guard – now if that had happened among the beautiful people on their beautiful cycles in front of the cheering masses .... These days the Elfstedentocht is also tackled by luxury cabin cruisers on the water, scooters, vintage cars and on foot although it is believed that the eleven cities were probably first skated in the sixteenth century.

One day later peace returns and we set off again. Because of the unexpected, nothing is going to plan. We decide henceforth formulate our route plans at the end of the day as opposed to the beginning.

From the hound of Vrouwe Johanna

At last! Open country and a change of scenery. Had enough of that boatyard for a while. Don't get me wrong, they're nice people but even dumbo here knows the idea of a boat is to actually move. They might as well have bought a shed (actually it is a bit of a shed but don't tell them).

Almost the last straw was when they watched a football match in the workshop! Yes, you hear me right. We haven't got a telly yet. But our friends have. Problem was that our friend's boat was in the boatyard's shed having some painting done. So, they set up the TV and an old sofa, borrowed from the office, in the shed. A lead snaked out of the door to an aerial clamped to a skip and there they were, a bunch of morons, sitting on a sofa on the floor of the workshop, drinking revolting supermarket beer, watching the European Football Championships. If only they could have seen themselves yelling at the England team on telly in a shed! I ask you. And they lost! Jeepers.

Anyhow, that lunatic episode behind us, we actually set off – and what a joy to have someone with us who actually knew what they were talking about. I was beginning to think this country they'd come to was only three-hundred metres square but as it turns out it's quite big – and interesting. So much so that other people speaking strange languages (in addition to the local one) come and boat here too. We were in a bit of danger from one tough-looking bunch when I..., well you know about that don't you – let's just say I lost concentration for a moment.

Now they really have stocked up with tins of things (some of them they will have recognised while others will be a mystery I'm sure) so I have a feeling the latest departure will lead to a somewhat protracted escapade. Mind you the first day's cruising was a bit conservative – Dad walks me further than that in a morning! In fact, we went such a short distance it was almost unnecessary to unplug the electricity lead!

Good job the exhaust isn't at the front or we'd never see where we're going!

Bye for now, Bonny

Lakes and Isles

The Fries bank holiday has come and gone so we return to our meanderings heading in the vague direction of Ijlst. It always 'focuses the concentration' when we see narrow channels combined with tight turns. Although the maps give you some indication, there is really no way of predicting the exact nature of what you will encounter till you get there – by which time it's usually too late to do much about it. Not only was Ijlst rather narrow and twisty it also had the added bonus of no available moorings so we had to go and turn round in a basin and retrace our steps.

We arrive in Bolsward where we made our first navigational cock-up. Our intention was to pass through and join another canal that would take us north. Bridge details are highlighted on the maps; information includes height, width and depth and these details are preceded by the letters 'BB' if the bridge is one that opens. Due to a map-reading mishap most of the bridges on our proposed route would have demolished our wheelhouse and it was an insistent, yet patient, local who pointed out our error so we had to turn round again and moor in the town basin. But a very pleasant and restful town mooring it was, soured slightly by the steely-eyed rent-collector who relieved us of 18 Euros for the night - but that did include all facilities including electricity.

Here we meet our first English couple. A large red barge creeps into town in the early evening crewed by Chris and June. Desperate for English company we dashed round and shared a couple of bottles of something appropriate while discussing the renovation of their barge and browsed our respective cock-up catalogues.

Bolsward is home to Sonnma beerenberg (same name but different brand to the brew that made me miss a morning a few months ago). It's a strong spirit basically flavoured by steeping 71 different herbs in gin for twenty-four hours. It is popular particularly in Friesland and is equally adept at staining carpets with indelible brown blobs and removing old paint. Actually, it is an acquired taste which I seem to have acquired, much to the delight of the head-ache tablet manufacturers.

It was on our way to the coastal town of Makkum that I first noticed the smell of hot rubber and after mooring up I noticed an ingress of water coming from the back end. Now, even I know that these two phenomena are unlikely to be linked but, for obvious reasons, the water leak had to tackled with some urgency. It transpired that the stern gland was weeping. Makkum is one of many places where the inland waterway meets the Ijsselmeer. It is a small enough town to make the transition very evident and if you pass through the lock you join sea-going craft. Before we saw all this we had actually to get into the place which was quite tricky. Once again a stiff breeze was our problem constantly blowing us towards a line of moored sailing tjalks as we negotiated a double 'S' bend. As we entered the harbour the bow-thruster packed up, probably due to over-enthusiastic application. Fortunately, we were close to an empty mooring to scramble to shore. I bought a suction pump from the superb little chandlery, sucked up some revolting grease-laden sludge from below the engine and sorted out our leak but still couldn't identify the source of the rubbery smell.

We didn't take the boat through the lock but cycled down to look. Landward of the lock is the familiarity of an inland harbour but to 'seaward' the transition is immediately obvious as a small fleet of fishing boats are readying nets for their next trip onto the Ijsselmeer; some nets are being repaired while others refract the sun as they hang from davits to dry in the wind. Moored to a nearby wooden jetty are a couple of large sailing klippers of the charter fleet which creak in the breeze awaiting their next customers. Makkum is close to the north-west shore of the Ijsselmeer over which it is a short trip to the Waddenzee and the world beyond. Access from Makkum's outer harbour to the lake is via a long channel down which there are boat-oriented businesses such as sailmakers and boat builders and near the channel mouth a huge yacht harbour housing some very expensive beasts. The air is fresh and clear and from a personal point of view it is a wonderful place and our favourite so far.

Opposite our mooring one tetchy local was taking an evening beer under his patio awning. With ever increasing vigour he would give the canvas a good stab with a yard brush to rid himself of visiting pigeons, pesky blighters that would alight and poop on his patio table. By the time he reached his third beer he was stabbing the awning with such vigour that he was in danger of trashing it altogether and in response to my cheery wave he snatched up his empties and stormed off into the house.

Direct channels across the lakes, some of which are quite large, are depicted by lines of green and red buoys but it is quite in order to set off at an angle towards a bunch of trees or reeds where you find the quiet island moorings. Our first such stop-over is on an island on a lake called Grote (big) Gaastmeer. As we approach it is not immediately evident where we can stop but we see a narrow channel between two small islands either side of which are well-tended moorings. Our island was notable not only for the marsh harrier that we watched for hours hunting in the reeds but also for the three sailing dinghies that pulled in nearby. Six German sailors alighted in pairs and trudged off into the undergrowth men to the left, women to the right. It was soon obvious that their brief stop was of purely a lavatorial nature as they returned to their dinghies with relieved looks re-fastening various bits of yachty clothing - the nautical equivalent of the splash and dash. Or launch and launch. The tranquillity of these island moorings is heavenly and as the chatter and twitter of the birds gradually dies away we are left with the rustle of the reeds, then, as the wind dies, total silence.

Insect management is important, particularly out in the countryside. Because the waterways are invariably bordered by reed-beds, trees or farmland flying things can become a nuisance. No, let's be honest, if you leave an unscreened door or window open in the evening you're in danger of losing sight of your aperitif. It's safer when the wind gets up (which it regularly does) when you can sit in relative comfort as air-borne beasts (of a goodly variety of design) are blown past like a swarm of buzzing rifle bullets. They have also gleaned some evolutionary benefit from their battle with man and have become worthy opponents. They dance gaily around our blue-lighted 'insectocutor' then replenish their energy by feeding on us before returning for another frolic round the lamp.

You are officially allowed three days on these moorings (although we have never seen anyone check), we stayed for two then left early on the morning of the third day. It was a sunny, windless day and had a fabulous cruise across the calm, virgin lake – like slowly cracking a giant mirror. Because of the flat terrain the skies are huge and we have a sense of total freedom.

We've encountered quite a number of 'firsts' - some more worrisome than others. Now on a canal on our way to Joure (to replenish our stock of meatballs) we were overtaken by a big commercial barge. We could see this beast from quite a way off but it crept closer with a threatening inevitability, dashing to collect its next load. We cruise at a conservative 6-7 Kph but these things do (at least) the maximum allowed on larger canals of 12.5. These guys take the centre of the waterway so Jan, who was steering at the time, correctly pulled over to the right. Although we were rocked around a little these empty barges look more threatening than they really are.

Worse by far is the occasion we are passed by a fully laden gravel barge. Because they are so much deeper in the water the effect it has on us is significantly enhanced. Just before it reaches us we accelerate on it's bow-wave which also pushes us off towards the right bank. As the bow of the ship draws level and begins to pass it 'takes the water' as it's powerful engine and propeller literally drag the canal water past and beneath it. As we fight this drag rushing past the barge's flanks we slow to a crawl (like water past a narrowboat in a bridge-hole but this was the whole canal). We not only sink about a foot in the water but also get sucked towards the barge so have to work hard with the wheel to keep us on some sort of course. As the hulk glides by we increasingly hear the grumble from the engine as its stern draws level. Then the water that the gravel-barge has displaced catches up with it from behind and we find ourselves riding its stern-wave. Consequently, our speed increases to almost that of the barge. At the same time we are sucked further towards the other ship. We go into full reverse and with the aid of the bow-thruster just manage to keep our bow away from his stern. We are within a metre of his back end as it passes us and we are left in a frothing, bubbling wake. We weigh around forty tonnes and have just been sloshed about like a piece of driftwood so it gives you some idea of the size and power of the big ships – no doubt we'll become accustomed to these encounters.

Some of these ships are new and shiny, worth literally millions, and some have obviously plied their trade for decades and are less well presented. One craft passed us the other day. Below the gunwales it was, well, like any other, but the superstructure was not designed with 'incognito' in mind – it being shocking pink and yellow. Quite frankly it looked rather fun and if it wanted to draw attention to itself, it succeeded – rather like putting a flashing light on a facial wart.

From our point of view meeting people is part of the joy of boating but here social interaction is very different by comparison to our experience of the UK canals where, because of the need to jump off the boat and do the locks, you are bound to meet other people. While waiting for a fill or an empty (or a queue or a cock-up) you pass the time of day and in such circumstances we met some lovely people, some of whom have become good friends. Here you very much stay cocooned on your boat as the locks and bridges are manned and communication is restricted to a quick wave or stilted conversations with the bridge-keepers via the VHF radio. We always try and chat to people when moored up and by making the effort we have met some great folks. Many though seem to value their privacy and I can see some people not talking to another soul during an entire trip – except perhaps for brief exchanges with dreaded 'rent collectors'.

Cease Fire

It has been a beautiful run across the lakes to Joure, sunny, quiet and until late morning, when we actually had to do some manoeuvring, virtually windless. A short distance from Joure there is a sluice (lock), which is permanently open except in times of high water, through which we must pass. By now the breeze had freshened and all was going fine until a cruiser, previously obscured from view, came charging towards the sluice from the opposite direction. Now, because they are pretty manoeuvrable and have a healthy power to weight ratio, they could have stopped within a boats-length to allow us passage - but they chose not to. We, being somewhat less nimble with stopping capability of a train, slowly ground to a halt ten metres or so from the lock then had to reverse to give them room to hurtle past. We were now not only out of their way but also going backwards and sideways in the wind. By the time we had got ourselves organised we'd used a couple of gallons of fuel and alarmed one native who feared for his greenhouse as we mucked about near his back garden. Most boaters are considerate but this chap, from a country a little to the east of Holland, will not be offered one of my (appalling) thirty-eurocent tins of supermarket beer. By the way, this cheap ale doesn't actually taste much worse than more expensive brands but due to both its anaesthetic and memory-erasing properties (and if you can overcome the vile taste of the first couple of tins) you can actually go on and have a jolly good night.

We motor into town past the Douwe Egberts factory (or one of them). 'Tabak, Koffie, Thee' the sign said. We knew about the coffee but the triple-whammy explains why some of the locals look a bit hyper. I suspect that it was both a subsidiary facility and we were looking at the back of it because I can't envisage hyped-up top brass working in what, in all honesty, looked like the rear of a builders merchants – and there aren't many worse places than the rear of a builders merchant!

Joure is a place that could have benefited from better signage. It's a good job that we decided to turn and moor where we did because round a blind bend the canal passed under a succession of low bridges, narrowed to a virtual point and ended in a brick wall. If we'd made the wrong decision we'd have had to hire a crane to get out. Luckily where we moored was fine and our old friends Chris and June crept into town - at least they would have crept in had we not recognised them and 'yoo-hooed' - much to the displeasure of a nearby fisherman having an early evening nap. He'd been having a mid-afternoon nap when we arrived so it was high time he woke up anyway.

At this stage of our adventure we are truly doing justice to the phrase 'aimless meandering'. Our route to date would look something like the track of a drunken figure skater dancing to 'Show me the way to go home'. I mentioned previously (at the time of our stern-gland leak in fact) that we had an unidentified smell of burning rubber. Well, we'd meandered to a tiny island on a small lake (just down a small canal off a large lake) and it is here I discover the cause. We'd had a clue en route when the battery monitor showed us to be charging at a fraction of its normal rate and it was in a mild blue-hued haze in the engine room I discovered that the fan belt was virtually shredded. How it had lasted so long I've no idea but it certainly wasn't going much further. To my horror (and due to my abject stupidity) the spare belt I had bought was the wrong size.

On arrival we had the place to ourselves and looked forward to a peaceful night - until a group of four sailing dinghies arrived. They moored two abreast on the opposite side of the island (a mere 15 paces away). The eight crew members pitched a variety of tents and transformed the island's small grassy interior into a sort of mini outdoor rock festival. They erected a BBQ, a table that groaned with alcohol, a portable hi-fi and camping stools. The centrepiece was a tall brass 'peace pipe' that they took turns puffing on. Fortunately, whatever was in it had a soporific effect and by four-o-clock in the morning they were all flat out. I was very glad I didn't rush out and lecture them on the evils of over-indulgence in 'dark matter' because it was these guys I would later rely on to help me procure a new fan belt (and a sermon would have been rather hypocritical; at least with regards to the alcohol).

The following morning I approached their leader who, despite obviously suffering 'the effects of the pipe', readily agreed to take me to a chandlery in one of their dinghies. He co-opted one of his troops, de-masted a dinghy (because the nearest shop was under a low bridge) and within an hour we were back with a new fan belt – I will be forever grateful. Needless to say, the repair took longer than it should have done and it'll be another week or two before I get rid of the grease smears. I get a sideways glance from the posh chap who has replaced the pipe-smokers and I can't tell whether he's envying me staggering out of the engine room looking vaguely competent or merely astonished at the mess I've got myself in.

Having had been told that the town of Grou was well worth a visit we headed off there the following morning with batteries now on maximum charge and me with a stubborn blob of muck over my right eyebrow. It is 10.30 am and there's not a spare mooring in sight, in fact many boats were doubled up. People looked on with a smugness that lets you know they have found a slot. We pretend that we are sight-seeing and not really bothered about stopping anyway. We actually need supplies and the only place to pull in is on a ferry stop. Our eagle-eyed skipper notices a sign stating that the ferry was not due for another hour so we slipped in and tied up. A guy dashed out of a hut looking none too pleased but the skipper sweet-talked him into letting us stay briefly while we dashed to the supermarket. I did have another ruse lined up, similar to the one used on land where in a busy town you put your hazard-lights on and open the bonnet while your accomplice dashes in to buy a lottery ticket. We didn't have hazard lights but I'm sure I could have found a genuine problem in the engine room without too much trouble. We pulled away just as the flag-bedecked ferry hove into view – he never realised how close he was to having to go and find an alternative stop for his passengers.

We felt a bit harassed and if there had been any hills we'd have headed for them. As it was we headed for an area that looked on the map like a confusing series of interconnecting lakes and channels – with lots of free moorings. Today is sunny and very hot and as we settle in we are subject to a roller-coaster of sensations from the ten or so moored boats and their inmates. Assimilating the sights, sounds and smells is undertaken as we 'take refreshment' and plan our own camp. Boaters have set up bivvies on the three-metre-wide strip of neatly mown grass. People chat and chuckle as the birds sing, mouth-watering smells from a number BBQs drift towards us (as do the fumes from a diesel generator) and a large lady passes by the assortment of multi-coloured parasols and waddles off into the trees with a roll of loo paper.

This is the first occasion on which we proudly display our new 5-Euro parasol purchased with optimism from a petrol station. Within a couple of hours it is worth rather less than 5 Euros because as we pull it out of the ground the bottom three-inches (and important pointy bit) remains buried in the peat - perhaps the eight-euro model was more robust. As we huddle under our parasol (it's a bit small in all truth) and wait for the lady to return from the woods before we begin our picnic, we discuss why we actually need to be in the shade at all. Most light-coloured surfaces reflect heat and light but due to an unfortunate quirk of physics the brilliant-white outer layer of the Northern European absorbs both with consummate efficiency. Consequently, our mooring is littered with puce body parts and the area looks like large, diseased cricket pitch infested with an assortment of giant blisters.

I encounter a friendly chap called Jan (Yan), in fact during the four hours it took us to put out the fire we became buddies. You see, late in the afternoon I'd noticed an increasing amount of smoke about thirty metres inland of our mooring and on investigation saw that a fire had crept about forty metres alongside a brackish drainage channel - and it was still creeping. Together we took a couple of buckets and, starting from the centre and working outwards, first stamped out the surface flames then chucked bucket after bucket of foul-smelling, brackish water on the fire. However, when the visible flames had been extinguished, the mound of dead reeds, dredged from the ditch and now bone dry, had begun to smoulder. When we thought we'd put that out it was obvious that the peat below had also caught so it was messy and hot work.

I was wearing work-boots but Jan's rubber sandals were gently melting out from beneath him – you could tell because every now and then he would perform a series of little hops and there was a smouldering rubber smell – not dissimilar to our disintegrating fan belt. Hot and mucky, we discussed the possible cause of the fire over a beer concluding that a cigarette butt was the most likely because the fire was adjacent to a path where we'd both seen a number of walkers earlier in the day. We both extinguished our roll-ups with extreme care and disappeared to our respective boats for a shower and dinner – followed by our dogs.

As evening falls amid the hiss of acres of cooling, sunburnt flesh we can just about make out the last beautiful bird calls of the evening over the over the racket of some tone-deaf idiot singing a medley of tuneless continental folk songs. We spend a while reflecting on the first few weeks of our Dutch adventure and decide that basically we've got a lot less cash.

From the Hound of Vrouwe Johanna

Well, this is more like what I expected. They look a bit 'working class' huddled under their umbrella, but they seem to have calmed down a bit. Nothing much seems to faze Mum too much but there's the odd 'technical issue' that get Dad in a panic – like when his beloved engine room started smelling like the bloke who was putting the fire out's melting shoes, but overall, he's less twitchy.

I never really liked the big waters. On the narrowboat I didn't like it when my lavatory was out of swimming range, but here it's another ball game. Some of these lakes are huge but despite that I feel ok with it. Perhaps they've put a dose of 'hang-loose-juice' in my snert.

There's not much social interaction going on – in fact I don't think I've come across another of my species for about three weeks. That's OK I guess but it would be nice to make some new friends. It's quite peculiar, the other boaters seem to keep themselves to themselves. Even when Dad goes to pester someone they seem anxious that he returns to his own country. Quite funny seeing Mum and Dad actually having to talk to one another. Having said that they're not much choice being huddled together under that brolly!

It's difficult to tell if we actually have a destination in mind or whether their Sat Nav is on the blink – we do seem to be just wandering about a bit. Nevertheless, it's relaxing and enjoyable.

I did get a rollicking for wagging a bottle of Dad's wine into a lake. It was perched very close to the side of the boat and I did try to explain that my wagging was in fact dog-semaphore, and an attempt to communicate with the outside world but he wasn't having it. Oh well.

Love, Bonny

Payback Time

We are in Alde Feanen, 'Old Fens' in the Friesian language. Formerly an area of 18th century peat extraction and the domain of hunters, turf (peat) diggers, farmers and fishermen, it is now a National Park and a maze of waterways - a land of lakes, islands, boats and bushes. We have been on one particular island for three days, pinned against the bank by a stiff wind. All the weekenders have taken themselves and unsavoury toiletry habits back home and we're left alone. It is still warm and the grass, neatly mown when we arrived, now looks in need of a trim. We know it's windy because a duck, flapping like mad, maintains station outside our wheelhouse. It eyed us with an expression that wondered how we were managing to keep up with it. Had it 'gone about' it could have been in Belgium within the hour enjoying exotic beer and chocolate.

Picking our way through the maze of waterways we arrive at the town of Earnewald, Alde Feanen's tourist centre. I nudge it a few centimetres west when I make a bit of a hash of mooring on a rather smart quay - which now has a red scuff mark on it. Provisions are purchased from one of those annoying mini supermarkets that has everything except what you really want and, not for the first time, the skipper will have to fashion a meal from an unlikely assortment of ingredients. What was more annoying was the attached petrol station which displays the cost of diesel on a large, double-sided sign – it was 10 cents per litre more expensive on the water-facing side!

While based in Zwartsluis I lost the little screw that held my glasses together, consequently the lens dropped out. The chap in the local chemist told me that they didn't repair glasses as a rule but if I would hang on he would see what he could do. He came back fifteen minutes later having repaired my specs but refused payment. I thanked him and told him that was a lovely gesture. He replied saying that there would come a time when I would be able to help a Dutchman.

Well, the time is here.

We return from shopping to find Jacques and Ilona, a Dutch couple we had previously befriended, moored close by. The male half of the partnership is partial to a glass of sherry and it was while I was enjoying his hospitality that we encounter an episode that filled us both with terror. We were sitting on his boat when we heard desperate cries for help. The shouting came from a cruiser about sixty metres away across the basin and we could see a lady crouching on the bathing platform. Jacques cycled and I ran around the basin perimeter to help. When we got closer we could see to our horror that she was leaning over the back of the platform holding a guy by his armpits. Only his head, shoulders and arms were visible while the rest of him was underneath the back of the boat. He was facing forward with outstretched arms, his hands clawing at the wooden laths trying to stop himself slipping as his wife tried to hold him. His wife was now near hysterical - and worse, as we got closer, we could see that the boat's engines were running. It was one of those instances where you feel sick at what you are going to find. I imagine red-stained water where the guy's feet had been shredded by the propellers – it was a truly awful moment. When we got there we could see the water bubbling from the back of the boat but thankfully the water was clear. I dashed up a ladder to the fly-bridge to turn the engines off while Jacques helped secure the man. We grabbed him by the armpits and hauled him out of the water onto the bathing platform where he was mercifully in one piece but we had to support him till his legs stopped shaking and he could stand by himself. His knees and front of his thighs were stained green where they had rubbed up underneath the boat. He was nearer seventy that sixty and close to the end of his tether but he did tell Jacques, while looking skyward, that in fact the propellers were not turning, the disturbance in the water was caused by his twin underwater exhausts bubbling away. They didn't speak English but the lady grabbed my hand and nodded her thanks, her eyes wide and her face ashen. The guy told

Jacques that he had merely slipped while adjusting a rope. He was dripping but the only visible signs of his ordeal were a cut hand and a pair of stained pants but, boy, it could it have been so much worse. It occurs to me only now as I write that, despite there being quite a number of boats about, we were the only four people in view in the harbour. It is hard to believe that nobody else heard the commotion and what would have happened if we'd not been about.

Jacques and I returned to his boat. He had spent many years in Australia while younger so spoke fluent English but with an Aussie inflection. As he upgraded our sherry glasses to tumblers and we sat he said, 'bladdy hell mate!' - which summed it up rather succinctly.

Before we left the following day I had an early morning cycle through the village. That didn't take long - even at my pace - but tucked out of the way down a side road, through some small industrial units is 'De Stripe', a museum specialising in traditional Frisian sailing ships called skutsjes. It was about 6.30 in the morning and sitting there, wrapped in a coat against the morning chill, was a lady sitting on a bench having a cup of coffee and a cigarette. She was probably as surprised as me to encounter anyone but we nodded a greeting and looked in silence over the assortment of beautifully kept little sailing boats surrounded by a jumble of spare parts. Some, a few leeboards for example, were recognisable and in good condition but there was also plenty rotting and rusting bits looking disconcertingly like some of the bits I've painted over on our boat.

We'd had enough of Earnewald so set the meaderometer to 'steady' and headed north – having extricated ourselves from the confusion of lakes and adjoining waterways. The Prinses Margriet Canal is the super-highway that runs roughly north-south through Friesland so we once again join the big commercial barges. We have to pass a huge railway swing-bridge that only opens periodically. Boats hover mid-stream to wait and when I enquired of an adjacent cruiser how long we would have to hold station, it came as something of a relief when he said that the bridge only opens when there is no train coming. We turn left onto the Harinxma Canal which heads west towards Harlingen right out on the west coast having stopped for fuel at a 'bunker-station'. The guy was livid because someone had mucked about with the calibration on his red-diesel pump and we were undercharged by ten cents per litre – it's pretty rare when boating that you end up on the right side financially so we set off with light hearts and wishing we'd asked for more than 300 litres. The weather made up for it mind you, it was horrid - we were battered by squally, slow-moving showers mixed with a bit of thunder and lightning.

Our boat is a bit short on ventilation and it was Chris and June (they of the lovely big red barge, Bernardus) who put us in touch with another Englishman, Len Barry. Len had helped them fit out their barge and thought he could handle making us a couple of pigeon boxes (or cuckoo hatches as I think they are known here). Opening, wooden roof boxes in effect. We'd moored in Franeker and paid our fee to the beady eyed rent-collector in return for a few rings in a wall and little else. By chance Len and his wife June would be passing us the following day on their narrowboat en-route to Harlingen, so we agreed to meet. They arrived at 1.00 pm for a coffee and chat and left at 9.00 pm after lots of chat, lots of coffee and a fair amount of wine – I think we were all short of English-speaking company because no-one would shut up! Eight hours chewing the fat and we hadn't even talked about the hatches. As Len and I were a little worse for wine we agree to meet the following morning having slept off the effects of too much Château Effluent. He duly took measurements and set off to have his boat bottom painted listing a little from the motley assortment of hardwood off-cuts I had handed over, from which I optimistically expected him to fashion our hatches.

Last time we were in Franeker it was well below freezing when we had visited by car during the search for our boat. While on that road trip a couple of years ago we'd arrived about 6.00 pm and we needed somewhere to stay. There was a rather smart-looking hotel on the outskirts which I considered too rich for our budget. Jan persuaded me to pull in anyway and she'd go and enquire. She came out beaming a few minutes later. She recounted her conversation with the receptionist:

'Could you tell me how much it is for the night please?'

'It's ninety Euros Madam'.

'WHAT? NINETY EUROS?'

'That's correct Madam.'

'Well, it's too much'.

'Oh really.' Pause. 'How much would you like to pay?'

'Forty. It's late, the middle of winter and there are only two cars in your car park.'

'Oh.' Pause. 'OK then, forty Euros'.

'Great,' said Jan, 'we'll stay for two nights'.

She even managed to wangle some morning coffee within the price too.

Today the weather was beautiful and the town was unrecognisable from the slippery, snow-blown place we remembered. The only place I could keep cool today was the air-conditioned library where I outstayed my welcome by looking at the pictures in the newspapers. I did have a (sort of) conversation with a passing local and gleaned that he was Dutch, his dog was German and he had once been to Scotland, near England. Looking at our boat he said it was 'vide for longht – goot!' Presumably he meant that it was unusual to have a boat with our length with so wide-a beam but gathered that overall, the proportions were beneficial.

We were moored near a lift-bridge immediately down-stream of which was a gentle 'S' bend and a regular flow of commercial barges negotiated the chicane effortlessly. This included one who had a load so large there was no way he could see forward from the wheel-house – his cargo was a large steel structure and he must have been navigating by radar and / or cameras. Presumably it is how they manage in thick fog but I have to admire once again the skill of these commercial skippers. One other thing you have to cope with on this stretch of canal is a periodic current. This occurs when they open sluice gates in Harlingen (around 8 or nine kilometres downstream); I believe the sluices are opened between the inland canal and seaward port at low tide to get rid of the low-lying inland water. It also helps flush out the silt to keep the waterways clear. The flow nearly caught us out while we waited for the lift bridge to open as the lights stubbornly refused to turn from single red to red/green to indicate that the bridge is about to be lifted for us. The bridge operator was standing outside his hut waving at us so vigorously that we thought he was trying to take off. When I judged him to be near collapse I called him on the VHF. Not having used the thing in anger before I was glad of it now because when the guy got his breath back he warned us of the current (that we knew about) and the fact that we'd have to reverse and pull in to allow a fully laden barge to pass upstream before we could go through (which we didn't know about). The flow wasn't very fierce but it was strong enough to mean that a heavy barge going against the current would find it difficult to negotiate the bends and narrow bridge without momentum - consequently he had to keep going while we waited.

    The contrast between this big barge rumbling by on a big waterway today and our pottering among the pleasure boats in 'lakeland' a few days ago could not be starker and we are thoroughly enjoying the pleasures and excitement of it all. In fact, the experience is so all-enveloping that we've almost forgotten that we can't find a leg of lamb or a decent pint of ale anywhere - almost, but not quite.

Lunch in the Engine Room

The skipper, perhaps nervous of my mechanical ability, asked me whether I was sure that we'd stopped water entering through our stern gland. Now that is akin to telling a child a horror story at bedtime. I knew we were down to our last couple of turns on the gland's adjustment nuts so decided to get it re-packed. The place to do this, according to a number of informed sources is a boatyard owned by a chap called Nieko. His yard is sited next to a scrapyard and some of Nieko's stuff looks like it's been dropped in the wrong location but among the detritus there are jewels undergoing renovation including a couple for English clients. He is a very nice guy, solid and trustworthy, 'old school' maybe, the type of chap with whom you'd trust your boat. He removed some nuts and an important-looking steel plate which, in my view at least, left a gaping gap as far as prop shaft security went – and then he went for lunch. I was a tad worried about water ingress so while he dined in his adjacent house, I sat in the engine room staring at my weak point. The skipper bought me a cup of tea and some towels, just in case. Nieko was a bit surprised that I'd lunched in the engine room but he duly came back and re-packed the gland, then adjusted the morse control, fixed something on the gearbox that had worked loose, then chatted for an hour – then went to make out the bill – which was actually very reasonable.

We set off in search of Leeurwarden, capital city of Friesland. It was founded in 750 AD so should have had time to get organised by the time we get there. Mata Hari, the world-famous spy, was born in this beautiful city which is home to more than 100,000 people among whom are a high proportion of students. It is a fabulous mix of tradition and trendy with fashionable shops and modern eateries are watched over by the city's leaning tower. In the 16th Century Leeuwarden's residents demanded a tower taller than the one in nearby Groningen but it soon started leaning and despite creating the odd kink to compensate, the builders gave up at 40 metres.

The main canal towards Groningen passes south of the city but we take a smaller one runs up the western side, through the city itself, before heading north. It's twists and turns require some concentration in a barge that, once turned, wants to keep going sideways but as we moor up against the steep grass bank of a park, we are no more than five minutes' walk from the city proper (ten minutes cycle!). We are relieved of cash for our mooring (four days for the price of three) but we've arrived at a good time according to the rent-collector because today (Thursday) is the final day of Avondvierdaags to be followed by a three-day music festival – 'good time' that is if you don't want peace and quiet. We'd had plenty of that so it was time for a boogie. Avondvierdaags is a traditional event where groups, particularly children, walk for four consecutive evenings over a distance of between 3 and 10 kilometres then, in Leeurwarden's case, hundreds of children gather in the shadow of the leaning tower on a car park (which, according to one local chap, used to be a pet cemetery). The kids gather in school groups then march through the city centre accompanied by their parents. The procession goes on for ages with blocks of revellers interspersed with five different marching bands dressed in their own particular uniform. Each band plays a variety of tat-tat, rat-a-tat-tat marching music – marching bands are big business in Holland and they take it very seriously. The beaming smiles and innocent, sparkly eyes of the kids is a joy to see - today they are the centre of attention and they lap it up. The skipper and I watch the festivities while taking refreshment in a side-walk café. We have a pint on the pavement and a pee in prison. You see, the café was formerly the city gaol and if you want 'powder your nose' the facilities are in the cells!

Friday is the start of the three-day festival though today is just a warm-up with the city only moderately crowded. Saturday is full throttle and an amazing spectacle. There are five stages dotted throughout the city offering live music from early afternoon the late evening; much of it was really good (covers of Springsteen, Bryan Adams, Abba for example), some local bands were playing local music which, to our taste, was ok but rather repetitive and one band was appalling, sounding like a lawnmower running over a stone then going back and doing it again, and again....

Street theatres would appear seemingly at random, at first with a knot of people, then a crowd and, if the act held interest, a throng. We didn't understand most of it due to language shortcomings, in fact there was even a mime act we couldn't follow so can only assume that it was based on some local fable. Periodically we would be passed by groups dressed in astonishing outfits either on foot or on some mode of transport. For example, a group of eleven girls are dressed in hooded, full length shiny, gold outfits with gold-painted faces, black gloves and black shoes – what on earth they were meant to be was beyond us but they make an amazing spectacle. A group of guys are driving vehicles cobbled-together from rejects from a scrap yard. They look like 'post nuclear holocaust' meets Mad Max and have obviously spent countless hours creating their vehicles reaching a point where they will frighten the most unimaginative child. By way of contrast, on the small, sunken canal that splits the main street, a group of nuns cruise serenely by - playing flutes! Their boat is skippered by 'the Pope' and he and his boatswain, a cardinal, wave enthusiastically to the crowds as they spread the gospel according to Saint Peculiar.

Thousands of people are enjoying the beautiful weather, some gather round the street theatres, many are sitting outside canal-side cafés and others, like us, just meander. We meander to a small, shady square away from the main drag where a smooth jazz trio is easing away the afternoon watched by a group of droopy-eyed enthusiasts. Perhaps it is no accident that the square is bordered by two 'Koffie Shops' (which openly supply soft drugs) and appreciation for the music is shown by whispered calls of 'yeah man' and 'haaay'. The air is thick with the smell of cannabis and one or two who have finished their enormous 'reefers' are taking advantage of the warm weather by taking an afternoon nap. I have mentioned before that the Romans were the first tourists to Friesland and one of their centurions is credited with introducing illicit relaxants for his cohorts as an antidote to indifferent Dutch weather. His name was Waccus Baccus and the jazz aficionados in our little square are paying him suitable homage on this lovely Saturday afternoon.

My version of the Elfstadentocht (an eleven city skating or cycle race) is to try and source frikadellen (meat balls) in eleven different cities but, despite having some previous success, I lucked out in Leeurwarden. In fact, the chosen establishment was so 'back street Istanbul' that I asked the proprietor the time rather than actually ordering anything. Instead, we sat in a café and had a toastie - not quite the same thing but satisfactory nevertheless. We were slightly put off our repast because across the road was a shop with the extremely unappetising name of 'Dick's Dumpstore'. For obvious reasons we avoided Dick's place and returned to the boat to plan our onward journey in time to see a double-masted, fully rigged Brigantine pass by - it was truly a magnificent sight. The ship was skippered by an elderly, white-bearded guy who was piloting his lovely craft to the accompaniment of 'hornpipe' music which echoes around the park and canal. You could hear his wonderful, diminishing refrain long after he had passed out of sight.

Caution is required when rounding Leeurwarden as the canal is twisty and there are many moored boats, some visitors and some permanent, so we headed slowly north. Our ultimate destination is Lauwersmeer which is about as far north as we can go without venturing onto the sea. We're travelling on the Dokkumer Ee which is a gentle river and blissfully peaceful after the chaos of the Leeuwarden festival. The only raised voice I hear is that of a fisherman vociferously grumbling about the state of Leeuwarden's football team. It's only when I tell him that I'm originally from Rochdale that he realises he's not so badly off after all. He returns to not catching fish and I go and look at an empty car that someone's driven into a ditch – perhaps it belongs to another football fan.

Not far up-river there is a fully operational windmill called De Zwaluw (the swallow) in the town of Burdaad. It was re-built in the 1980's following a fire and flour is milled daily (except the day we were there when they were cleaning it!). It brings back memories of one of my previous incarnations as a baker but our guided tour is not exactly relaxing as we sneeze continually in the flour dust and have to scrabble up and down three very steep sets of wooden stairs. The newly installed internal workings of the mill are very impressive and imposing. The milling stones are connected by huge oak beams and a series of giant wooden cogs to the sails that power the mill. Venturing out onto the veranda halfway up the mill we walk on a slatted floor that doesn't look strong enough but the view is amazing. Attached to the windmill itself is a sawmill that, although it now only works for demonstrations, is also wind-powered. The mill supplies flour to bakeries and restaurants and the skipper buys a bag of strong white flour from the proprietor who looks ghost-like covered in fine dust. Jan will later make suet pastry – ideal fayre for a boiling hot summer day!

We showed a genuine interest in the workings of the mill and because the lady who was due to show us round didn't speak much English she dragged her teenage (and reluctant) son away from his Nintendo to help translate for us. It was this act of kindness that persuaded the skipper to lash out on a bag of flour. Our visit was also accompanied by the bizarre spectacle of a trio of accordion players across the river, playing away while sitting outside a garage in the afternoon sun. It's weird and wonderful moments like these that we'll look back on if we ever reach the 'armchair stage' in our dotage.

From the Hound of Vrouwe Johanna

Well, if we'd had a quiet time beforehand, Leeuwarden made up for it! Never seen so many lunatics in one place at one time – and living with this pair I've seen plenty! Great fun though although I was a bit disturbed by all those children gathering on a pet cemetery – that was a bit close to the bone.

He's had an epiphany – a bloke mended his glasses so he fished a chap out from under a boat. Spooked him a bit I think, the way the glass-repairer said he would return a kindness. Karma Mum called it – though why he and his Austro / Dutch mate had to polish off a bottle of Bristol Cream to celebrate is a bit of a mystery. Mind you, it's made me watch out while mooching about the deck.

I am impressed with this part of the world though, lovely country and a real mix of manic and not-a-lot-at-all. It's funny, even though we were in a busy city, we still didn't really speak to anyone (save for ordering a sandwich). And everyone else seemed to know what they were doing and where they were going except us – like we were flies on the wall watching some crazy drama.

I'm not sure where we are exactly but I know we're pretty far north. I'm on the lookout for reindeer – in fact I'm on the lookout for anything not blundering around on two legs. It's peculiar when you see more windmills than cows – and this is Friesland after all.

Time to prepare for the next challenge – whatever that is.

Love Bonny

Northerly Limit

As we cruise up the Dokkumer Ee, heading north east, we have been wondering why the waterways are so quiet. Where are all the boats? Ok, there are thousands of kilometres of canals and rivers in Holland and we all go roughly the same speed (except hire-boats) but it is still strange. Well, when we arrive in Dokkum, we find them – its bedlam and this is the first time we've encountered facilities that are anything but really spot-on. It is the height of the season and a substantial proportion of the moorings are under renovation. I'm reminded of our travels in the UK where, each time we visited a National Trust property, it was invariably cloaked in scaffolding. We arrive in the early afternoon and are fortunate to find a mooring; unlike many boats which pass us, then go by again in search of somewhere to stop – and there are early indications of a native uprising. We well remember the occasions where we have endured the smug looks of people who have found a prime spot (probably having moored up shortly after breakfast) while we end up mooring on a weed-infested patch with no bollards by a sewage works, but now it's our turn. Some folk really do look rather irate and we wish we had moored within the ramparts of this pretty fortified town, guarded by its pair of immaculate windmills, rather than on the outside where we are most vulnerable to attack.

As these homeless boats drift to and fro, one thing we do notice about many of the crews is how well clad they are, particularly on the 'double-chin palaces' which predominate. This must be partly because from casting off to mooring they never leave the confines of their boats - unlike the UK where at least one of the crew is attired to sweat over locks and bridges while the other dresses in sympathy. We tend to dress down, so much so that when we join a couple studying the menu in the window of a local restaurant, they move swiftly on.

We are approaching the most northerly point of our trip in mainland Europe, a lake called Lauwersmeer. The lake was only created in 1969 when a dyke and lock was completed (as part of the Delta plan devised following disastrous floods in 1953 to alleviate the risk of flooding) blocking off what was until then an estuary. From the lake you can access, via the lock, the Waddenzee and the ring of islands that sweep round the north-west coast a little way offshore. We have neither the required insurance nor qualifications to head to sea so our plan is to head up the lake into the northerly wind, turn east for a couple of kilometres then head south to join the Rietdiep which will take us down to Groningen. It is windy, the lake is large and we are a little nervous. As we travel the tree-lined channel that takes us to the lake I'm trying to look relaxed while the skipper 'who would rather have something to do' hangs on to the wheel. Then we see a narrowboat! It has come off the lake and is flying a Dutch flag. Our nerves are settled somewhat as it is the right way up (the boat, not the flag) and there are two people standing on the back. We take some photographs and wave to them. They wave back but when they see our red ensign they REALLY wave back. We will meet the owners at a later date and discover an amazing coincidence.

The lake really is pretty rough. Because it is shallow the waves are short and choppy and we bounce about. This becomes a roll when we have the wind on our beam while doing the easterly leg and we have to put the dog below so she doesn't fall off. I can only presume that the narrowboat we passed must have come straight down wind as I would not have fancied going across the wind and waves in one of those. The only other boats we see on the lake are a few yachts which are suited to the conditions.

We find our way off the open water with some difficulty. The channels through which we must pass to cross the lake are marked as usual by red and green buoys. (Incidentally, you will find the green ones to port as you head downstream). As the skipper is clinging onto the steering wheel and has a manic, dead-ahead stare, I'm in charge of navigation. Our difficulty is that there are a number of channels that we don't want to take and the buoys keep disappearing between the waves so by the time we've checked the map and sat-nav (which is showing signs of 'agitation' at just the wrong moment), we are not sure if the buoy on which we were originally checking is the same one as we look out next time! (I'm also a bit red / green colour-blind which doesn't help). Also, because the lake is quite large I am finding it difficult to judge distance and the channel we must eventually take is at an angle to our current position so hard to spot, consequently the shoreline appears to be an unbroken horizon of trees and reeds. Despite the fact that we are well under a metre draft we really don't want to turn south too early and end up beached on a sandbar in a stiff onshore wind. In addition to all these amateur fumblings we're having enough trouble just standing up so there is a bit of ripe language before we eventually scuttle off the lake up the right hole. Talk about making a drama out of a crisis.

The little port of Zoutkamp marks the start of the Reitdiep, a gentle river flowing north through the province of Groningen. Zoutkamp is a charming place with sailing barges, fishing boats and small multi-coloured wooden 'cottages' and again we get the feel of the inland waterways meeting the sea (and after the experience of the past couple of hours we're glad to be heading inland). As we pass the village we are in turn passed by a fast-moving storm with the sun peeping out from below the clouds. I take a photo and I announce proudly that it is probably my best one yet - to which the skipper unkindly replies, 'well, one of them has to be the best.'

After a couple of days pottering south, we arrive in Groningen, a lovely city which we have visited twice by car but this is our first time by boat. When we arrive we look at our city map for a central mooring but, as far as we can see, the six municipal swimming pools outnumber the moorings. There is one spot but we are just beaten to it by a cruiser who presumably can now sit there and look smug for the remainder of the afternoon. We are forced to moor outside an Aldi supermarket but get a rollicking from the officious waterway patrol lady so have to move on a further kilometre. Actually, the reason she was so irate was because she had followed us on her bicycle from the previous bridge in order to open the next one for us only to find us waltzing around a supermarket in search of meatballs. We are a moored bit out in the middle of nowhere and as Groningen is the birthplace of the pirate Roche Braziliano, we can only hope his relatives have pursued an alternative career.

Groningen itself is truly 'boaty' city and as we had cruised through we had seen literally hundreds of residential barges so the only way to have a proper look is to cycle back into town. It is Sunday lunchtime and although the shops are shut there are plenty of bars and cafés open. But it is the boats that really fascinate me. Our barge is a Groningen Boltjalk and although it has been substantially altered, the original shape of shell (casco in Dutch) remains. I cycle in the shade of manicured trees down cobbled streets which run alongside the smaller 'residential canals' (non through routes which would normally be bypassed). I see a number of boats whose hulls are virtually identical to ours, though most of these have their original sailing rigs in place. There are barges of all shape and size, some in beautiful condition but others sadly appear untended and unloved. Many are residential boats and 'hard-wired' into the city's water and sewage system so have probably not moved for years but still, what a marvellous way to live in the heart of a fascinating city. There are also some extraordinary 'bespoke' models of futuristic design, possibly creations of imaginations enhanced by the 'wicked weed'. One in particular, built on a floating pontoon, looks like a 21st century Nissan hut about to be swamped by a giant wave. Then, as I cycle round the next bend I see on an adjoining waterway, a masted sailing barge under motor chugging slowly between ancient buildings and I'm transported back to another time – it is absolutely fascinating.

Almost equally fascinating to the tradition and majesty of this boat-fest is a beach volleyball tournament being contested by teams of girls clad in bikinis. A patch of imported sand had been dumped on a car park in the shadow of a large Church and perhaps unsurprisingly, a respectable crowd has gathered. Before I go and watch the tournament I sit in the sunshine outside a café to reflect on my morning. I order a coffee and on the spur of the moment decide on an Amaretto (Italian liqueur) as a restorative. It is the first occasion I have ever had to stop someone in the act of pouring me a drink – the barman was nearly at the half-pint mark before I called a halt explaining that I not only had to be able to be able to focus on the volleyball but also cycle home along the canal towpath.

The Dutch annual five-week general holiday approaches so we are going to head back to home port to avoid what we are promised will be a swarm of private and hire boats. It will also give us the opportunity for a mid-season re-hash. This re-hash is something for which I'm going to have to mentally prepare because it will involve a number of major projects; for example, replacing the head-gasket and skimming the head on the generator - something I have never tackled before but will do with the help of my English friend Peter, who is undaunted and fearless while working on somebody else's expensive equipment. Next we'll re-vamp the wheelhouse which will include some re-wiring and re-plumbing in order to move the washing machine into the disused shower tray in the loo so we can make space to improve the seating and generally make the area more user-friendly before sanding and varnishing the interior and exterior. Then I'll install a couple of wooden pigeon boxes (built by our English friend Len Barry) above the two bedrooms as the ventilation is badly lacking and finally we'll paint the exterior of the boat. When we come out of the clinic for the totally knackered we plan set off again in another direction.

As a consequence of this daunting schedule our journey back, which is via the Drenthe canal linking Groningen and Meppel, will be tackled with due lack of haste in order to put off the inevitable as long as possible. I know these jobs need doing, indeed am being enthusiastically encouraged to tackle them by the skipper in the hope of disproving the maxim 'you can have anything but not everything'.

The locks on the Drenthe canal are only 24-metres in length hence this is not a waterway for commercial boats so we are looking forward to a serene potter. The northerly section of the canal is very pretty and we pass a beautiful white windmill, fairly isolated, and positioned on a stretch of forest-lined waterway. Set against a dark, stormy sky it is lovely. Our first port of call is Assen, or it would have been if there'd been a port to call in at. This is 'transition harbour' where an approximate mile-long stretch of town-centre access canal is at the concrete and 'wires-hanging-out' stage so we have to tie up to a tree and get the bread knife out and defoliate in order to get the dog off.

There is a popular staging post called Hoogersmilde where we are absolutely inundated by flies. Agriculture is abundant in the countryside. This area is a bit more arable and crops such as corn for animal feed is grown. They also cultivate flowers and we see many dairy cows and sheep (for wool presumably as they don't eat them). This is the first time however we've come across a fly farm. The swarm of black 'house flies' is annoying and unpleasant but when the wind changes we are nearly overcome by an ammoniacal pong. I don't know what it is about the Dutch, probably their natural stoicism, but they seem to have the ability to ignore these difficulties and just carry on with their BBQs – if you can't do anything about it, just ignore it.

Drenthe canal has many long straight stretches and is rather tedious in places with many lift bridges and a handful of locks with many of the bridges operated by folk who live nearby and open the bridges on request. The protocol is to honk your horn and someone will materialise to help - which usually happens. At one bridge though we have a fifteen-minute wait as we honk then sit mid-stream then honk again. Out of a wooden shack adjacent to a nearby cottage emerges a chap with a newspaper under his arm doing up his trousers. We reckon he'd probably nodded off while doing the crossword! Unabashed and unhurried he waves as we pass but at least these bridges are free unlike many in Friesland where you have to pop a couple of Euros into a clog suspended from a stick.

The canal is narrow compared to the commercial ones we have encountered and we have to take care when passing other boats particularly when the wind blows and the banks are reedy. We remember the narrower, shallower UK canals where it is sometimes difficult to get out of the shallows and away from the side. On several occasions while passing other boats we have to steer the boat into the bank to get the stern away while simultaneously using the bow-thruster to keep the bow out. It is quite tricky because you get nudged towards the bank as the other boat approaches (usually too quickly for the circumstances) then sucked towards the boat as you draw level so we have to keep out wits about us.

So, we're back to Zwartsluis. Anyone with any valuable equipment I'm likely to borrow has stashed it under lock and key safe from yours truly, ham-fisted Harry, who would doubtless return each expensive item in a number of pieces. They've allocated us a mooring out of the way on the town side of 'long-eared-owl island' – a splendid spot lying alongside a pontoon as opposed to nose-on like before. Now I really have no excuse for not working on the boat. Actually, we are welcomed back enthusiastically by owner Klass – I'd forgotten to pay him our last month's rent!

So begins another round of prodding, poking and hacking in preparation for another voyage.

From the Hound of Vrouwe Johanna

Thank goodness for that. He's calmed down now we're tied up again. No more panicky dashes to the engine room when he hears a strange noise or outbursts of foul language when his battery monitor fails to register the reading he's expecting (or hoping for!). He kept tapping it and fiddling with the wires – even Mum couldn't convince him it might just have been the batteries that were knackered. This is not the main batteries you understand, no, we changed them before we set off – in fact the proceeds from the car went towards them. No, this is another set – goodness knows what these ones do but I suppose they must be there for a reason. Mind you he does a lot of things without reason.

Still, it's nice to be back – the folk really are very nice here – particularly when Dad's not on the scrounge. Actually, that's not fair, he's very rarely on the scrounge – he normally takes things without asking. Not that I'm trying to paint him in a bad light, oh no. He can do that for himself. Overall, he's all right, in a sort of grumpy, panicky way.

Where do we go next? Don't know, but hopefully I'll have time to have a haircut before we go. Mum'll do it – wouldn't trust him!

Just a couple of weeks ago we were bouncing about on a big lake when I was banished to my bunk, frightened stiff. Seems like another life now we're back. Wasn't half exciting though – perhaps that's why we do it. Love Bonny

Bye bye Zwartsluis

Part Two

Our little barge has undergone a facelift. I didn't use Boatox, relying rather on various skills gleamed from fitting out a couple of narrowboats - which is probably why it looks such a mess. I've spent most of the last two years, in among various trips, hacking about with the interior so the neglected extremities looked a bit mottled. It is a ship in wolf's clothing, but it has become our home. Mutterings that we would soon be leaving attracted much interest. This turned to near delirium as we announced our imminent departure for pastures new. I would finally stop pestering people for advice or borrowing tools that would be returned covered in grease – or bent.

The day dawned fine - 3rd April 2009......

We're off to France.

We'd said goodbye to Richard and Jenny – there were gifts a plenty and tears.

We'd said goodbye the previous evening to Klass and Metsje from the boatyard – an enormous Chinese take-away in the company of the staff and assorted friends from the marina. All paid for by Klaas – there was a huge pile of food, enough in fact for doggy bags for breakfast – unfortunate turn of phrase that.

Sadly, we'd had a bit of a falling out with Rob the imitation policeman so he merely watched, alone again, from his wheelhouse. The daft thing is I can't even remember what it was over – only I'm sure it was his fault!

Dave didn't shout anything rude this time but perhaps he should have done. I fired up the engine but hadn't even untied our ropes when the main water-pump failed. The impeller had disintegrated sending bits of petrified rubber down a pipe into the oil cooler. Fortunately, we were only popping down to France so a 2-hour delay was of little importance.

Eventually, in a cloud of filthy exhaust smoke, we left Zwartsluis followed by Baz and Ally who would accompany us on their pretty barge. Our intention is to travel through central Holland, eastern Belgium and on to Burgundy in France. If we'd realized the forthcoming trip would be as frightening as it was wonderful we would have been far more nervous but we set off feeling a mixture of sadness and exhilaration. We were aiming ultimately for St. Jean de Losne on the junction of the River Saone and Canal de Bourgogne, six months and many miles distant.

St. Jean was actually our second choice. We'd previously phoned the port Captain at Roanne to be told, 'tuh, you murst pherne before January if you wish to stay here for the following winteure'. A 'power-mad bureaucrat', king of his little world, who lost us as potential moorers for good. (He actually called later in the year offering us a mooring – one of many unfilled slots that winter I learned subsequently).

We rounded a bend on the Zwartewater river and our many friends, made over two wonderful years, were left behind to reflect on our legacy to their town. That wouldn't have taken them long! By the time we had traversed the small Ganzendiep link canal and joined the River Ijssel at Kampen heading for Ketelmeer, we would have been just another transient visitor in their long, water-dependent existence.

We have been on the Ijssel before, at the end of last year in fact after we'd finished another phase of our never-ending catalogue of phases, when we joined it from the Twentekanaal which runs down the Dutch / German border. On that trip I nipped into Germany for the first time. I cycled, and the only reason I knew I was in Germany was an 'Achtung' sign by a mucky ditch. There is no border as such on the small cycle track, but despite their being no physical checkpoint the architecture changed from low-slung Dutch to high-pitch, saw-toothed German. I bought a bar of chocolate at a filling station. The choccy-bar had German writing on it to prove that I'd travelled internationally – in the small print, after all the e-numbers - 'Made in England'.

The Twentekanaal was unremarkable really, despite being rural and attractive. Except Almelo perhaps, which had a large market, the kind where you could by just about anything, including a live cow or dead goat. But it was when we entered the Ijssel just down-stream of Zutphen that we had our first taste of a 'big river'. We had to battle the 6/7 kph current to get to our overnight mooring upstream in Zutphen Marina – as our boats maximum speed is barely 10, it was a bit of a struggle. After we'd paid too much for very basic facilities we headed off downstream the following day. Now we zipped along of course pushed along by the current, our only concern was having to stop for something (which to be fair is unlikely as the river widens considerably the further west we go).

Big commercial ships, well over 100 metres in length use this waterway which links the Rhine (Nederrijn or Dutch Rhine) and the Ijsselmeer. To give you an idea of the size of the river, at one point we were being overtaken by a laden 100-metre ship which was in turn being overtaken by another empty one of similar size. If that wasn't enough there was a further one coming up-stream - so at that point we were virtually four abreast. We kept well out of the way to the right bank and it was a bit alarming for a moment.

Despite their size there was not too much turbulence (due largely to the width and depth of the river) but we were really rocked about when a 'Police launch' passed us doing 25 kph or so – a boat very similar to Rob the imitation policeman's, burning about 50 litres of diesel an hour – at the taxpayers' expense. It's probably rushing to the dead goat stall to procure one before they ran out (not that a dead goat can run out).

There are few better feelings than zipping down a river carried by the current. We pass the odd village or pretty windmill or the occasional knackered native ploughing a lonely furrow.

In Kampen last time we saw a 'replica' of Noah's' Ark. It's gone now, probably sitting atop a mountain somewhere – but not in Holland, because there aren't any. Being in an ark or on a boat is not a bad place to be when about a quarter of the country is below sea level. It's also flat and we descend one of the few locks to enter the Ijssell. This time there's no ark, instead multi-masted, multi-coloured sailing ships moored on the quay - charter boats at rest awaiting the start of the season. In full flight these ships are an extraordinary sight out on the lakes. Gangs of people pay good money for a week to crew one of these beauties. They haul ropes and defecate in a bucket in the name of team-building or personal discovery, often discovering that life aboard a sailing klipper is hard.

We're spat out of the end of the river into Ketelmeer where we turn left (port) and travel down the 'inland' waterway to the east of Flevoland polder. The water here is wide and inviting and part-way we descend our fourth lock in three years.

We stop for 'elevenses' and de-camp to deck chairs on the bank. Basking in the sunshine to get some colour into our winter-white extremities, a fishing boat passes. Drying fish-traps strung from the rigging look like bejewelled spiders' webs in the sun on a dewy morning.

Baz and Ally are experienced boaters having skippered a passenger narrow-boat in the UK for many years. We're into our 6th year boating so between us we've learned plenty but both crews feel the reassurance of companionship. Baz is a big guy, well over 6 feet, a gentle chap but with a certain 'presence', so he's head of security. Ally is the brains of the outfit and voice of reason. My wife Jan is a joker who will calm us down after nervy encounters. And me, well I'm a short, portly bloke who will probably get everyone else into trouble.

Had we been travelling 90 years ago our passage would have been very different. Instead of cruising this inland waterway we would have been hugging the coast of the Zuiderzee (South Sea) a shallow inlet of the North Sea. It's pretty extraordinary because pre 1920 Elburg and other towns such as Hardevijk, Spakenburg (all to our left as we head south) would have been on the coast. Their outlook is very different now over a wide waterway to the new polder of Flevoland.

We moor at Elburg. It's a postcard-pretty port that relies largely on tourism these days after it was bypassed by the railway when local landowners refused to accept 'low' offers for their land. We moor well back from the town-side port - mainly because we thought it would be free there – it's not. Across the waterway are some rather smart boatyards catering for rather smart people in rather smart, multi-thousand Euro motor cruisers. Four 'Eengleesh' people of various sizes stand out in their jumbled assortment of charity-shop clothing.

Having done a bit of this sort of thing before, one thing you can predict with certainty is uncertainty. Namely various challenges that crop up, particularly when you are relaxed and really enjoying yourself. We set off in a mysterious fit of optimism the following day with Baz and Ally leading. The sun shone and there was barely a breeze as we headed off down the wide waterway. Then the fog came rolling in, pretty thick stuff too, so it was navigation lights on as we all peered into the gloom. There are usually some big ships about so we have to be vigilant. Being in the fog is very disorientating so when Baz steered the wrong side of a huge dredging boat at anchor nobody was surprised, certainly nobody blamed him. The dredger was festooned with lights so it was nigh impossible to ascertain which side to pass. Unfortunately, as Baz crept down the starboard side of the ship (the correct side) he rammed a sandbank and got stuck. We waved happily as we reversed and sailed on... ..no, not really, we helped pull him off, but he was a bit sheepish, calling himself all the names under the fog.

Further south is the port of Spakenburg, another delightful little town. (From here on in I'm not going to use 'delightful little town' again – instead, we'll presume it's delightful unless I tell you different). It's home to a fleet of Botters, purpose-built wooden fishing boats designed to ply their trade on the Ijsselmeer. They are wide for their 13-metre length with a rounded, up-swept bow. The forward quarter houses a low cabin with basic loo and bed for overnight trips and the remainder is an enclosed flat deck for the landing and storing of fish. The first botters were built in the 1860s so were exclusively sail-powered but most now also have motors and are largely 'historic' ships and ornamental. I'm not sure how many are still in existence but there are enough to have rallies race-weekends out on the lakes. Our friend from Zwartsluis, Richard, rescued what is believed to be the first ever botter built. They found it part-submerged in Amsterdam (in the 1960s I believe) being used as a giant flower tub outside a restaurant. With the help of personal money and local company donations, they restored it and now take groups, up to a dozen or so at a time, on evening trips complete with picnic and sometimes music. When we had a trip a chap was hacking away on an accordion which accompanied our evening smorgasbord. Botter ZS 13 is run as a trust and to keep the first ever botter in service, income received from paying guests and local sponsorship just about keeps it afloat – mainly thanks to the voluntary efforts and skills of enthusiasts who do the repair and maintenance work.

Hardevijk (pronounced - hard e vike) is our next port of call (nautical expression there!). A large former seafaring and fishing town its now more yacht harbour and tourist centre. As with other towns along here it's raison-d'etre changed dramatically when the Ijsselmeer was created. As a testament to its former fishing glory-days, they hold the annual Aaltjesdad which translates as Eel Day where people indulge that well-known pastime - the purchasing and the consuming of eels! Eels look foul but smoked eel is really good – particularly after a couple of dozen beers. Hardevijk is also home to Hanky Panky – aka Hendrikus Johannes Everhardus "Henk" Schiffmacher – tattoo artist to the stars apparently! I opted out of a tattoo mainly because whenever I go on one of my regular sorties to the engine room, I emerge covered in so much oil and grease, you wouldn't be able to see the tattoo anyway. I should really be nicknamed Herr Inkblot. In the early morning, before we leave, the net-bedecked fishing boat slips out quietly for another day on the lakes.

Right, we need to get on with this saga a bit or it will be longer than the actual trip. Left out of Hardevijk we head for Muiden, a few kilometres east of Amsterdam aiming for (yet) another lock onto the Vecht for a short run before turning off onto the Small Veesp canal. It's at the end of this we encounter our first major panic. We have to cross the Amsterdam Rhine Canal, literally straight over it, at right angles to its course. This is a major highway carrying some very large ships. We have to wait out of sight of the canal before passing under a bridge and rounding a slight corner before crossing the canal. I use one of the skills learned while planning this continental odyssey and contact the bridge-keeper via VHF radio - and he completely ignores us. We wait a further 20 minutes and try again with the same result. I'm about to get stroppy on the radio when the bridge swings. Jan goes to the front as we crawl through so she can see if the way is clear. It's only 50 metres or so across but it's obvious that the water is turbulent. Four big cargo boats, two in each direction, have just gone past. This is obviously the reason for the delay and why we start rocking about when we approach the canal from the narrow end of our funnel. When we get out onto the canal I lose control immediately, the boat pitches and rolls and Jan has to cling to the mast to save herself being thrown into the water. Not only that but one moment the boat is facing in the right direction, the next off by 25 degrees, pointing at the wall. I can't believe the water can be so disturbed and powerful and I seriously wonder whether we can hit the fat end of the waiting funnel across the canal. Baz, who is following, tells me later that our propeller was regularly out of the water and we look like a toy duck in a bath. It really is by as much luck as judgement that we enter the short lock-cut opposite and it is a sincere relief to get into the shallow lock that will take onto the Trekkvart.

We head briefly west towards Amsterdam and moor close enough for me to cycle in – maximum range on a bike at this point is 10 kilometres each way – with a bit of a rest in the middle. Holland is a country of bicycles. Train and bus stations have row upon row of them, literally thousands, as commuters cycle to the stations and take trains to work. There are dedicated cycle paths and woe betide a car driver who injures a cyclist because the cycle is king – even if the cyclist is 'under the influence'. I join a tidal wave heading into the city at rush hour, they are going a bit quick for me but the peloton induces me to new feats of endeavour. I rest on a bridge traversing one of the many smaller canals. As a trip boat glides by I notice an 'Erotic discount Centre' near a 'Sex shop / DVD Cabin' near a……..well, you get the picture. A local walks past eating a pasty which all seems a bit normal.

Now we head south onto the River Amstel which incidentally is my favourite

Dutch beer (Amstel, not river). Hopefully we'll come across a town called Kebab and life will complete! Actually, we're heading for Gouda so at least I'll get some cheese.

Communication with the outside world is by phone, it's just very occasionally you can pick up a stray Wifi signal. We moored on the riverbank in the middle of nowhere, the only building anywhere near was a farm about a quarter of a mile away – and lo and behold we picked up a signal. While surfing the following morning the fog had descended again and we had the ghostly sight of a big cargo barge passing us in the gloom. It must have been travelling on radar.

Baz and I chat together via VHF – it's good to tell someone about your rattles and squeaks, even if we don't have the technical nous to sort them out.

The Amstel leads into the Aarkanaal which becomes the Goouwe after crossing the Oude Rijn (Old Rhine) and it is at Waddinxveen shortly afterwards that we have our first mechanical hiccup. A Morse cable snapped on Baz and Ally's boat as we were approaching a bridge leaving them unable to select a gear. (Morse cables connect your throttle leaver in the wheelhouse to both accelerator and gearbox). We were lucky that there was a 'lay-by' 50 metres back so we roped the boats together and we towed them back. This is a large canal and within a few minutes a big ship goes by. Because the bridge is on a slight bend he's going slowly – thankfully, as we are still making the boats fast when he arrives. Via the bridge-keeper Baz finds a mechanic who arrives on his motorcycle a couple of hours later. He has a look, and with a shake of the head and a good mutter he disappears again to return within the hour with a replacement cable.

Holland is a country of bicycles but it's also a country of boats, both commercial and pleasure, and consequently there is an infrastructure in place to repair and service the armada. In fact, it's fair to say that everybody knows someone who can fix a boat - if they can't do it themselves that is. You never quite know what's going to emerge from inside a motorcycle helmet but Baz's knight soon had him selecting gears with gay abandon.

So, we arrive at Gouda – cheese city. To be honest we found the Dutch cheeses generally rather bland and a bit samey. I was treated to a cheese tasting soiree last year by a chap from our boatyard in Zwartsluis. He offered me a variety of small lumps of cheese on a filthy tasting black bread. Frankly they all tasted very similar until we got to the 'old' cheeses – the real specials. These were different admittedly, largely because they were saturated with salt. So much so in fact that they nearly masked the taste of the bread. Perhaps it didn't help that my cheesy host had a severe psychological disorder due to problems at work and relationship re-alignments so I have left with a prejudiced view the Dutch cheese. We bought a little piece of Gouda cheese 'just for the record' and turned east towards Utrecht and Nieuwegein. Also, for the record, Gouda is twinned with Gloucester – they have yet to produce Double Gouda, which would be doubtless doubly bland.

We lock down onto the Hollandse Ijssel, the river that services and skirts Gouda. We pass locks and sluices that give access to, and protect the town from, this tidal river before locking up again into a small canal, also called the Hollandse Ijssel. Reminiscent of the canals in the UK (without shopping trolleys or water gypsies) we immediately feel a little relaxing of tension and celebrate with yet another glass of wine - and a piece of cheese.

We wind our way east through small towns with narrow bridges. Although everything works efficiently, this is not a major commercial canal which is obvious from the old skeletal ironwork on the 'praying mantis' lift-bridges and (sometimes) disused canal-side buildings. Dare I say it but it is slightly 'run-of-the-mill' here, attractive and gentle, yet uninspiring. If we were doing similar for the first time, yes, great, but we've done this before and there are no tingly nerves to remind us that we're alive and buzzing.

But we start buzzing again when the waterway widens and commercial ships come back into the equation as we approach Utrecht and Nieuwegein. The former is a fair-sized city serviced by the Amsterdam Rhine Canal and the latter gateway to the big Lek river and access to the major European waterways network. West to Rotterdam (and the world), east to the Rhine and Germany and Switzerland. I guess it can be all rather intimidating and you have to keep your wits about you, watching navigation markers and keeping out of the way of the big boats.

Sadly, it's at this point that Baz and Ally decide they've had enough. Whether it's the thought of traversing the big rivers (which you must do to go south) or the news of the impending arrival of their grandchild, and desire to be close enough to get back to the UK easily, I'm not sure. Hopefully it's not us that's put them off. In any event we are really sorry to leave them behind and when I get our first glimpse of the River Lek there's a bit of 'turning back' in us too! But we have a dream to fulfil so after a last night with our companions, we head on.

I've written a letter – here......

From: The Captain's dog
MV Vrouwe Johanna

Dear Mr Mayor of Zwartsluis

Can I say what a delightful two years we spent as guests in your town.
Almost without exception your subjects treated this old dog and his parents to a hearty and sincere welcome. For the overwhelming majority of our stay we were made to feel very much at home, particularly when spending money in one of your fine assortment of shops. I feel I should mention however the Jack Russell who urinated on our ropes back in August 2008 – behaviour most unbefitting an intelligent, if strong-minded, breed. I have to say though, this crass display of piddling was wholly unrepresentative of the vast majority of the natives. Also worthy of my irritation is that mottled cat who lived on Mastenmarkerstraat who wouldn't keep still long enough for me to attack it.
May I, with all due respect, point out one or two things that may enhance the visitor experience. Firstly, you can't buy lamb - which is one of our favourites. I understand your view of them, being little fluffy things that gambol around a field, but if you are prepared to eat snert (that explosive pea and ham soup you seem so fond of), is a little lamb so out of the question? Dad did manage to buy a saddle of lamb in Staphorst but it was very small (a rat saddle perhaps) and very expensive – and there were no leftovers.

Another thing is all those infernal two-wheel contraptions. I really would have thought that a wonderful country, so advanced in many ways, would have embraced a more suitable form of transport, particularly when you have so many natural resources just off your west coast. Every family appears to be a multiple-contraption household which makes it all the more inexplicable that someone should thieve Dad's old run-about – purchased I might add (at little expense) from one of the fine contraption emporiums in your town. I am amazed at the risk car-drivers take every time they venture out on the highways and the apparent disregard these two-wheelers have for safety. I saw one where a mother was transporting three young children on the same machine – one in a basket on the front, one in another basket on the back and one in a trailer – and this was winter when the temperature was well below freezing.

My only other 'bone' of contention (I've emphasised the little English quip there in case you missed it) is your method of communication. I'm not quite sure why you have so many consonants in your language, delivered with a series of guttural throat-clearings. We have tried to master it I promise you but poor old Dad spent hours practising in a shower of spittle and was still quite unable to converse in your native tongue. It got expensive too because both he and Mum, in an effort to purchase goods from your emporiums, tried to order in Dutch but frequently got entirely the wrong item. It was only so as not to offend your traders that, instead of trying to exchange the offending item for the right product, they came home with something wholly unsuitable. We have a 'mistake' cupboard full of unwanted and largely unrecognisable artefacts which may be of historical interest in years to come but not much good in the here and now.

Now, I don't want to appear a grumbler, far from it, because we have had delightful experiences in Zwartsluis. Take Mother's art group for example which lasted for four hours, yes four hours, one evening a week. The reason for this protracted painting was 'Vine Time'. She explained this to Dad as the hourly halt in proceedings where one of the students would open a bottle of wine, and on the hour, every hour, the leader of the group would insist that everyone downed brushes and had a slurp. Now Mum doesn't drink, instead she was awash with coffee when she returned home sometime towards midnight. Had she been a drinker she would quite possibly never found her way home having downed enough wine to immerse a sheep (if you could find one). But the friends she made there were lovely people and she was readily accepted into the colourful world of Zwartsluis artists - all ladies I might add – future Dutch Mistresses perhaps?

Overall, thank you Mr Mayor. We have enjoyed a wonderful two-year sojourn in your town and although I doubt I shall return – age catching up – I'm sure Mum and Dad will.

Fondly
   The Hound of Vrouwe Johanna

BIG Rivers

Access onto the River Lek is via an enormous double lock totalling 220 metres in length. We're like a tiny pea in a barrel as we gently descend. The huge gates open as we fire straight across the river into another big lock, this even longer at 240 metres, on the south bank. The Lek is one of the 3 big rivers we'll have to tackle, we're only going straight across this one so it's no problem as long as we don't get side-swiped by a one of the cargo ships that motor on here at some speed. We do drift downstream a little on the current but it's not as bad as we had feared.

The town of Viannen guards the lock at the northern end of the Merwerdekanaal. It is an ancient place and a potter round on the bike sees you pass through the remnants of ancient castles and fortifications. Mobile sales emporiums (Dutch equivalent to burger vans) line the main street selling the likes of Kip, Kaas and Kibling (chicken, cheese and chunks of white fish nuggets in seasoned batter).

We're doing a faux snakes and ladders manoeuvre working our way south and gradually east across Holland - our next target is Gorinchem. Another riverside city, this one is on the banks of the Waal. Now this IS a big river. It is the main distributary branch of the Rhine carrying 65% of it's water from Germany east to Rotterdam. We moor in a nature reserve a few kilometres north of Gorinchem and I cycle in for a look at the river. For any relative novices, like me, this is quite a sight. It's huge, perhaps a couple of hundred metres wide, milk-chocolate-muddy and a highway for a fleet of big boats, some huge. Often you have a 'rooster tail' of water emerging from the rear of a boat when it is running hard against the current. One that I saw was a pusher-tug (which is basically an enormous engine housed in a flat-fronted shell) pushing 3 caissons full of coal against the current – which we were told was flowing at a steady 2 / 3 knots. This combination was followed by seven rooster tails gradually diminishing from something over a metre in height to a tiddler bringing up the rear. The combination was being chased by a churning, foaming river monster. You could hear and 'feel' the low growl of the powerful engines from over 100 metres distant as it headed up river to the east. In addition, there were eight other large cargo boats in sight zipping left and right, so this is quite obviously a major artery. The remaining boats are just 'normal' 100 metre ones ferrying coal, oil, gravel and the many other products that help keep Western Europe ticking.

On my return to our boat on wobbly legs I decide not to tell Jan what I've seen I case she decided to follow Baz and Ally back to the UK. Instead, I decided to repair to the engine room and have a large whiskey - then another. Then I check every nut and bolt I can access to make sure a that nothing will drop off when we get on the river. We only have to travel about four kilometres up stream but I have to admit to being a bit nervous.

I know, I know, it sounds like I'm being a bit wimpy but anything new on this scale makes me excited and anxious. Anyhow, the following morning, we lock down in the company of three other boats. A small Dutch cruiser, an empty 60-metre commercial barge and an ex-hire boat being piloted by a chap whose gear box is on the blink. It's Fergy and Audrey's first boat and I'm not sure he's aware of the foolhardiness of travelling anywhere with an integral piece of equipment in that condition, never mind on a waterway of this size. Anyway, out we go and from 'sea level' it looks even wider than yesterday when I was perched up on the wharf.

We head straight across to the right bank (left bank technically as they are categorised when looking down-stream) and basically get out of everyone's way. We head east against the current and only make about 3 kph so it's not long before two barges we had seen in the distance catch us up and thunder by. As I've said previously they don't really make that much wash, just leave us a moderate swell. It's because their wake is contra to the flow of the river that the water surface looks jumbled long after they've passed. One, that looks like a fuel carrier of some sort, is so laden and low in the water that it's gunwales are awash.

Our 4-kilometre trip takes over an hour before we turn off into a tributary that will take us down our next 'ladder'; the Afgedamde Maas. Audrey and Fergy of the dicky equipment are ahead of us somewhere and have planned a similar route towards the Mass river.

As we moor up we see the setting sun, an orange globe speared atop a church steeple in distant Woudrichem. It's so tranquil, calm and beautiful that we wonder what all the fuss was about - unlike Fergy who phones to tell us that they are at anchor on the banks of the Maas with a gear box in shreds. They are understandably panicky and looking for someone to tow them to a safe haven - and a mechanic. By the sound of it they was lucky to get as far as they did but it's still a poor situation.

We leave our Yachthaven the following morning – they were a friendly bunch, the port captain was a cheery soul who smiled a lot even if he was dressed in 'Mr Toad' trousers. Our next proper challenge will be the Maas River and we lock down on to it near Huesden. This river, and it's extension through Belgium into France, will be home for a good few weeks.

Although a big river it doesn't somehow feel as threatening as the Waal. It still has similarly large ships and we'll have to cope with some big locks. Maybe it's the vegetation on the banks that soften the look and the fact that cows are mooching about in the shallows having a drink. We'll be travelling many miles against the current and although our progress is fairly slow it's actually relaxing. One of the main differences between here and the UK canals is the relative isolation you can feel. Yes, there are quite a number of boats about, largely commercial, but you don't communicate, unlike the canals, and to a lesser extent rivers, in the UK where you are constantly chatting at locks where you have to get off and operate them yourself.

We spot Fergy and Audrey anchored in a shallow inlet and stop to see if they are alright. They re-assure us that someone is due to arrive shortly to tow them to a boatyard a few kilometres upriver.

Samuel Johnson compared sailing in a ship to being in jail with the chance of being drowned. I suspect this is how Fergy and Audrey feel. Despite our offer of a tow, we all agree that it's perhaps best left to the experts and we leave them. A while later they phone and tell us they are under tow and approaching safety.

Despite trying to call them on a number of occasions over the next few days, we never hear from them again.

It's April 21st, we've been going less than three weeks and feel to have had a major adventure already. Another major adventure is our first lock (sluis) here on the Maas. It's pretty intimidating. Two pairs of concrete towers stand tall against the sky at each corner of the lock. A high-level gantry connects the two fore towers, likewise the rear, across the lock gates. We are funnelled into the lock by a four-metre high steel wall to port and a 50-metre long floating waiting pontoon to starboard. Further back to starboard we wait on another 300-metre floating pontoon and watch as a commercial barge heads for the lock before us. We await the lock keepers call on the VHF radio and creep in at the back of the lock. Basically, we want to keep out of the way as much as possible and prefer to enter the lock at the rear as there tends to be less turbulence. The lock is roughly 250 metres long and 16 metres wide with bollards set into the wall at 2.5 metre intervals up the wall. As we rise we have to move our ropes up to the next bollard – which is not straightforward as our boat is washed fore and aft, as well as rocking from side to side with the turbulence.

But manage we do, partly thanks to Jan keeping calm. The stern of the ship in front towers over our bow and it must be intimidating for her. We stay tied up till the commercial powers out of the lock before we trundle behind in it's wake.

We get an idea of how well the Dutch make use of their waterway network when we see a lorry tipping topsoil straight into a barge. A 50-metre steel ramp had been built out from the bank supported on a large floating pontoon anchored in the river. The lorry reverses to the end of the ramp and tips its load straight into the ship that has moored directly below. It's peculiar seeing a big truck perched in mid-air.

We thought we might struggle to find suitable moorings on the rivers but if we don't happen upon one of the infrequent pleasure-boat harbours we can stop above a lock on a waiting pontoon. Particularly good mooring spots are what I believe are the sites of gravel or sand extraction, now flooded to form artificial lakes. They are safe and accessed via a channel off the river. We pulled off into one such lake and lo and behold a narrowboat arrived! Peter and Barbara on Oxford Blue are wanderers supreme and seem unfazed by trundling round on a boat that some say is unsuited to large continental waterways. They seem to manage just fine, as do others who we've come across.

Then suddenly, a hill!

In the distance to the east, a lumpy apparition appears on the horizon. We haven't seen a proper lump for a while so this is pretty exciting. It's not exactly a snow-capped Himalayan peak but it's the biggest thing we've come across in 2 years. The Dutch landscape is indeed rather featureless but this is compensated for by interesting waterside towns and big skies. You can see a storm approaching from the Urals and prepare yourself - unlike our former home in the Pennines where filthy weather creeps over the hilltops and douses you in a good old northern downpour almost before you can raise your brolly.

Before we crash into the hill we turn south at Nijmegen and arrive at Roermond, a large city on the river's eastern bank. Across the river is the creatively titled Maasplassen (loose translation – Maas pee or Maas puddle) where we moor up for a few days on a safe, clean mooring on another large lake. Here we meet Noel and Barbara on their barge Henrietta – we had dinner with them in Zwartsluis not long ago – our first social evening for a while. Then a lady arrives from Southport, Lancashire – not directly you understand, she's actually now living in nearby Venlo, but she's originally from the same part of the world as us so we can chat freely about kiss-me-quick hats and black puddings – you can't do that with everyone.

The water here is gin clear (Dutch waterways are generally very clean). As we pull away a couple of days later we can see our 'deposits' lurking in the shallows including vegetable peelings and, well, other bits and bobs. I position the boat, stern towards the bank and a healthy burst of throttle disperses things a bit! It's still early season but I can imagine this place being packed during the holidays or at weekends. It's the equivalent to a city-centre park where high-rise residents imagine they're in the country and lounge around in dog muck while idly swapping tales of investment strategies while drinking flat beer.

Following the German border south we ascend a huge lock which has floating bollards. These are set into the wall on runners and rise or fall with the water – much easier than the 'bollard-in-the-wall' arrangement, and we arrive, via Maasbracht and the Julianakanaal, in Maastricht. It's here, in perhaps the flattest country in the World, they held a summit.

There is mooring on a stone jetty which splits the river longitudinally for 200-metres or so mid-river between two bridges but because of all the steps this is not ideal for an ageing dog. We moor instead in front of a 'wacky-backy' café boat. It's in effect a Koffie Shop where the purchase and consummation of products 'wacky' is permitted. Periodically a whiff of something drifts our way, which is why the skipper can be found on the rear deck, relaxing in her chair, nostrils aflare. Because the quay is high we need a ladder from the cabin roof to get off which is a bit precarious, particularly when a recent cloud from the Koffie Shop has left us feeling a bit giddy.

Maastricht is the junction of some large waterways including the Albert Canal and the Maas River (which will soon become the Meuse) so we need to keep a sharp look-out as we head off towards the Belgian border immediately south of the city. As you enter Belgium you stop to inform the authorities who you are and where you are heading. Or rather you are supposed to - we just fired straight through the border blissfully unaware of our international indiscretion. You don't have to pay for a license if you're shooting through on the super-highway to France, but if you detour to sample the beer, choccies and Eddie Mercks Museum in the Belgian interior, you have to pay for the privilege. Whichever way, they take your name to ensure you actually do what you said you'd do. In our case they don't know we're here so they won't know what we did.

Consequently, we sneak into Liege under cover of our smoky engine and moor up in a wholly unsuitable yacht harbour. It's a spur that runs parallel to the river and unsuitable because once we're in we can't turn round. Helpfully there is a 'maximum turning 12m' sign halfway down the spur so we'll have to reverse 200 metres round a slight bend down an avenue of expensive boats to get back on the river. This manoeuvre is contemplated in a very nasty bar in a miserable suburb after we'd taken the wrong route into town. I understand that Liege is known for its beauty and in particular it's markets, but we failed to find them. I'm sure we'll return to do it justice but if you want a 'city guide' you won't find one here - there are plenty on the web.

Sensing our proximity to La Belle France we sneak out at 07.30 and are soon in a lock that we share with a huge commercial boat carrying scrap metal. The skipper looked down on us from the comfort of his air-conditioned wheelhouse with a haughty look, bordering on disdain. It probably took all his self-control not to winch our scruffy little old boat onto his scrap heap.

Soon after leaving Liege and it's numerous bridge crossings the Meuse becomes really beautiful – excepting the odd 'scar', primarily the Knauf factory, which is huge and gypsum-dusty. It looks like the Shell oil refinery at the bottom of the river Weaver in Cheshire, England, except this one's covered in a ghostly white sheen. It reminds us of that early Windows screensaver with all it's re-generating pipework. Gypsum is used in plasterboard walling and the Knauf brand is one that even I have heard of having done a few bodgy renovations in a past life.

Typically, there is a narrow flood plain next to the river before wooded slopes rise gently a hundred metres or so. Some impressive properties adorn these hillsides and every now and then a magnificent citadel is silhouetted against the sky. It really is lovely territory and our view from the river is indeed a privileged one.

We're in the land-locked region of Wallonia, the southern and predominantly French-speaking area of Belgium. Taking up roughly half the area of the country it houses only a third of the population but due to its coal and iron industry and transport links via the Meuse and Sambre rivers, it was second only to the UK during the industrial revolution in terms of wealth. Huy is one of the cities on the Meuse and the vista of huge religious buildings and old fortifications on the hills above the city are awe-inspiring and testament to its former wealth. I believe one particular fortification was built by the Dutch in the early 19th Century replacing a 16th century castle that was dismantled by the locals. They were supposedly sick and tired of it being attacked due it's symbolic strength and important strategic location in the region so they just removed it!

Leaving the city there is a 4-metre wall to starboard, flood protection I would think. Set in this wall is a steep concrete slipway. At the bottom of this slippery-looking slope is a chap washing his Audi motor car. We hope his handbrake is in good condition – Vorsprung durch gurgle.

Huy was also home to John Joseph Merlin, inventor of the roller skate. I mention this purely for the nautical connections of roller and skate.

Namur is the confluence of the Sambre and Meuse rivers. The former flows west toward Charleroi as the Meuse turns south. Namur is the capital of Wallonia and a stunning place. The modern, fully serviced mooring has wonderful views of the citadel perched on the hill-top across the river. The citadel sits directly above Walloon's parliament building on the junction of the rivers and is originally Roman, although it has been extended periodically since. Witnessing the floodlit citadel guarding the floodlit bridge in the foreground by night is truly amazing.

We stay a day or two and explore the town. What a market! After the limited choice we found in Holland, this is foodie heaven. I bought some jellied tongue for a sandwich – turns out it was Pâté de tête which is all the soft bits of a pigs head mashed up and re-constituted into a block and sliced. But it looks just like tongue. Luckily I found this out after lunch so enjoyed it - on buttered brown bread with a smear of mint jelly! We could envisage trouble ahead on the weight front.

It was here too that we met Geoff and Jenny on their Linssen Dutch Cruiser. A friendly, cheerful and smart couple who we soon brought down to our level. We'd cruise with them on and off for the next few weeks. This arrangement works fine if there's not too much advance planning, in which case you may feel obliged to compromise your own strategy and habits in favour of keeping the peace. We spent many evenings together and often cruised in train. But we also did different things individually and sometimes moored in different places. No pressure to please or oblige – just a natural friendship, which was ideal. A friendship that endured through that summer and still does – despite living in different countries. In fact, they have sold their boat!

The scenery continues to be stunning, huge riverside houses, wooded hills and occasional cliffs line our route as we approach the home town of Adolphe Sax, inventor of the saxophone. Dinant is another bustling, fortified town squeezed within the confines of the river valley. Devastated regularly over the years, it suffered particularly badly during World War 1. Consequently, it's a mixture of ancient and relatively new buildings and is also home to the 'couque', Europe's hardest biscuit!

We head off in the rain towards France. Just prior to Givet we pass the 'Douane Belgie' (Belgian Customs) where a bemused official is unable to rubber-stamp our departure from Belgium because we never officially entered - but it gives him a good excuse to have a mutter. So, after a month and a day through half of Holland and all of Belgium we arrive in La Belle France.

Overall impressions; Holland? Marvellous. Belgium? Well, it's not fair to express an opinion because we weren't there long enough – and for that brief period we were illegal aliens.

I've written another letter.......
  From: The Captain's dog
  MV Vrouwe Johanna

Dear Nicholas the Wonder-worker

I'm sure this epistle will reach you despite addressing you by your alternative title. As patron paint of sailors under your more familiar guise, Saint Nicholas, you have guided us safely into our third country in a month. As someone who has watched over seafarers for aeons I would have expected no less. I believe in this sort of thing you see. I'm superstitious, respectful of tradition and pray to Dog regularly.

  It's the Wonder-worker aspect of your persona that I focus on in this letter because, despite your ethereal guidance, there are limits to your powers when it comes to dealing with the stupidity of the earth-bound species – namely Mum and Dad and the extraordinary assortment of misfits with whom they share the waterways. They just seem to launch themselves into an adventure knowing bugger all about what they are letting themselves in for, and more importantly me! I have no say in the matter, I'm excluded from life-altering family decisions; potentially life-ending indeed. They charge out into huge rivers with suicidal abandon. These massive, muddy serpents are patrolled by leviathans. One brush with one of these beasts could spell catastrophe. And they go against the flow! Why for goodness sake. They're revving the mutts off the engine and barely moving.

Between you and me I don't blame Baz and Ally for ducking out. I enjoyed their company and miss them but fully sympathise with their desires to see their grandchildren grow up. If I thought that Mum and Dad could manage without me I'd have gone back to Blighty with them!

Lots of pleasure boaters seem to go far too fast, their sole purpose seems to be to get to the next mooring as fast as possible then fall asleep. Not wanting to cause an international incident, I'll not specify which country the main culprits come from but they do seem a bit pushy. Having said that, we're now approaching France so we'll be able to travel for four hours during the middle of the day when the locals are at lunch.

I know as patron saint of mariners you have our best interests at heart but we've been passed by some of your apostles, covertly patrolling in Police boats. You couldn't ask them to slow down a bit could you, they don't half knock us about.

Overall though, thank you for safe passage thus far, although I'm pretty sure we'll be turning round to go home soon.

Much love

Bonny

La Belle France

Just before leaving Belgium we passed the hamlets of Lustin, Dave and Grotte! Now in France we bypass Chooz and Ham. Nothing internationally distinctive about the two nations place names then. Ham has a tunnel though, the first one we've encountered, which is unsurprising really, they don't need tunnels in Holland, there's nothing to dig through.

There are locks before and after the tunnel (which is about 600-metres long). We're now into to 'Freycinet' territory. A Freycinet barge was built to a gauge not exceeding 38.5m x 5.05m (126 x 16.6 feet), and the locks are sized accordingly – in other words much smaller than we have been used to. The locks look a bit unkempt, like some we encountered in the UK. The old barges were the workhorses of the canals and a few are still in use commercially today. Others have been converted to pleasure boats but the vast majority have disappeared altogether. It's largely because of the commercial boats that the canals are kept open and they carry for, example, logs and grain, unlike our boat that carries a fat chap and his wife – although the quantity of vin rouge could be considered commercial.

There is one distinctive change though - in France you have to pay a Vignette (cruising license) whereas in Holland it's free. Again, this is probably due to less to the benevolence of the Dutch but more the amount of commercial traffic and the need to keep the waterways flowing.

Haybes is a magnificent mooring on the Meuse where we have exclusive use of a fully serviced pontoon. The view looking down from the river bridge is breathtaking. Our little boat is nestled on the riverbank by this lovely town, set within rolling, forested hills. The town is dominated by the Hotel de Ville (town hall). As is often the case it is the best kept building in town and just in case we weren't aware which country we are in, it has a dozen Tricolours flapping in the breeze from it's first floor balcony.

When we cycled to the nearby town of Fumay we got wrapped up in a march for 'The Freedom of France'. It seemed to be working as there wasn't a single person in handcuffs and a local Gendarme was standing on a corner eating an ice-cream. Perhaps the march was organized by the local Thrush population because historically the songbirds were snared (when they came in search of rowan berries) plucked and cooked in butter and sage. The Thrush population is safe these days and thankfully the town is better known for it's white pudding with onions.

We were making steady southerly progress when we encountered an unfortunate delay. Entering a lock behind Geoff and Jenny we duly rose 2 ½ meters. Our friends exited the lock then the gates shut — then we started going down again! Geoff looked a bit bemused as he sailed away and turned to see us disappearing down behind the lock gates again. When you approach a lock there are various methods for setting it in motion. You either turn a chord which dangles over the stream from a 'gallows' situated a couple of hundred metres from the lock (like this particular one). Alternatively you press an automated 'clicker', given to you at an earlier lock and which you carry with you. Thereafter the process is automated — the lock sets itself and you are bidden by a sequence of traffic lights. What we didn't realize was that EACH boat has to turn the chord so the lock recognizes how many boats are in the lock, hence a 'magic eye' can count you out and close the gates behind you. We didn't twist the chord a second time so the lock gates closed and we had to be rescued by a laughing lockkeeper. Actually, I'm not sure why he is called a lock keeper because all the does is keep the grass mown and try to flog you his home-made thrush wine, all the rest is done automatically — unless he has to rescue an idiot.

We've been lucky with the weather thus far, but now we pay for it. It rains for much of the next 6 days. The town of Château Regnault is little to sister to Bogny-sur-Meuse, directly across the river, and it's here we hole up for a week as it rains and rains. The river rises and the flow increases, fewer and fewer boats pass us upstream. We're OK though safely tied to a floating pontoon; there's a butcher, baker and épicerie (grocer) nearby. It's in the butchers that Jan's early attempt at the French language got a bit bogged down. We wanted some minced beef, translated as boeuf haché (pron. burf hashay). I instructed her in the finer arts of meat procurement and she set off for the shop. As she walked she muttered and practised her little speech all the while. It was a bit of a 'Chinese Whispers' situation because by the time she got there here instruction to the butcher had morphed to a 'kilo of hashish please', which, on a rainy weekday, cheered up the meat-man and his assistant no end. She's delaying a haircut.

One morning (7.45 ish) I'm in the wheelhouse fabricating my memoirs. Outside it's lashing it down, blowing a gale and generally fairly miserable. Something distracts me and I look up and see a small face at the window. It's a young lad who's just standing there in the rain peering in at me. Poor thing is drenched so I invite him in. His name is Thomas and he's a bit early for his school bus which leaves from the lay-by just up the steps from our mooring. He tells me he is eleven, though he looks younger, and that he lives with his Mum across the river in Bogny (pron. bon yee). We chat and he asks me, with genuine interest, about our boat. Is it a house? Why is the steering wheel so big? Where are we going? Where are we from? Soon some of his mates arrive at the bus-stop so he leaves and trots up the steps to join his pals.

Later that day I take a walk over the bridge to Bogny but what I see leaves me quite disturbed. The main thoroughfare is fairly typical of riverside towns we have seen previously with tabac, bakery and butcher but I investigate the little hillside town a bit further. One street back it's a very different story. Crumbling houses some of which have cracks you can nearly walk through, boarded up shops, rickety pavements and a general feeling of undignified decay. There are pockets of resistance and many people live here quite happily I'm sure but the general trend of the town feels to be down. My (very limited) intuition proves pretty accurate when I discover the industry that used to be here, based largely around metal including the manufacture of nails and bolts, has shrunk. Many fewer people are now employed in this sector and I wonder what a place like this holds for young Thomas and his mates. If they leave to find work a generation will slip away and the town will be starved of it's lifeblood. Historically industry was present here because of the river as raw materials were shipped in and finished goods shipped out. Now the river just creeps by, unaware of the crumbling town above.

There's a knock on the boat door late in the afternoon. It's my young friend and he's been hard at work at school and has produced a mini boating dictionary for me. French words written on a torn piece of paper against their English translations. He's beaming and tells Jan and I that teacher helped him. We get the impression that he and his Mum are not well-off but an eleven-year-old lad is happy to please us and has no concept that his town might be withering away. I guess he'll find out soon enough.

Bogny and Château Regnault sit astride a loop in the river and high on a bluff on the western side is the site of a legendary 'Hermitage'. Here there is a memorial plaque to ten resistance fighters who prevented the German army destroying a bridge over the Meuse in September 1944 thereby allowing a company of US soldiers to cross and join up with forces in nearby Belgium. They used a Mittrailleuse, a multi barrelled machine gun, that was found in nearby forest four years earlier and restored by local resistance fighters. The bluff towers over the river, a perfect strategic position from which the local resistance fired their gun at the Germans way below. It's sobering to imagine the danger of this act of defiance, one of many throughout war-torn France. The staccato chatter of the old gun would have echoed through the beautiful landscape of hills and forests – utterly at odds with the beauty and peace now.

The weather has relented and the river slowed a little as we motor on to Charlesville-Meziéres. There's the International Institute of Puppetry here and they hold Festival Mondial des Théâtres de Marionnettes every three years. The town is obviously big into performance art as right outside our boat we have a young man juggling three large daggers, the kind of things Errol Flynn would wield while wearing silly trousers. Our juggler is a member of a 'Troupe', a travelling circus, and if lobbing daggers is not enough, he is accompanied by his pet rat, Nestas, who weaves around the guy's shoulders during his performance! Nestas is a white rat who keeps jumping off his master to scuttle away in search of a titbit, so our juggler has to repeatedly stop his practice and recapture his pet.

Later in the evening a group of lads arrive and sit on the grass nearby drinking too much. They get quite boisterous and the language becomes flowery. Unacceptable? No. The only difference between us is that I'm on a boat.

The hills are flattening out a little as we progress through the department of Ardennes in the region of Champagne-Ardennes and the landscape is dominated far and nearby steeples and cows respectively. Every town or city seems to have one claim to fame, puppets in the last place, here in Sedan we find the largest fortified medieval castle in Europe. Like so many towns on the Meuse, it's ancient centre is built in a loop or curve in the river. We had a brief flirt with the real world here where we picked up our mail at the Poste Restante to be told, quite unnecessarily, that we'd no money left and where we could buy a half-price sofa.

Besides fortifications, the other buildings prevalent in towns and cities are religious. The huge Gothic church in Mouzon seems disproportionate to the size of the small town. It's twin steeples, vaulted roof and enormous organ are awe-inspiring and it never ceases to amaze me how our forefathers could construct such mighty, complex structures without the machinery used on today's buildings.

It's near Stennay that the river morphs with the canal and becomes the Canal de La Meuse. As the river is much smaller now, man-made canal replaces unnavigable stretches of river. I've been looking forward to Stennay, not least because it has a Beer Museum. It's a highlight that would take so much self-control to avoid that I don't even bother trying. The walk round is interesting and informative but only a prelude to sitting in the bar at the end and actually tasting the filthy stuff.

Here we encounter petanque (pron. pettonk), otherwise known as boules. Adjacent to our boat a number of matches were taking place on what is normally a car park. It's a great game, played by anyone who can throw a metal ball towards a target known as a 'cochonnet' (piglet), a 30mm target ball, usually made of wood. It appears to be a gentle, delightful way to pass an hour or two in the dappled shade, but look closer and there's a seething undercurrent of vitriol – rather like croquet where you can legitimately crunch Aunt Maude's ball into the undergrowth because she's threatening to cut your allowance. The game I watched was being taken very seriously and even to my untrained eye these players are pretty determined. During the match there was little jocularity and the local supremo stood out - a chap with a casual, yet steely, air wearing a flat cap. A cigarette dangled from the corner of his mouth giving him a mean-looking one-eyed squint as the smoke curled up to stain his hat. He appeared to wait for the other 5 players to throw their balls, then with a hip-wiggle and a cough, he took careful aim. Slowly alternating between a crouch and fully erect, like a predatory animal waiting to charge on it's prey, he gauged range and wind-speed. Then with a vicious underarm whoosh he launched his 700 gramme ball towards the 'head' - it landed flush. With a series of staccato clacks the other balls, placed so carefully and accurately over the previous few minutes, were scattered all over the car park. I'm not exactly sure of the outcome but there were appreciative murmurings as measurements were taken with chord and calliper before everyone wandered around collecting their balls. Our hero had a magnet on a string so he could pick his up without actually bending down – after all the highly-trained athlete cannot afford to risk a cricked back.

One thing every petanque player want to avoid is Fanny - 'Il est Fanny' (he is fanny). This is an ignominious and potentially expensive state of affairs for a player or team beaten 13 – 0. Not only must the losing player traditionally kiss the bottom of a girl named fanny but also buy a round of drinks for the opposing team. These days girls called fanny who are prepared to have their bottom kissed are few and far between so paintings or statues are kissed instead. But the alcoholic forfeit remains.

As we leave the following morning the scene of heroic battle has reverted to a car park and almost immediately we encounter a minor irritation, a lock that won't work. We've been stuck twice now, left sitting like lemons in a drippy, empty lock while we await the super-heroes from the VNF (Voies Navigables de France), the organisation that manages the French waterways

– very efficiently I might add.

We moor later at Dun-sur-Meuse, a beautiful little place. Way above us is a wooded hill on top of which is a church – a wonderful spot from which to take a photograph of our mooring and the countryside. I cycle up a very steep hill and arrive, knackered, to find my view completely obscured by a wall of trees – so I cycle down again. We have climbed steadily since mid-Holland so rather than looking up at citadels and castles we now look down on endless countryside with little villages, set in a patchwork of shades of green, identified by church steeples and curls of smoke.

We also pass a walled cemetery, the resting place of a few of the many souls who tragically perished in the great war – this is a prelude to one of the most moving experiences of my life. We are nearing Verdun.

This is the site of the terrible Battle of Verdun. Known also as the Hell of Verdun, it is here in the hills to the north of the city, between February and December 1916, that an estimated 260,000 lives were lost - that's nearly 850 men every day for 10 months – it's almost impossible to imagine.

I tend to cycle round cities in the early morning when there is nobody else about, and the hour I spent alone, after dawn, in Verdun moved me to tears. The Monument to the victory at Verdun is at the top of the steps linking lower and upper Verdun. Down the centre of the steps flow a series of mini fountains. As I look down towards the river, the only sound I can hear is the hiss and trickle of the water. Below is the Monument to the sons of Verdun depicting five soldiers representing different branches of the armed forces, a memorial to 'des enfants de Verdun mort pour la France, - 'Children of Verdun who died for France'. In upper Verdun there is a building at the bottom of a slope racked with bullet holes. Today in the silence it is difficult to imagine the din and desperation of the soldiers fighting for this tiny bit of territory in a small square in a tiny corner of France.

Nearby the The Douaumont Ossuary is a monument below which are the unidentified, jumbled skeletons of 130,000 men, both French and German, who died in the battle. For me, nearly one hundred years on, it is extraordinary and appalling. God only knows what it was like to live it.

For the French, Verdun and it's horrors have become the defining memory of the First World War. French historian Antoine Prost writes appositely; "Like Auschwitz, Verdun marks a transgression of the limits of the human condition".

After that recent deluge it's now turned hot. So much so in fact that it's melted our candles in the window (could be a song there). I wonder whether the good Lord notices that I only go into a church when it's hot. The 17th church in St. Mihiel is magnificent - quite stunning stained-glass windows throughout and amazing, intricate sculptures (by Ligier Richier). Although I'm a weather-dependent visitor, I appreciate how these places typify the wonderful architectural and spiritual heritage of France. I say a little prayer, asking politely for an easing of the temperature.

My wish to cool down is granted on the last day of May. Our engine is cooled by water pumped direct from the waterway and circulated round the engine. It's then mixed with oil and smoke before shooting out the back. The water inlet has blocked so I have to get into the canal to unblock the pipe from underneath – bit of a design fault here. We're fine on rivers and deep water but when we get close to the bank on a weedy, muddy canal, all sorts of stuff gets sucked up into our system, occasionally blocking the pipe. Despite risking Weil's disease (a water-born malaise spread by rat's urine) I am cooler, if ratty – the Lord works in mysterious ways. This is Pagny-sur-Meuse and I'm further irritated by country and western music blurting out of the nearby village hall. Thigh-slapping, toe-tapping (and annoying) natives dribble out of the hall till the early hours until finally, about 2.00 am, we can perspire in peace.

Black Kites are prevalent. We see many of these medium-sized birds of prey as they soar above a rubbish dump near the town of Toul. Not the most romantic setting but it's exciting to see something new – disappointingly my photographs show various ill-defined dark smudges on a dappled sky - quite frankly they could be dead midges stuck on the camera lens, but I know what they are. They are recognizable by their forked tails, but even in my most imaginative mode it's impossible to confirm the shape from my smudgy snapshots.

Toul's kite-infested rubbish dump services a magnificent town. White stone ramparts encircle the old town which contains, among other things the imposing Gothic St Etienne Cathedral – in a state of some disrepair. Although conservation and repair work is ongoing it is an enormous undertaking. From a distance (the port for example) the edifice is stunning, threatening and enormous against the skyline. Close up however it's obvious neither time nor the elements have been kind to it's intricate masonry.

France and wine are synonymous. In Toul there was a monastery with an impressive wine cellar. The monastery has gone but the wine cellar remains – accessed via a camera shop I believe – got their priorities right there then!

It's early May and we are here with Geoff and Jenny for a few days and it's here we first meet Mike and Paula with whom we'll also become lasting friends. I find it pretty easy to meet people, if you go along and compliment someone's boat they'll soon start chatting. We're naturally drawn to the red ensign, largely because of the language factor I guess, but I do try out my school French on other boaters and locals. If they are prepared to converse like a 4-year-old and speak slowly, as if talking to an idiot, we can get on quite well. What you miss though is the colloquial language and humour associated with a jolly time in a bar, so I'm restricted to talk of the weather and directions to the bakery. I was talking to an English friend recently and he buttoned it quite well. He said that if he's chatting with a single Frenchman in a bar there's no problem. With a mixture of basic French and some patience it's possible to have a good conversation. The problem comes when another French person joins the conversation. Instantly, without thinking about it or deliberately trying to cut out the foreigner, the two French speakers revert to colloquial and fast-spoken French, at which point the outsider is lost. It's the quippy, colloquial bits that make for amusing and in-depth conversation that are missed.

The Moselle river is beautiful and we join it having passed Lorraine Marine, based on the outskirts of Toul, one of the few boatyards that caters for the mooring and repair of barges on the canals in France. The region of Moselle is synonymous with wine. The river is a tributary of the Rhine. We're aiming for Nancy on the Marne au Rhin canal which heads ultimately out to Strasbourg in Eastern France. Shortly after joining the river we pass through a large lock and when the gates open we're faced with an enormous commercial barge that looks to be taking up the whole waterway. We have to squeeze past and once again are reminded of how tiddly and vulnerable we are.

Having overnighted at Pompey, a steel town which, I am told, produced the rivets for the Eiffel Tower, we join the canal to Nancy leaving the Moselle which swings north-east on it's way to Mets, Luxembourg and Germany.

And another letter!..........
   From: The Captain's dog
   MV Vrouwe Johanna

Dear Belgium

I must sincerely apologise for the behaviour of my father. He showed complete disregard for your regulations and virtually ignored your fine country and it's inmates. Having trampled straight through your immigration process he clattered and wheezed through your wonderful landscape at what can only be laughably described as wharf speed. It seems the more racket the engine makes, the slower it goes and the more filth gets churned out the hole in the back.

One can only presume that this apparent ignorance is driven by his desire to arrive in your neighbour, France. He (and mother cannot be entirely blameless here) believe that getting to France will see an upturn in culinary satisfaction. I'm not so sure. After all, a country which eats just about anything that moves, stuff that even dog-food manufacturers turn their noses up at, sounds like a recipe for disaster for me. What about choccies and beer, the production and purveyance of which, you are peerless?

Quite frankly I wouldn't be surprised if you excommunicated them under your strict Walloon-avoidance laws.

Can I at least try and set the record straight. Now that they have given me a lap top I can freely express my views, shared I may say throughout the canine boating community. We love Belgium! The DBA (Dogs Boating Association) have nothing but praise for Belgium and on our wag-site will continue to endorse your country as a wonderful place to frolic and defecate without fear of persecution.

I can honestly say that wherever I have been dragged on their wanderings, I have happy memories and made good friends. Sadly, this was denied me in your country.

Let's end on a happier note. On one of the rare occasions that I popped up on deck I spotted one of your citizens running along the towpath. He seemed to have developed a brand new exercise routine because, as he ran, there was such a blur of random activity from his limbs, he looked like he was trying to fight off a flock of hornets. If you can find this chap (indeed if he has not been stung to death) his regime may become a sensation on the internet as a dance craze or wacky fitness routine and give your country a third reason to be recognizable.

Yours, rather sheepishly,

Bonny

The Magic of Nancy

By some margin Nancy is the largest city we have visited on our European trip. The short cruise into the city from the Moselle is increasingly urban and all that is associated with humans en mass - billboards, assorted rubbish and increasingly fraught-looking urbanites grabbing a moment by the canal.

There are two ports (basins) in Nancy, one free the other not. We're in the free one - in effect the commercial port with less facilities. We're separated from the posh one by a road bridge which carries cars and trams to and from the centre of the city, two lanes for each. We are next to a big boat called Niagara. Once I mistakenly took some pills of that name believing they would enhance my libido but they just made me pee all night.

A French guy helps us moor up and I invite him in for a coffee. He's Michel, married to an English lady called Lucy, who is an opera singer. She calls him 'Rabbit' – not, I'm assured, for his sexual proclivity, more than he has an attractive bottom. I must admit I have never regarded rabbits bottoms as distinctively attractive and the briefest study of Michel's rear does nothing to augment my views on the correlation of the two sets of cheeks. They are a delightful couple (Michel and Lucy, not the cheeks) who live on a big old barge in the posher Bassin St. Georges over the bridge.

They show us a great act of kindness in relation to our immediate concerns, that being the dog, who has a problem with her tummy. We need to see a vet and the nearest one is about 2 kilometres away. I found the vets on the internet and cycled in to make an appointment having failed raise them on the phone. Lucy immediately threw her keys on our wheelhouse table and said that we could use her car as long as we needed it, she would walk to work. We'd known them barely an hour.

Unfortunately, the vet diagnosed what, in all likelihood, was a cancerous tumour. Bonny is 16 now but really fit despite her discomfort and we were warned that she may not survive the operation. The feisty old girl in effect told us not to give up by her demeanour on the examination table so we all agreed she deserved a chance and we left her there. They operated and she did survive. They kept her in overnight and I picked her up again the following afternoon swathed in a huge 'wrap' bandage. She acted like a puppy again, so much so that we thought she'd do herself a damage. The vets, 2 ladies and a female assistant were absolutely brilliant – we couldn't have asked for more. Including a follow-up appointment a week later to remove bandages and stitches, the total bill was two hundred Euros. We'll be forever in their debt for their skill and compassion.

I made friends with a homeless guy who slept on a bench up the steps from our boat. Having made him a cup of coffee I wondered whether he would think me presumptuous, but he thanked me and shook my hand. His hand was big, but soft and clean. He's a tall man and, though a little unkempt, looked pretty fit. He carried his belongings in a faux-leather case, the type used to carry a portable computer. One day he arrived supporting it from below as it had obviously succumbed to life on the street. We gave him a strong shopping bag, a fabric-weave one from a supermarket. Another evening he arrived and laid on his bench to sleep. Just as he was settled it began to rain and though not apparently angry, he sighed and raised his eyebrows in resignation. I went out with a tarpaulin and laid it over him, he even raised his boots so I could cover his feet and legs. He smiled again and I told him it was a cadeau (gift). Early the following morning he was gone, to wherever a homeless man spends his days, and the tarpaulin was neatly folded on our rear deck. He explained later that evening that it was just too big to cart around permanently, but thanked me anyway. There was a night-club boat moored one hundred metres down the quay and though some clubbers were boisterous they never bothered our friend. It appears that homeless people (at least some of them) are treated with respect, maybe because they've had a bum roll of life's dice, any of us could be there.

Lucy gave us tickets to the opera, a production of Idomeneo, in which she was singing in the chorus. It was dress-rehearsal night where they perform the whole opera but without full costume. The auditorium was full to bursting and we felt pretty haughty in our private box! Written by Mozart when he was just 24, this production is rather 'dark' and probably for the aficionado – not that I've seen any other productions, indeed any other operas. We're not opera fans. I suppose it would have helped if we'd seen one, it's just that we never fancied it having seen snatches on television. We tend to prefer the less severe theatre of musicals or plays, but it was a great experience and we felt proud of our new friend. Fortunately, I was able to pass off a brief, snarling snore as an attack of hay-fever and the professional singers were not overly distracted from their endeavours - though I did 'get a look' from a lady in a hat from the box next door. Following the show we had a drink with Lucy in one of the bars that border the square – very civilized.

By day or night Place Stanislas is the most beautiful square, some say the most attractive in Europe. Over one hundred metres square it is bordered by the Opera House, The Grand Hotel, a Fine Arts Museum, and the magnificent Hotel de Ville which occupies the whole of the south side. In the centre stands a bronze statue dedicated to Stanislas Leszczyskni. The completion of the square realized Stanislas' dream of linking the medieval old town to the new one built in the 17th Century. We enter the via a huge gilded, wrought iron gate, one of four at each corner of the square. By day the gilding glints and shimmers in the sun and the ochre-stone square is alive with tourist and local alike, munching, drinking, snapping and chatting. By night it is even more impressive, aglow from lanterns on the gates and subtle, indirect lighting on the buildings. At 10.45 pm each evening the lights are dimmed throughout the whole square and visitors are treated to a light show projected onto the wall of the mighty town hall. It depicts a colourful, magical 25-minute history of Nancy and Lorraine.

Our pals Mike and Paula are moored against us and we're chatting as a large boat moors up nearby. It's skippered by a chap who I am to discover who is a former submarine commander. Short of stature but not on confidence he soon approaches. Now, you instinctively know when someone is on the scrounge by the way they begin a conversation, commenting on the weather or beauty of Nancy for example, while obviously interested in neither the subject nor my reply. In clipped English he soon gets past the unnecessary and asks if he can borrow some allen keys. Of course, it's not a problem but he could have saved himself some trouble if he'd just stated his business in the first place. His German wife, of considerably greater stature than he, falls into the 'long-suffering' category. Despite being physically capable she's patently had enough of hauling ropes and being shouted at. Long sighs and mountainous bosom heaves depict a lady at the end of her rope. She is ready to quit life on the water and buy a house back home – whether the commander agrees is probably of little consequence.

Lucy and Michel invite us to dinner – not at their house but at someone else's! They tell us their long-term friends, Mark and Natalie, won't mind, they do this sort of thing all the time. We take them at their word and agree to meet them at their mates' canal-side house two days hence, so we set off on the boat in the direction of Strasbourg.

It's an amazing evening which includes our hosts, surrogate hosts and two lesbians with their 10-year-old daughter. We learn throughout the course of a fabulous meal that one half of the female partnership used to teach French in Russia. It was while she was teaching in a town she describes as 'between somewhere and nowhere', that she had visited one of the five orphanages. Many of the parents are incapable of raising children through either abject poverty or alcoholism and there are hundreds of children without a home. This we are told is just one example of a phenomenon found throughout Russia, particularly rural Russia where the post-communism existence has left many without a guaranteed lifestyle, however basic, and they are now desolate.

Simone (name changed) adopted Tania two years previously. Now 10, she has had corrective surgery on a hair lip and although Simone said she still has issues stemming from her dire start in life, she is making steady progress. After dinner while we chatted Tania was clambering over the sofa and playing quietly. She is a lovely young thing with bright eyes and now, a bright future.

It really was a heart-warming evening and just one of the unexpected chapters we would never have dreamt of writing when we set off.

We returned to Nancy briefly to have the dog's stitches removed and while there decided we needed a large parasol for the back deck. I'd seen one previously in a superstore so cycled the 2 kilometres and bought one. I cycled back (with the odd rest) with a huge box under my arm. Then I cycled 4 km in the other direction to buy some brackets (the type that secure a TV aerial to a wall) and 4 km back again. Having bolted the brackets (with some difficulty and flowery language) to the rear wall of our engine room, I inserted the stem of our new parasol down into the 2 brackets. I proudly raised our sunshade which stood out in all its glory like a huge red splat on a blue lagoon. We drew gasps of admiration and murmurings of envy as we took our places in the shade – for a few seconds that is, till the merest breath of wind turned the parasol inside out. Despite moving with the speed of a striking snail, I couldn't get to it before it had collapsed into an assortment of matchsticks. Admiration and envy had turned to sympathy and smirks. Not best pleased, I stuffed all the firewood and canvas back into the box and cycled 2 km to the point of purchase where I had protracted conversations with a number of increasingly senior employees about why their parasol was not fit for outdoor use. They finally conceded and with my forty Euros back in my wallet I cycled back to the boat where I could admire my perfectly installed TV brackets, while getting sunburnt. I'd ridden 16 km, four of them with 100 cwt of driftwood under my arm and ended up at point zero.

'Stopped in a nice spot,' Jan had written in her log – which wasn't awfully informative. We had in fact moored in a lay-by a kilometre from the village of Maixe when we were boarded by the waterways police. A white van pulled up and two uniformed men demanded to be invited aboard. I wondered if we were in trouble but all they wanted was to check our boat out. My bodyguard had gone for a walk with the dog so I felt vulnerable. They checked insurance documents, proof of ownership, waterways driving licence, first-aid kit, life jackets, VHF qualifications and fire-extinguishers. All was in order except the extinguishers which, they politely pointed out, were roughly a century out of date. They gave me a form stating that I had a month to rectify the problem or I would face a 1,500 Euro fine and would be wheel-clamped. The only thing they didn't check was my diesel tanks, the configuration and pipework of which I had had altered at considerable cost in Holland. You are only allowed to use white diesel, basically fully taxed fuel similar to the stuff we put in our cars, for propulsion. Red diesel (which is much cheaper) can only he used for heating and to fuel the generator to generate electricity on board. If you are caught using red diesel to fuel your main engine there are substantial penalties.

Lucy came to our rescue again and took me to a specialist fire-extinguisher shop. The guy told me that ours were so old that he couldn't even refill them – another 200 Euros for new ones. Let's face it though they are lifesavers so, at the very least, it's false economy to skimp on them. I called the police who arrived within 20 minutes and struck us off their most-wanted list.

Leaving lovely Nancy behind we cross an Etang (wide part of the canal, translated literally as pond) and arrive at a lock that can safely described as a concrete shaft. From a distance the structure looks like a stained concrete trapezoid built into a hillside with an operator's hut perched on the top. The lock is 10-metres deep and you enter (when ascending) through a guillotine gate that drips on you as you pass below it. You look up the sheer sides to a 40 x 5-metre rectangle of sky. It's not as deep as many large river locks but its relatively small dimensions combined with its height do make it a little claustrophobic.

We have climbed steadily since leaving central Holland and are now, on the summit stretch of the Marne Rhine Canal, at roughly 1000 feet. We travel past lakes that are presumably feeders for the canal, though they are largely hidden behind grassy banks and the landscape here is green and forested with endless skies. Passing through two tunnels (one 475m the other 2306m) we arrive at an amazing piece of modern canal architecture – the Saint-Louis-Arzviller incline plane.

We have ascended many locks on the way here but the first 17 of our descent have been replaced by the incline plane that lowers us 44.5 metres. It takes roughly 20 minutes from entering the caisson through a guillotine gate at the top to exiting at the bottom. The descent itself takes about 4 minutes. Compare this with the full day it took horse-drawn barges to traverse the 17 locks and you see what a huge difference it makes to commercial traffic on a time budget. It opened in 1969 and at that time the only other structure operating on a similar principle was the Foxton incline plane on the Grand Union Canal in Leicestershire, UK.

The 41-metre caisson weighs about 900 tonnes and is counterbalanced by two huge concrete blocks. The caisson, supported on a massive steel frame, slips 100-metres down the slope driven by two winches powered by electric motors. Initially two identical planes were planned but only one was built due to the general decline in water transport. These days the vast majority of passages are by pleasure boats but the lift also attracts 150,000 visitors a year. Unsurprising, as it really is an impressive beast set in a wonderful landscape.

As we pull up and wait we watch Geoff and Jenny go down in the caisson before us. There's sign that states you must stay on your boat in the waiting area, which I ignore and take some photos. Photos, I might add, that emerge spectacular from the depths of my camera even by my appalling standards. A native walks over and points out that I am breaking the rules and tells me there is a sign telling me to stay on the boat.

'I can't understand it, I'm English,' I reply.

'It's in English,' he says.

Sadly, these days the stock excuse of being a foreigner rarely works – despite there being a sign in my native language and I speak French and I'd parked the boat strategically right in front of the sign.

(On 4th July 2013 a tourist barge, 'Paris', was entering the caisson at the top when the caisson suddenly moved trapping the boat and it's 21 passengers in the gate. This released a huge amount of water down the unprotected plane and threatened dangerous flooding down the valley. A campsite and restaurant were evacuated in Lutzelbourg 3 km or so downstream until the flow could be stemmed but thankfully nobody was hurt.)

We stayed in Lutzelbourg for two weeks. It is a magical place situated at the junction of five valleys and whose architecture appears German influenced.

A Polish lady who grows fruit and vegetables on her nearby plot comes round each morning, her bike laden with cherries, green beans and other delicious goodies picked daily. A semi-ruined castle overlooks the town and the view from its (former) ramparts is spectacular. A multitude of shades of green shimmer on the forest-clad slopes of the Vosges Mountains, the town nestled way below by the canal and you can see the TGV (train) as it slithers and snakes along the valley floor.

I cycle up the flight of locks that have been replaced by the incline plane. Derelict until recently, the lock keepers' cottages are now being renovated and a trickle of water is maintained to keep the water fresh. Fish swim among a host of gorgeous plant-life – it's like Eden in a magic forest. The lockhouses are picture-postcard pretty, as will be the price tag in years to come.

Geoff and Jenny are here with us and I have a photo of them and Jan trying to sit in the shade of (another) new parasol. This one's horrible. I came across it at a petrol station (bought after I'd lost part of a previous one in the peat in Friesland) and has been kept in reserve. It is really cheap and nasty. However badly I mistreat it, it refuses to turn inside out or collapse. Had I bought the 5 Euro version rather than the 8, I may, by now, have found justification to chuck it in a bin. It's a piddly blue and yellow stripy affair; the sort you would find on a beach. In fact, if you died under it on a beach some sympathetic soul would cover you with a sheet to save you the embarrassment of being associated with it. It was an impulse buy before you ask, I'd only gone into the garage for some head-ache pills.

Lutzelbourg is as far as we're going on the Marne au Rhine canal. Strasbourg is only about 50 km east but we need to think about getting down to Burgundy.

Before we leave I help our friend Mike bring his boat up the 10 locks from Saverne. He's got a bit of a problem – one unfortunately of his own making. A guy (who is the previous owner of Mike's boat) sadly has had difficulty adjusting to the death of his mother two years previously. Mike was aware of this but only realized how serious his psychological problems when they were on the way from the UK in Mike's car. After a couple of days he was driven to distraction by his friend's unwillingness to help out with the cooking, cleaning etc. and constantly drinking and smoking (and leaving mucky bandages from leg ulcers lying around). We set off and when Mike gave his companion the helm he promptly drove the boat into a wall so it was left for Mike and me to look after the boat while the poor guy sat cocooned in his infuriating dream-world stewed in whiskey and surrounded by a cloud of smoke.

He did have moments of lucidity and constantly thanked us for giving him a wonderful time, quite oblivious to the fact that his behaviour was driving everyone mad. He cut a sad figure and is now getting some professional help.

Living with someone on a boat full time, even for a couple of weeks, is not easy. Even with the likes of Jan and I who get along really well, you have to respect each other's 'space' and Mike and his companion were a couple of battling wasps trapped in a jam jar.

Yet another letter..........
  From: The Captain's dog
  MV Vrouwe Johanna

Dear Mr boat-driver instructor

I don't know what you told Dad but I have had the opportunity to compare his driving with that of professionals. Did you really advise him to pinball around inside a lock, clacking about, sounding like a blacksmith hammering a horseshoe? Or drift feebly into the bank while waiting for a lock in anything but a light breeze? To be fair he is improving. Initially he used the ginerator (a noisy distillation machine that shunts the front of the boat into a wall) to pirouette a sort of smoke-shrouded waltz. He's tried to explain how this awful beast makes 380-volt electricity to drive something else that makes a filthy noise at the sharp end but I'm not really bothered. Thankfully he now he rarely turns it on. This is much to the relief of local wild-life conservationists who have lodged a formal complaint over the thing's pollutive characteristics. He leaves huge acreages of
  countryside swathed in a nasty fug and an irritating (if pretty) multicoloured scum on the water.

We have days when he travels in his work overalls because of the boats 'engineering inconsistencies', constantly disappearing into the engine room to make things even more insufferable. He tells us he's saving money by doing it himself – but at what cost to mother earth?

Compare this shambles with the elderly couple I saw piloting a full-size (39 x 5m) peniche into a lock the other day. Both, I would estimate, were in their late 60s and had an air of professional competence, performing what looked a very awkward procedure with skill and calm. She drove while he gently lobbed a rope over a bollard and brought the boat to a halt with barely a hairs-width all round. She even came out of the wheelhouse and mopped the side-deck while the boat was going down in the lock. What a joy to see – I thought of asking them for a job but I really don't think Mum could manage Dad on her own.

Anyhow we've turned round and are heading back. Be home soon I imagine.

Love

Bonny

New Friends

So, in the company of Mike and his mate we re-trace our steps to Nancy where we meet Bob, a former miner from Derbyshire travelling on his narrowboat, Woodpecker. His second name is Woodcock and I can't believe there is no correlation between his name and that of his boat. He's accompanied by Dozer, a young English Bull Terrier who is both lovely and a complete lunatic. Bob is strong as an ox, but so is Dozer, but it's the latter who appears in compete charge of their relationship.

Overnight there is a terrific electrical storm, one that will come to typify the summer cycle, and today is July 14th, the commemoration of the storming of the Bastille, the beginning of the French Revolution. We moor in St Catherine's Basin again. Alongside us is Bob in his narrowboat, and alongside him Mike and crew. We're just nicely settled when we are all booted out to make way for a hotel boat. I'm secretly relieved because Mikes mate has just got his guitar out and unless he's actually learned to play the damn thing in the last week, we've been saved a tortuous few minutes. We have to slum it on the canal bank from where we watch the fabulous Feu d'Artifice (fireworks display) unleashed to frighten the dogs and enrapture visitors and locals alike. The French love their fireworks as much as they love their public holidays and the two are synonymous.

Following the display our homeless friend walks slowly by with his new shopping bag. It begins to rain again so I beckon him onto the boat out of the deluge. He raises a hand in acknowledgement but continues on to shelter under a nearby bridge. The man who's name I (shamefully) don't know was willing to accept a coffee and a shopping bag but drew the line at sheltering in our wheelhouse. When I look out again a few minutes later he is gone. We never see him again. I hope people continue to show benevolence to this gentle man.

We turn south on the Canal des Vosges named after the mountain range. Though barely mountains, as the highest point is only about 1,400 metres, it's pretty.

There's a tidal wave of 'Northern European' cruisers heading south, pushing us along on their bow-wave. They appear to shun the philosophy of golfer Walter Hagen's when he (supposedly) said, 'You're only here for a short visit. Don't hurry. Don't worry. And be sure to smell the flowers along the way'. They seem to have a desire to leave when the locks open at 9.00 am, cruise till lunchtime and sit on the prime moorings for the rest of the day. Occasionally they'll have another early afternoon sprint, arriving in a swirl of endeavour to prepare food that they have bought with them from their homeland.

When we narrowboated in the UK we liked to leave early (6.00 am for example). It's the best time of the day to us – fewer boats, more wildlife and soft early morning light. Of course, we operated our own locks there and in effect they never closed. Here we are governed by opening hours as, on some canals, they are lock keeper operated. Where they are automated, a member of staff has to be available in case of emergency so even these have restricted hours, which are generally 9.00 am to midday and 1.00 pm till 7.00.

Our dear old Ford motor smokes (like Wigan in the late nineteenth century) so a subtle getaway is impossible. We sometimes still like to set off as early as opening hours permit, so start the engine at 8.45 am. This allows for a 10-minute warm up and slow potter to the lock in order to arrive as it opens. However – when our competitors see us engulfed in smoke it's obvious we're up to something. Frantic instructions are yelled and ropes are untied as two cruisers shove off and dash up to the lock before us. Each lock passage takes about 20 minutes, depending on whether the lock is set or not when you arrive, so by the time we are ready to go the first two cruisers are on their way and there's usually at least one more sneaked off before us too. When we finally get into the first lock it's nearer 10 than half past nine and as we only amble slowly, the morning's cruising is somewhat curtailed.

The following day I start the engine at 8.30 in an effort to steal a march on the opposition – who incidentally will be different to yesterday's lot who have charged south over the horizon and are probably somewhere near Morocco. However, not to be outdone there is another mad dash to the first lock and a new generation of sprinters have beaten us – once again we are relegated to the bronze medal.

Looks like the only way we will secure an early get-away is by chaining other people's door shut but perhaps there's another way, so.......

..........next morning I creep out and fire up old smoky at 7.30!! This'll muck 'em up! True to form, out they rush. We've got Fritz in his slippers and Agnetha in her nightdress elegantly slithering around the dewy deck desperately loosing their boat from the quay. They charge off with a smug grin. As they pass I have already stopped the engine and we have just settled down to a leisurely breakfast on the back deck – steaming coffee and fresh croissants. Their smug grin fades a little. As we chat and take in the morning air Fritz and Frau are hovering around in a narrow, stone-lined lock cut 60 metres away. They will be there for an hour and a half before the lock opens but I'm sure it'll all be worth it.

I don't want to give the impression that all 'Neuro' (Northern European) boats are pushy and self-interested. Take for example.........., no, can't think of anyone. They do tend to stick together though and I suspect the jungle drums beat to inform one another of the juiciest spots to moor. To be fair we have met and will meet some lovely people of all nationalities, it's just that some have garnered a certain reputation.

We are heading for Epinal which I excitedly declare is the Champagne Capital of the world. Jan doesn't drink so couldn't give a hoot, but I'm licking my lips at the prospect of sitting on the blunt end sipping a chilled glass of genuine bubbly. It's rather disappointing to find that the Champagne Capital is actually Épernay, roughly four hundred kilometres west. Epinal is a former industrial port now given over to plaisanciers (pleasure boaters). But at least there's a supermarket nearby where I buy a box of Bordeaux red with which I can drown my ignorance.

It's now August and it can be insufferably hot – around 40 degrees sometimes, so keeping cool is a challenge. Swimming costumes and a dosing with a hosepipe is one way before sitting under a tree in the shade. Hose-dousing is not too practical at night as the bed gets damp so we have a large desk fan pointed at the bed that helps stir up the humid air. We're on our third fan now. They seem to make increasingly unusual noises before packing up altogether. This I am told is due to a technical deficiency in one of our electrical appliances – the one that converts low-voltage battery power (24-volt) to mains power (240-volt); namely the inverter, which is an item of historical interest and delivers an inexact electrical current to our sensitive fans. I did take a fan apart once to mend it but ended up with a pile of detritus, which was soon scooped into a bin bag, and dispatched.

We're still in the Vosges so there are plenty of locks with the associated frustration of malfunctions and bad manners. Our next waypoint is the town of Corre where we will join the Saone river and the downhill run to St. Jean de Losne.

We moor with numerous other boats at Corre, it's peaceful, approaching aperitif time (which is a self-determined hour dependant on how thirsty we are) when a barge comes past on the narrow canal at warp speed. Everybody is thrown about by this idiot and some, moored on the towpath, have their mooring pins pulled out of the bank. The English skipper is subjected to a volley of abuse and his response is that he has a flight to catch. 'Any faster and you'll take off yourself', yells one of his victims (although I've toned the language down a bit). It's a bit sad really that I actually remember incidents like this because the whole Vosges trip is beautiful. Pleasant towns and villages with fine food, friendly folk and stunning scenery.

We see our first Coypu – a large rodent-like beast related to the rat, but the dimensions of a small, fat dog. It's a semi-aquatic herbivore imported from South America and is considered a bit of a pest. Known as a Ragondin in France, it's a rather splendid-looking animal that gently glides through the water, mostly submerged, before being slaughtered for it's fur. The French tend to eat most things but I think Coypus are one of the few exceptions -

unless that's where ratatouille comes from - or that well-known Indian dish, Rodent Josh.

One interesting thing we have come across are Lavoirs or Bassin Publics. They are basically shallow, stone troughs, usually with inward-sloping sides, which were used by local communities to wash and rinse their clothes. Originally washing was done on stone slabs on the riverbank but that practice largely ceased due to polluted river-water during the Industrial Revolution. Public (or private for the wealthier townsfolk) lavoirs were built, often fed by a spring (or clean river or canal water) to provide a constant supply of fresh, clean water which flows down a gradual incline. They are not commonly used today but many have been preserved and are housed in intricate, sometimes ornate, open-sided buildings. I came across one chap washing his dog's blanket. 'Best to do this here', he said with a smile, 'wife not too happy in kitchen sink'. In days gone by lavoirs were important socially too, the news-hub of the community, where gossip was exchanged. They were also an exclusively female haunt. A bit like Weight Watchers these days without the washing. Local legends were concocted to frighten the children into staying away and any breech of the strict rules, such as illegal religious gatherings, prompted the intervention of the local Gendarme.

Another construction you still see are pissoirs which were first introduced in Paris in the 1830's to discourage the needy from tinkling against important public buildings. Even the new, and rather more private, public loos are still called pissoirs. A friend of mine who was visiting France a number of years ago was told that the little, stone-built constructions in many town centres are pissoirs. He duly availed himself of one and was mid-stream when someone popped their head in and asked what time the bus was due! Yes, he was in a bus shelter. Seems a little care is required when picking your little stone construction. Mind you, if he'd been waiting in a pissoir for a bus he really would have got nowhere.

The River Saone is tree-lined and serene with an abundance of birdlife and fish. It's clean, gentle waters flow south and now back on deeper, wider water our boat thrives. The name Saone derives from Souconna, the Gallic river goddess and it flows for nearly 500 kilometres where it joins the mighty

Rhone. Although relatively small as we set off, it gradually widens to become a major waterway. You can travel down through eastern France all the way from Corre to the Rhone delta, the Carmargue, on the Mediterranean. It's like the A1 in England but with better service stations and more fishermen.

Roughly 40 km down is the town of Port-sur-Saone. This is an interesting place, in particular the Fresco painted on a wall depicting figures including Gandhi, Mother Theresa, Anne Frank, Martin Luther-King, also founder of the International Committee of the Red Cross Henri Dunad and strangely, Gavroche, who was a character from Victor Hugo's classic Les Miserables who died on the barricades in June rebellion in Paris in 1832 and who, for many, typifies the spirit of disenfranchised youth of Paris in those days. This Fresco of Human Rights is immediately behind a testament to human wrongs – a memorial to the local casualties in the First World War. Poignantly a young soldier, dressed in camouflage fatigues, is sitting on the memorial plinth as I pass smoking a contemplative cigarette and staring into the middle distance.

We begin week 19 of our trek and arrive at Savoyeux. This is Bob the Narrowboat's home port and we moor with him for a few days. Much of his time is spent coping with his dog and to witness this battle of wills is entertainment of the highest order. Bob is a big guy who sits on a 3-legged milking stool, which he swamps. He's reading a paperback with a huge bite out of it so he has to imagine the text in the lower right portion. Dozer snoozes nearby with a grin on his face.

Bob decides to take the dog for a 'good' walk. Due to his old mining injury Bob limps along the pontoon, pulled along by Dozer. Thirty metres to the bank, left along the port for 400 metres, over the bridge across the canal and off down the opposite towpath before disappearing round a bend nearly a kilometre away. Half an hour later they hove back into view finally making it all the way back to the pontoon – where Dozer promptly has a huge dump right outside Bob's boat! 'Well you bloody animal', he says, as he unravels his hose-pipe.

Christianne is Bob's lady friend, and a delight she is too. Speaking limited English, with what my wife describes as a sexy French accent, she has a house nearby but spends much of her time around the boat refereeing skirmishes between one man and his dog. One evening she cooked us a wild boar casserole. Bob was heartbroken to have run over it in his Land Rover a few weeks previously but came to terms with that and the whole family (including Christianne's 2 sons) had many tasty meals.

Gray is somewhere we'll remember. It's where we had our mooring ropes cut. The flow on the river is gentle and we were moored facing down-stream. (Normally you would moor with your nose up-stream to prevent debris getting stuck in the vital components of your rear end). I woke at 1.00 am. Something had disturbed me, so I dashed up to the wheelhouse to see two teenagers just about to cut the last of our four mooring lines. As I shouted they ran off and drove away in a car with their 'giggling' girlfriends. We were hanging on by the fore-most rope and the stern had already swung out 30 degrees from the bank. I could see a tangle of ropes as the three lines they'd chopped were hanging in bits from both our boat and the quay-side bollards. The only way I could get back to the bank was by starting the engine and driving against the surviving front line. This is a common-enough technique whereby the front of the boat is held by a line as you set your rudder to steer the rear of the boat into the bank. The problem is that with ropes dangling in the water there was a real danger of one getting wrapped round the propeller which could stop it dead. Luckily we got back in and we re-tied with the odds and ends of rope - and a length of chain.

To be set loose on a canal is aggravating but not really too much of a problem. There is no flow and you'll not go far, but a river is a different matter. Had we not woken up we could have travelled quite a way, hitting a bridge support or, god forbid, ending up on a weir. Really not very amusing – so much so that I cycled to the police station the following morning to report the incident. Although a large town with plenty of commerce, a chunk of that is water-born trade along a quay which has moorings for perhaps 20 boats and can be particularly busy in summer. The Gendarme took me seriously but I was unable to give him any specific details of the plonkers that set us free so there wasn't a great deal he could do. He did promise to order more patrols down on the quay as a deterrent. It's a shame as this is the first really unpleasant incident and I'm pretty sure they are few and far between – we do however now always moor with a chain on rivers.

I have to say that generally the youngsters, at least provincially where we have experience, are very polite; often saying 'bonjour Monsieur' in passing. The only mickey-take is out of our accents, but that is in good humour. Adults too are friendly and accommodating, offering a 'bonjour' or a 'bonjour monsieur-dame'. Monsieur-dame is the joint greeting for a male and female, a shortening of 'Monsieur et Madame' – as opposed to greeting me singly because they are unsure what sex I am. The beard and revolting, hairy legs give that away – not that they are an exclusively male trait.

Gray has a lot to offer but, after our experience, we didn't feel like accepting so we headed down-stream, soon passing out of Franche-Comté into Burgundy. Even we've heard of Burgundy so there's a tingle of excitement as we near our destination.

Mantoche is en route and the most beautiful mooring. A well-maintained quay is backed by manicured willow-tree-shaded grass. Fixed picnic tables are well used by boaters and landlubbers alike and are a common feature and popular wherever we go. They are respected, invariably clean and usually in delightful spots. Behind an adjacent wall is a lovely old château – this is the kind of place we could stay for ages.

Then Bob arrives and we all begin another round of jousting with Dozer. This time it's doggy training. Bob wonders why the dog does what it wants and Jan explains that it's probably the way he speaks to it. 'Will you go over there and sit under that tree out of the way so I can read my book in peace'. The dog of course doesn't move. Jan trains Dozer to sit then walks away a few paces before beckoning him forward to receive a biscuit. The dog's doing fine but Bob soon gets bored with this and tips a pile of biscuits in front of the dog and goes to read what's left of his book.

We stay here 5 days and may well have been there still if the local mayor hadn't come up and politely told us it was a 3-day maximum. I could have pulled the old 'bonnet-up-mechanical-problems' trick, but I didn't. We'll come back here and I don't want blackballing. The mayor accepted a glass of beer and my apology and we left the following morning – but not before Jan had taken a swim in the river in her lifejacket (she's not a strong swimmer), to the alarm of a group of natives who thought she was in trouble. They jabbered about calling for the emergency services before we re-assured them that her behaviour was quite normal.

We pass the town of Pontailler, where the Canal entre Champagne et Bourgogne (re-named from Canal de La Marne a la Saone) heads north towards Reims. A few kilometres further on to our left is the entrance to the Canal Rhone au Rhin which heads north-east towards Germany and the River Rhine. Between these two canals is Auxonne where we stay the night and are buffeted about by water skiers slaloming between buoys on the designated stretch of river opposite our mooring.

If anyone hears of, or investigates, the inland waterways in France, the chances are they will have come across the company H20 and the town of St. Jean de Losne. Some weeks previously I'd telephoned them to request a winter mooring. 'Yes, we'll probably be able to find something for you', I was told. Well, we were about to find out.

After four and half months, roughly 1500 km and an experience we will never forget we arrive at St. Jean de Losne and moor on the 'steps' on the river, the town quay in effect. It's hot, the cafés on the river frontage are busy and I go in search of H20's offices, situated in the nearby Gare d'Eau (literally water station). It's suggested by the 'Capitain' (the person in charge of the ships and mooring in the port) that we motor down to the 'old lock' (Écluse Ancienne) to see how we like it. The old lock is literally that, a disused lock cut, now redundant after the course of the river was altered. It is where many of the larger barges reside and is around 3 km down river from the town itself. It is accessed from the downstream end and closed off at the other. There are perhaps 40 barges moored here permanently and space for us if we want it.

Because it's so hot we drape or wheelhouse in a couple of old sheets to keep the worst of the sun off. I'm not surprised the locals were a bit wary when our old barge, draped in Laura Ashley's finest, moors up in a cloud of filthy smoke - must have made a 'bit of an impression'. The only thing in our favour was that the cloud of smoke kept the worst of the sun a bay for a few minutes. Residents have little gardens here and I can only hope that we haven't permanently damaged the delicate ecostructure. Roy and

Carol kindly help us moor up then ask if we need a lift into town to do some shopping. This is either mighty neighbourly or a way to get rid of us at the earliest opportunity.

Road access to the old lock is via a dusty, gravelly track running alongside the river. We don't have a car and the thought of cycling 3 km for a baguette, particularly on a winter morning, does not appeal. Nice though the moorings are we decide to request something nearer the town. H2o oblige and we are allocated a mooring on the fourth of five pontoons in the Gare d'eau – but not for a while until the spot becomes vacant.

An appeal to the Lord
 From: The Captain's dog
 MV Vrouwe Johanna

Oh Lord

Was I really once like this beast we've encountered? This whirlwind of muscle-bound misbehaviour that does exactly as it pleases. It portrays an air of joyful contempt at any effort to point it in the right direction, both physically and mentally. Fortunately, one of the few people on the planet strong enough to handle it is Father Bob, but even he can't have his eye on the ball every waking moment. In fact, when his back is turned the ball is shredded into a sort of plastic pasta.
 If I was like this let me apologize immediately for past sins.
 They seem excited. We appear to have come to the end of our journey.
 Hope it's all that it's cracked up to be.
 Bye for now
 Love Bonny

Sad footnote:

Our beloved dog is gone.

Bonny had a large tumour removed in Nancy and against all expectations recovered to near-puppy state. Sadly, the cancer returned (as we were warned it might) and we were forced to take that dreadful decision. We were both with her when she was put to sleep and only yesterday we scattered her ashes on a grass bank overlooking the marina where we moor. Saying goodbye to our faithful friend was utterly heart-breaking.

We set off from Holland with the intention of reaching St. Jean de Losne for the winter and she made it all the way with us. We took her from a rescue centre fourteen years ago (when she was nearly two) and she helped us through some dark times when Jan was fighting her own battles but she also shared our very best years on the waterways.

My first morning walk without her after more than five thousand in her happy company was one of the saddest and loneliest experiences I have ever had.

A snapshot of winter in Burgundy

It's the shortest day.

In England sack-cloth Druids cavort around Stone Henge getting covered in mud to celebrate the winter solstice. As the last of the smoke (wood fires and wacky baccy) drifts away over the Wiltshire downs, 700 kilometres away in St. Jean de Losne it's difficult to tell if mankind has ceased to exist because it's pretty quiet here at the best of times – at least before 8.00 am.

The sun makes a misty appearance and begins it's half-hearted arc across the winter sky – or it would if it wasn't hidden behind dead trees and a newly-built block of flats (cunningly designed to look like a railway station). All appears calm and tranquil, or dead perhaps. But lift a corner of this winter blanket and you can spot life. Not life as you would know in the world beyond the water, but life nevertheless. Pond life, as my brother calls it.

In the Gare D'eau, the main port in St Jean de Losne, there are about a dozen boats that support life throughout the winter; mainly Dutch barges but with a couple of wide-beam narrowboats and the odd Dutch-style cruiser. Within a few kilometres there are other pockets of habitation including moorings at the start of the Rhone au Rhin canal at St. Symphorien (4 km up the River Saone) and the Ecluse Ancienne (a disused river lock 3 km south). Between these and further moorings at the start of the Bourgogne Canal there are perhaps another dozen boat dwellers. In addition, there are half a dozen British (or English-speaking) families who live in those peculiar constructions called houses. PLUS there are a few natives, an indigenous tribe who speak a peculiar language. A few of we English-speakers communicate with them in grunts and hand-signals originating in cave-dwelling times.

We boaters are mainly English but a few antipodeans and the odd American do decide to test their resolve against a mid-european winter.

We're an eclectic bunch.

We are perched on the end of 'D' pontoon in the Gare D'eau. We're at a funny angle because this spot is not designed for boats our length and we have to straddle a couple of boats and tie up with a selection of old car tyres and a few granny knots. There are roughly 30 boats between us and the passerelle (walkway) linking the pontoon to the Rue du Port. There is one space about half way down into which pull Terry and Sandra on their newly-acquired Dutch cruiser. He is large, she is petite; there's probably about 12-stone between them but at least we'll have company during the winter. There is a French guy living on his boat right at the shore-end of the pontoon but we haven't made his acquaintance yet.

Just after lunch the following day I hear a scream. The kind of primeval noise that you hear when someone dies and raw emotion is released. What the….?

I run from our boat towards the noise and the French guy runs from the opposite direction.

'What on earth's the matter?' I ask.

'My fender', wails Terry, 'my bloody fender's fallen in the water'.

Now a fender is a sturdy, inflatable ball that protects paintwork; you see them everywhere.

'For God's sake,' I tell him. 'They are designed to float and you can buy them at a boat-jumble for a couple for Euros each'.

'No, it's a guitar, a 1974 bass guitar – that Fender. Worth a bloody fortune'.

It was something of a classic instrument apparently and he'd stripped it down to refurbish it. He was taking the wooden bit up to the back deck to paint it when he tripped and dropped it. It was wood and it did float. With some huffing and puffing we retrieved it but it would mean a trip to the guitar doctor in Dijon to replace the metal bits.

Terry is also a recently retired, 20-stone (conservative estimate) athlete.

He's a hammer thrower – a skill at which I also excel having regularly thrown one while failing to repair something in the engine room! Terry and Sandra are to become good friends.

December through March the temperatures range roughly between 15 above and 15 below zero. 15 above is not so bad but 15 below can be a tad irritating, particularly when accompanied by a wind straight from the Arctic. We get snow too sometimes but it rarely lingers more than a few days. More frustrating are the periods of mist and fog that can also last for days when it stays cold due to lack of sunshine. Its flat, grey light and accompanying soupy atmosphere is perfect for those wishing to develop a bronchial disorder. At the moment we are in the midst of a round of winter bugs, one causing intestinal chaos, another catarrh related. Some of us find it hard to differentiate between 'a bout of something' and the succession of thundering hangovers induced by 2 Euro-a-litre wine – taken medicinally, naturally.

A fair proportion of the winter is spent just keeping warm. We have a multi-fuel stove and a 'domestic' oil-fired central heating boiler. We burn coal on our stove in addition to wood that has to be chopped and brought aboard. My wife allows me to look after that side of things and despite suffering from log-choppers droop I enjoy being out in the fresh air (when it's not foggy – or 15 below – or chucking it down). France is a major player as 'the lungs of Europe' due to the huge amount of woodland and forest. Wood is burnt in great quantities on domestic fires but despite that the forests are still expanding.

Other winter inmates include Ken and Rhonda; Kiwis and good fun. Because there aren't many sheep to chase here in Burgundy they have to keep warm like the rest of us – with a wood burner. Ken likes his warmth and has the fire so hot that not only is the boat kept at around 30 degrees but the tiles are coming adrift in the adjoining bathroom. Rhonda however is not as keen on this excessive heat, mainly because it melts her chocolate. She goes round opening windows then Ken charges round after her snapping them shut again. She reckons that Ken is unaware of her chocolate addiction so she secretes choccies in various knicker drawers and cupboards. Sadly her 'little treats' often come out in a soggy lump due to the heat - and the washing machine was going constantly to wash Dairy Milk out of her underwear.

Ken is partial to Chinese food so he organized a lunch out in Dijon, 30 kilometres away. It turned into a popular outing as there were about 25 of us.

'Follow me,' said Ken as we piled into our cars, 'I've got a Sat Nav.'

It all started off well enough but then we encountered a potato harvesting machine. It was on a single-lane farm track that bisected two enormous fields. I'm sure farmer was a bit surprised when he encountered a convoy of cars driving through his potatoes – like a wagon-train throwing up a plume of dust on the prairie. When we eventually arrived, covered in soil, we suggested that the 'shortest route' option on the Sat Nav was not the wisest choice. Ken just told us his maps needed updating a bit.

The meal was poor and we all made our own way home, full of monosodium glutamate, on real roads.

The 'community' in St. Jean is perhaps the nicest thing about being here. A melange of vastly different people drawn together by common difficulties such as misbehaving lavatories or dribbly windows. We help and support each other and socialize together, whether at organized (and I use that in the loosest possible interpretation of the word) events or popping round for a cuppa or a meal. We have activities such as a weekly organized walk (although I prefer the disorganized walk as far as the shop to top up on wine), quizzes, BBQs, First-aid instruction, card-making etc. etc. In fact if someone's prepared to organize something, others generally join in. For example, Jan set up a ladies debating group where they talk about a multitude of things over a coffee on Tuesday mornings. 'No bickering about husbands' is about the only rule, which to my mind severely limits the potential of the fairer sex to dominate the world through a 'unification of minds', but they seem to enjoy it.

On sub-zero winter mornings the air is crisp and still and smoke from wood stoves drifts lazily across the port. As we walk out to buy our daily baguette (that's bread, not the local newspaper) we encounter the distinctive sweet smell of burning oak and see cormorants and kingfishers hunting for breakfast. Of course, the port can freeze up, you can tell it's frozen because there are little piles of vegetable peelings sitting on the ice outside wheelhouse doors. Furry animals scamper across the frozen wastes in search of fresh veggies. The authorities turn off the water supply on the pontoons to prevent the pipes freezing so in extended periods of very cold weather we have to manage our water usage. The longest we've experienced during our three winters here was about 2 weeks without fresh water so we had to monitor our on-board supply diligently – in our case, 2000 litres. Plus of course you don't know how long the cold spell will last so you tend to be over-conservative – cleaning your teeth in Chardonnay or having a quick shower in your clothes are two ways to stretch your precious supply.

When a Burgundian day finally gets going life is really pretty normal, except that everything is crammed into about 7 hours daylight. Shops, open for brief periods either side of a protracted lunch, are well stocked with winter fayre – like sprouts and parsnips. One thing summer visitors may miss is a cheese called Mont D'or. This is a creamy, mild offering that comes in a small, circular wooden box (like Brie for example). This one though is popped in a low oven for half-an-hour, with a dash of white wine on top (if you are so inclined) and eaten rather like a Swiss fondue where chunks of fresh bread are dipped in and dribbled all over the tablecloth and into your lap. It's great winter food and is often followed on our boat by a casserole that has been simmering on top of the wood stove for a couple of days.

Because we are all of a certain age, we have more arthritic hip parties than Bar Mitsvahs, more deaths than births and more goings than comings - but overall, we do pretty well. It's not easy sometimes to live in such close proximity to your spouse for extended periods (one or two couples have indeed capitulated) so you have to create time and space for yourselves. For example, I have a large radiator in the engine room so it is to there I repair after a blazing row to have a glass of Grouse and contemplate engine repairs or write my memoirs.

St. Jean is a small town and the French generally seems to close their shutters at about 7.00 pm and that's it for the day. They appear to gather in family groups behind closed doors rather than cavort around the town. Empty streets can be a bit eerie; echoes from your shoes clatter around narrow streets between high-walled buildings under sodium streetlights. You pass the odd bar where a dirty, yellow glow struggles out through steamy windows onto the pavement. These customers are without family perhaps or maybe still finishing lunch.

Some villages you pass in the summer really are dying on their feet as the younger generation has moved out in search of work leaving their crinkly elders to shore up crumbling farms and houses. Many don't even have a boulangerie. There seems little future for these rural places but St. Jean does. It is at a waterways carrefour (crossroads) and, to me, really should make more of itself. There are few B & Bs or hotels but with the natural draw of the waterways and attendant boat-related businesses, they could promote the town much more fervently. I can only conclude that the locals are happy with it as it is but the people who organize civic events are once again the elder generation and the town is perhaps in danger of suffocating itself in the present and past. That said, there are four supermarkets plus independent butchers, bakers and restaurants which all seem to do pretty well – where all the customers come from goodness knows.

Local civic events are organized in a particular 'laisez-faire' manner, for example the Remembrance Day Parade. We spectators, locals and foreigners alike, gather at the cenotaph in untidy groups and wait patiently for the official parade to arrive. Published starting times are irrelevant as the clock ticks on (and on); the River Saone meanders by and autumn leaves drift to the ground, in fact we've waited that long that the trees themselves are in danger of expiring. Just when we think we must have the wrong day the parade arrives. Official bodies in full 'regimental colours' march down the street. Gendarmes (shiny-buttoned uniforms, foreign Legion-type caps) and Pompiers (the fire-brigade in pristine shiny gold helmets), many playing brass instruments and rattling snare drums, hove into view. All of a sudden everything falls miraculously into place and the mayor delivers his speech via a speaker balanced in a nearby tree (the speaker not the mayor). The ceremony is as moving as anywhere worldwide, sombrely respected by all. Suddenly the band strikes up again and the procession 'rat-a-tat-tats' off towards the Marie and free aperitifs for those not frozen into a lump.

Jan went to a Christmas Eve midnight mass a couple of years ago. The service was Catholic and pretty High Church – a dour affair which lasted a couple of hours too long during which she understood little. This year she's going to the 6.00 pm service, which is supposed to be a more light-hearted nativity-type do. There were rumours that last year it was thrown into some confusion as the innkeeper, a staunch socialist, was unable to open the inn to Joseph because he was attending an industrial tribunal.

Jan and I have toyed with the idea of organising a winter pantomime but have decided that nothing could top the general shambles that is everyday life.

The St. Nicholas Parade is another event held locally, although it also occurs throughout much of northern Europe. The format varies a little from place to place (we have seen an equivalent in Holland) but generally St. Nicholas, looking uncannily like Father Christmas with a Bishops' mitre, is the star of a parade whose helpers (whose origin I understand to be young Moorish kids from Morocco) distribute sweets and little presents to the substantial crowds. St. Nicholas is patron saint of Children, Amsterdam and sailors and with the latter in mind the boating community is invited to head the parade. It's quite an honour really and we dress in layer upon layer of goose-down clothing encased with a large white sheet all held together with a dressing gown cord. Oh, and pointy hats. We carry flaming torches and look like an order of fat, slow-moving monks. This festival however is one (of a number) that binds the local community together and the natives come out in droves so support.

In conclusion winter in St. Jean de Losne is great for us but it's not for everyone. You have to make sure that both your boat and personal constitution are up to the challenge. Don't expect to wear shorts, or if you do make sure your affairs are in order. The sun is often battered into submission by the other elements but you do get beautiful, crisp, frosty days when its a pleasure to be hacking logs or warming up in casualty with a broken limb after a tumble on the ice.

Like anywhere really, you get out what you put in and overall it's the people that make the difference – some of them even make it a bit better.

The Grand Fete

There is a boaty, social festival planned for the end of April. Historically hoards of stalls surround the Gare d'Eau offering anything from mattresses to household bric-a-brac. The odd beer tent and burger 'establishment' complete this smorgasbord of delight. We've delayed our departure to savour this social highlight. Only someone either hasn't read the script or everyone has had a communal memory failure because there are only a dozen stalls, all selling household relics they probably bought at the previous 'festival'. For some reason it takes us a month to get overt this disappointment and it's not until June 14th that we finally untie and set off on another trip.

The morning we left it was partly cloudy with some sun. By the time we arrived at the fuel barge 300m away it was mostly cloudy with very little sun. By the time we moored up a further 150m up river on the town quay it was chucking it down with no sun. So, we stayed there for two days to re-acquaint ourselves with the creaks, clicks and buzzing noises that tell us that we are once more independent of shore-based support.

We had a good winter. Safe in a large marina off the river and we made new friends, some of whom were so impressed with us that they had set off at the earliest opportunity towards the furthest navigable point. Many good folk who we were sorry to see go. They left behind the ghosts of wine-sodden evenings, some of which we could recall.

We were serenaded on our way by a Swiss chap who entertained with his Alpine Horn on the roof of his hire boat – a haunting, mournful racket that mirrored the weather.

Down river is the town of Seurre, accessed immediately after a lock. There's no room here – or rather there is but the visitor's pontoon has red tape all over it so we push on to Verdun-sur-Doubs (pronounced doos) where we moor illegally against another boat that's also moored illegally. We've had to turn off the Saone up the Doubs river and there is a strict 15-metre limit – I guess it's because time is getting on and we are only 4 metres over the limit the port captain shows sympathy – as long as we leave pronto in the morning.

Nearby there are flood-height markers on the buildings – some are astonishingly high, perhaps 5 metres or more above normal levels. The river Doubs is known for being a bit feisty, rising quickly at times of heavy rain and not the place to be on a slow old barge. I understand that the highest flood marks were in the days before barrages (weirs) were constructed up stream to control the flow, but apparently it's still a bit dangerous at times.

The locks are bigger here again on the River Saone, well over 100 metres, and are used regularly by commercials carrying, amongst other things, cereals loaded from riverside silos. Down another such lock and we arrive at Chalon-sur-Saone. This is a lovely-looking city and huge river cruisers (holiday boats) are moored on the town walls. We're looking forward to stopping here and sail confidently into the Port de Plaisance – where we are confidently waved out again by the port captain – 15-metre limit again; oh well. Consequently, we moor on a concrete quay a couple of hundred yards up river in the company of a Danish couple on their Skutse (a type of barge, and a pretty one too). It's a beautiful spot though, and at dusk we see a sickle of moon creeping low across an ochre sky above the ancient river bridge.

From Chalon we ascended the 10-metre lock and start the route Bourbonnaise which connects the River Saone (and all points south) to the River Seine (and all points north). This route consists of four consecutive canals namely, the Canal du Centre, the Lateral a La Loire, The Briare and the Loing. In total it is 414 km in length incorporating 149 locks.

A couple of kilometres up the Canal du Centre is the village of Fragnes. Due to the wonders of modern technology, we are able to connect to the internet, via wifi, at various strategically situated locations. We have to make the most of these wifi 'hot-spots' because although strategically located they are also sparsely located. Thus, this particular Friday I was to be found huddled under an umbrella in the drizzle outside the 'Capitainerie' (Port Captain's Office) with my lap-top balanced on a wall. The huge workforce needed to keep the port running efficiently was having her day off so the village natives who visited the adjacent bakery must have thought an idiot had landed among them.

By evening it had cleared up enough for us to try out our new BBQ. We produced clouds of smoke trying to light our damp charcoal and eventually cooked the chicken in the oven on the boat. Fortunately, because we made such a lot of noise and smell, nearby boaters thought we were having a good time. We obviously made an impression because the lady next door, on a rather new and posh cruiser and apparently overcome with envy of our sumptuous feast, repeated at regular intervals how 'deelateful' her champagne cocktail was. If only she'd known that our supermarket chicken thighs had been cooked in the oven and the BBQ had left a lingering smell of kerosene she may have come round and offered us a brown ale instead of trying to show off.

Adjacent to the mooring is an impressive open-sided wooden structure, perhaps 20 by 15 metres, a modern version of an historic community hall in which ancient Gauls would probably have frolicked and sacrificed an unwilling animal. There was a 'Grand Fete' advertised for the following evening so we dressed up joined the fray. It's not often we put on the old glad-rags and we had to retrieve them from the depths of some musty cupboard and give them an airing. We don't need many clothes, especially during the summer when we rotate a few combinations of shorts and t-shirts, so when a fellow boater complimented Jan on her nice wardrobe she replied, 'Yes, thank you. But I haven't a lot to put in it!'

A friend of ours, David, has discovered a clothes shop – no that's not the right description – a 'seller of clothes' is more accurate, called The Kilo Shop, where you buy clothes by weight – 7 Euros per kilo. There is lots of second-hand stuff, probably obtained from dead people, but there is some new stuff and there are genuine bargains to be had. You can buy 3 or 4 brand new short-sleeve summer shirts for example for 6 or 7 euros. The designs can be a bit off the wall but at that price we don't mind making a talking point of ourselves. David indeed obtained a couple of pairs of trousers for 10 Euros. The fact that they made him look like Rupert Bear was incidental to the sheer quality of the garments. In fact, an internet search revealed that a similar pair from a fashionable city shop would set you back about 80 Euros. The only problem with buying high quality, durable gear (with a pattern quite disproportionate to the value for money) is that you have to put up with sniggers and pointing for that much longer.

  I digress. We joined the festivities adjacent our boat in search of a glass of something suitable - but we were immediately invited to leave. Unfortunately, this was a private wedding. The Grand Fete was 2 kilometres away in the actual village hall so we cycled. Joining a large audience at fever pitch of anticipation. The hall lights dimmed, the stage lights went up and we were treated to a bunch of 4-year-old school children waving their arms about dressed in tutus. I'm sure the lone boy among 20 of his female peers will treasure the photographs in years to come. We thought it couldn't get much better but then the local (adult) line-dancing group took the stage. A dozen substantial ladies with buffalo-bearing hips moved conservatively in ever decreasing circles. The only real bit that moves in line dancing is the feet – and we couldn't see them over the sea of captivated (and captive) watchers. There was the occasional clap from the dancers which only seemed to startle the older participants into getting even more out of sync. Next it was the 5/6 year-olds dressed in home-made animal costumes (lion dancing?) followed by another bout of bovine line-shuffling. So, after 4 of a scheduled 20 'turns' we took our leave feigning indigestion. But not before I encountered a bloke in the gents lavatory wearing three belts. No, I didn't ask. Quite unable to sleep after this fevered excitement we retired to the rear deck for a glass of Benedictine to calm down a bit. It was still before 9.00pm and the wedding party had already gone – in fact not the type of do I would really wanted to be part of anyway. I'm glad we were booted out.

  What the village hall night was all about was local folk getting together to augment their sense of community. After all there's bugger-all else to do in these little places.

The occasion from which we were summarily dismissed reminded me of a friend of mine who turned up at a wedding in his dressing gown which was as near as he could get to a morning suit.

Now, I'm partial to a drop of red. Jan doesn't drink at all so can unfortunately remember everything about the previous days cock-ups. So with my taste buds tingling with anticipation I visit a local Cave (pron. carve). Wine distribution and sales centres, these places are renown for being purveyors of some fine (but not necessarily cheap) wine. The lady of the cave was almost overcome by my knowledge of supermarket boxed wine and agreed (with rather a 'bitter-lemon' expression) to allow me to sample each of the ten red boxes available. If she expected me to spit them out she was mistaken. My philosophy here is that it important to ascertain the severity of crushing hangover one may end up with as part of the wine tipplers art. Jan was with me and later said she was very proud that I decided not to buy anything at all. I'm absolutely no expert (as is patently obvious) but they all tasted the same. It was as if a tanker full of 'off-cuts' had filled a hidden reservoir somewhere in the depths of the ladies cave and the same wine poured into different coloured boxes.

By contrast, at the other end of the cave was a humidor-type cabinet where the 'real' wines were temperature controlled. I'd had a (very brief) look at these before I assaulted the boxes and noted that the cheapest was 50 Euros a bottle (there was plenty of choice in between mind, just that the humidor housed the crème de la crème). As we were leaving a chap (in rather smart loafers) was completing an order for two dozen cases. I'm later informed that this wine is for laying down – probably in the cellar of a château. For me (in the words of Monty Python) it was a wine for laying down and avoiding.

We set off again after my headache had calmed somewhat and found ourselves following a hotel boat. These are of 'canal-max' proportion, in other words just able to squeeze into the 40 x 5 metre locks. The canals are relatively narrow and shallow and as these boats are deep drafted they travel at barely 3 kilometres an hour while churning up all sorts of foul stuff from the canal bed. In fact, following a hotel boat is like following a horse with diarrhoea down a single-track road. Unless they pull in somewhere to allow the group of (usually) Americans to go and eat another mountain of food you may as well stop and moor up for the day and give them a chance to get well ahead. To be fair, these guys are just earning a living and we inevitably show them respect. Mind you charging around 50,000 Euros for six people for a week, they must be doing OK.

One place a hotel boat may pull in is Santenay, a beautiful little town nestling below vine-covered slopes in a shallow valley. Access from the canal is down a steep slope and across a lovely, flower bedecked, stone bridge. The town is centered on a square (as if often the case) perhaps 100 metres across. Sculptures, flowers and a circular fountain are set on pristine, stepped, limestone plinths; a fitting backdrop to immaculate shops and wine caves selling local Pinot Noir-based red wine with some Chardonnay. We're in the Cote de Beaune commune in Burgundy, deep in world-famous wine territory. Sadly, it's largely wasted on a fiscally challenged and vine-ignorant peasant like me – but it's a beautiful place just to come and witness a wine-dependant community. You can almost taste the pride the locals have in their town. I did actually buy a corkscrew as a memento and, as Jan pointed out, it would come in very handy for opening my boxes.

At Chagny, a town a few hours up the canal, we were told by a fellow-boater to visit the 'best French market' she had ever seen – fabulous food, beautiful clothes, African leather goods etc etc.. Sadly, when we got there it had finished but judging by the amount of scrap paper and brown lettuce leaves in the gutters it would have been quite an event. Echoes of the bustling market whispered excitedly in the deserted streets. Once again we retired to the rear deck for a Benedictine to try and conjure up images of what the 'best French market' might have looked like.

Our next stop was St Leger where nothing happened. The journey there though was punctuated by running aground twice and squashing the satellite dish under a low bridge much to the amusement of two local fishermen. It's bent but works better than it ever did.

We encounter Rob and Kathy who seemed disproportionately delighted to be asked on board for a cup of tea. Turns out they are not boaters but a couple on a camping holiday having a drive round the area. 'I don't want to harp on.....' was Rob's favourite intro, but he did, obviously overcome with emotion that someone spoke the same language. He regaled us with tales of their gardening business back in the UK. 'I don't want to bore you......' he said - and he didn't because they were an enthusiastic and engaging pair who'd found their niche and spoke of it with real gusto. They only left when Walter, a Belgian chap with his big dog, a 'Belgian' something, came to see us. We'd met Walter the previous year when his dog was totally out of control and he'd sworn that a firm hand was the only way to calm it. Well, that obviously hadn't worked because in the intervening 12 months his wife, Nicky, had taken over the training while Walter recovered from various dog-related injuries. What Walter had was total recall of all the places he'd visited to this point and marked on our map every water and electricity point for the previous 200 kilometres. There were only 4 but it was still impressive! Veteran boaters and a great couple.

The small town of Blanzy had a butcher whose award-winning sausages even we couldn't ruin on the BBQ – they were truly superb. You'd have thought we'd have learned our lesson regarding 'Grand Fetes', but no. This was advertised as a grand parade and fair followed by a live rock band due to perform at 9.30 pm. We must have read the poster wrong because at the appointed hour we went to see the band but they were still in the process of setting up a small make-shift stage under a scabby tree in a memorial garden. To reach the stage we'd had to go through the fair-ground (optimistic description) where the dozen attractions had attracted only about 15 people and that included the 'attraction managers'. We hung around for a while hoping for an upturn in activity before contemplating retiring to the rear deck for .... well, you know. By now it was dusk so we set off home. But joy! Marching down the street in the distance was a brass (type) band carrying flaming torches. I hope you can imagine the scene because it made quite a spectacle in the gathering gloom. As the progression approached we could tell there was quite a number and the chap we talked to, who had driven 25 kilometres with his extended family to be entertained, became quite animated. He and we were a tad disappointed when the parade passed our position because there were 2 trumpets, one trombone, two drums and a cymbal. The 'band' was accompanied by 12 under-age torch bearers, numerous ladies pushing prams and an assortment of agricultural workers carrying 'implements'. They were all on their way to the fair ground then on to 'let go' with the rock band. We nearly invited our new friends back to the rear deck but decided that the skipper and I could critique the evening's entertainment adequately without assistance.

  The following morning however we hit pay-dirt. A real, adult brass band set up right outside our boat and they were really very good. They played for an hour or so but kept sidling off into the trees (so the performance was a bit disjointed) because the temperature was in the mid 30's and climbing so approaching mid-day they packed up their sweaty instruments and retired to a local restaurant for a 7-hour lunch.

  I regularly cycle early in the morning – it's the best time of day because it's not yet insufferably hot and the wildlife is foraging. In fact, I regularly see insomniac locals staggering back from the boulangerie under a sheaf of baguettes. Early afternoon onwards we're getting stifling temperatures of near 40 degrees and that's not the time for a portly chap, whose peak of physical fitness was 30 years previously, to coax his steed around the lanes of central France. I've seen red squirrel, kites, coypu, hare, beaver and a myriad of birds I don't recognise. Most animals are very nervous of their human cousins – largely because the French eat just about anything that moves. When in Holland I had the ignominious experience of being beaten by a 12-year-old schoolgirl while leading the Tour de France on my bicycle. I am now in another country and my self-esteem has taken another knock. I'd worked out a four-kilometre circuit round country lanes beginning and ending at the boat. Half way through the third 'lap' (once again going 'at some pace!') I was passed by a group of 8 portly gentlemen, the youngest of whom was well into his seventies. They muttered bonjours, then au revoirs, as they eased by, dressed in enough orthopaedic equipment to stock a modest shop. They wore bulging, logo-bedecked suits and trendy shades; a lingering whiff of liniment the only evidence of their passing. Fortunately, they turned off my route shortly after overtaking so I wasn't able to embarrass them by catching up and shooting past – leaving them with a lingering whiff of red wine and fags.

We are now going 'downhill' – that is the locks are descending, which is far easier than going uphill, and we now have helpful (if largely unnecessary) assistance from lock keepers. Struggling uphill there was no sign of anybody so work that one out.

And so we arrive in Genelard, a pretty place with plenty of mooring round a large basin. It is now World Cup football time so when a boat pulled in behind us with a German flag I helped them moor up. I told the couple how lucky they were to be progressing in the tournament and they must have bribed the referee! (Remember this time, the Frank Lampard shot that definitely DID cross the line and bounce out again!?) Frankly they looked a bit blank and didn't respond, not a word. I sloped off back to our boat. The man, grey-haired, slim and a person of few words later wandered over to our boat and said, 'Ve are in fact Belgian!! And yes, encounters with the Germans can be tiresome. Historically we have had two and that was quite enough!' The German and Belgian flags are very similar, differing only in orientation – you have to be a little careful!

The temperature was up around 40, in all honesty not a time to be out in the sun for any length of time. The Belgian lady was even thinner than her husband, almost to the point of emaciation. She was dangerously sunburned, REALLY dark brown and looked like an assortment of charcoal twigs dressed in a leopard-skin bikini. All rather nasty; in fact, she could have been a specimen of early humanoid brought back from Africa by Livingstone.

Now (as I regularly point out) our dear old boat is a bit smoky, especially on start-up – but the English-registered (and owned) barge we witnessed here was in a different league and the exhaust came out of the side of the boat rather than the rear. When leaving Genelard to ascend, one has to traverse the basin and turn sharp to starboard to enter the lock. A small (8-metre?) cruiser had arrived late the previous evening and moored immediately outside the lock. The occupants were still in bed when our English barge approached. Barges don't do right angles easily especially at low speed, they just tend to drift. This is what happened here as 40 tonnes of barge slipped slowly sideways, belching smoke, towards the lock and the little cruiser. There was a lot of shouting from the barge skipper until the cruiser's curtains twitched open revealing a wide-eyed, horrified stare. 'FEND HER ORF!' yelled the barge skipper as terrified cruiser man dashed out in his underwear. He was a ghostly figure largely hidden in the plume of grey smoke - and disappeared completely when the barge skipper gave a burst of 'opposite lock' and a thick plume belched out of the side of the barge. Cruiser man, his wife (who had by now also dashed out) and the barge crew desperately tried to avert a complete cock-up in near-zero visibility frantically moving fenders and shoving with boat-poles. There was contact but happily the cruiser was steel and survived the encounter (not that we saw much of it through the smoke). Had it been fibreglass it might have been a different story.

A little further along we stop at Paray le Monial a city known as the 'Sacred Heart' where pilgrims, up to 300,000 per year (according to some accounts), come and worship where Christ (allegedly) appeared to a nun, Sister Margaret Mary. Paray is twinned with Bethlehem and is a real mix comprising Churches, Basilisk, Museums, Kebab shops, a canal, a youthful River Loire and acres of marquees to feed and house pilgrims. Pope John-Paul II visited in 1986, preparing the ground for us 14 years later – I bet he didn't have a kebab. We also met Aussies Andrew and Laura who told us in detail how to cycle around in circles before NOT being able to find a supermarket. Mooring 11 Euros, spiritual uplift free. Leaving Paray the canal was lined with Plane Trees and put me in mind of photos we've seen of the Canal du Muddy. Very pretty in the morning sun.

I can now relate an incident that is (vaguely) amusing in hindsight. Just shy of Digoin we moor for lunch on an isolated stretch. It is stiflingly hot so I suggest the skipper takes her chair outside to sit on the bank in the shade while I make a sandwich. While in the galley I hear a cry and looking out the skipper is nowhere to be seen, so I dash outside. She's backward-somersaulted, chair and all, off the towpath down the bank. When I reach her she's a few feet down suspended and tangled in a thorn bush! It took a good few minutes to disentangle her and get her back up the hill. She's covered in scratches and shaken up but after a good wash and being smeared with antiseptic cream she's really no worse for wear. Had the bush not been there she'd have travelled another 20 feet or so into a brackish stream – all in all it could have been an awful lot worse.

I had a fair few scratches myself (but nothing like Jan) so bloodied but unbowed we set off for Digoin. Here the Canal du Centre becomes the Canal Lateral a La Loire and the Roanne Canal branches off to the left. Just before Digoin to our right there is a thin (20 metre) strip of land on which someone is growing vines. We try to think of a name for the wine produced from this 'mini vineyard' sandwiched between the canal and the railway and come up with Château Nooga Choo Choo!!!! Good eh?

We don't stop at Digoin because to risk sneaking on to the inadequate finger-pontoons in a stiff breeze may have resulted in carnage so we motor on in search of Bill and Rosemary (with whom we wintered in St. Jean). We find them at Beaulon, after which the count of migraines, merriment and mishaps is upped a few notches!

As we descend the lock at Beaulon the canal opens on the left into what was presumably once a commercial quay – quite what was transported to and from here I never found out (timber or cereal crops maybe) but nowadays it is a 300 metre plaisance mooring with free electricity and water, which is why it is quite busy! Awaiting our arrival are not only Bill and Rosemary but also our English friends Jane and David who we first met in Zwartsluis, Netherlands just after we had both first bought our barges. (We last saw Dave pottering off with a midge in his hair). At the time our barge was unpainted (or neglected) and, because the timing was wrong on the engine, it smoked even worse than it does nowadays. Well, we had sorted out the timing and given Vrouwe Johanna a few coats of paint so David (in particular) was really quite surprised that I could have made her look even worse! It was lovely to see them all again, quite extraordinary really bumping into friends, each in our floating homes, in the middle of nowhere.

Old Pals, New Pals

On arrival at Beaulon our friends helped us moor and there followed a bout of hand shaking and French-kissing. I had previously warned Dave about this but it seems to have gone unheeded. Poor old Bill had some nasty scabs on both his forehead and cheek and gentle probing gleaned that they were in fact the result of something common among the boating fraternity, the U.D.I. (Unidentified Drinking Injury). This is a syndrome where a boater wakes to find a bruise, scab or some such other uncomfortable ailment whose origin is shrouded in the mists of the previous evening's Merlot. Bill's had occurred when he fell off a buffet, face-first, onto the carpet! The truth was unearthed after we told him to stop fibbing and stop lying about a rock-climbing incident!

Anyhow they all made us welcome and there followed at least a week of communal frivolity. Dave is an accomplished musician (guitar) and he and I have a very different take on music – he takes the applause while I take my leave. The musical soiree we had (very loose description) was a moderate success, Dave had not got any 'sing-along' music with him and my turgid renderings had people reaching for more anaesthetic - but it was 'different'. It didn't help that Dave's wife (a delightful yet nutty (and drunk) Swede) kept shouting at me to shut up and let the expert (Dave) have a go. Well, I did and retired to a distant corner of the mooring with a bottle of Château Nooga Choo Choo.

We had BBQs a plenty, one of which was planned on the lovely stone-built barby constructed by the local commune for the use of both boaters and the local community. The morning of our planned conflagration (quite a few boats were 'up for it') the local Mairie came along and stuck a sign on the barby: 'reserved today for the commune of Beaulon'. Great! Luckily it turns out that the Commune barby was lunchtime – the long lunch for which the French are famous. Actually, it was lovely to see families including small kids making use of the local facilities without the fear of a bunch of hooligans vomiting everywhere!

Good plaisance moorings often have a 2-metre-wide hardcore key with bollards, electric and water, then a stretch of grass bank where you can plonk your tables and chairs under the trees. It's very social and people (generally carrying a touch too much weight) march about in too little clothing wearing silly hats, all too late to protect puce skin. There are quite a number of such moorings up the Route Bourbonnaise en route to St Mammes (and the Seine).

It was here we also met Gordon and Gwen. They are a remarkable (and very likeable) couple considerably nearer 80 than 70 who travel with a self-built boat (that's virtually everything including the shell where much of the steel was obtained through scrap yards), a small car and a motorcycle. They 'leap-frog' with their various modes of transport so always have a means of getting to shops / doctors or wherever. Without being condescending in any shape or form, are a credit to the 'get up and get on with it' philosophy.

Gordon knows an awful lot about boats. I (with Bill's help) was replacing a Morse cable (the one that connects the lever with a knob on it in the wheelhouse to the gearbox) and I was nearing the end of connecting the fiddly nuts to the control in the wheelhouse when Gordon appeared, took one quick look and said, 'You've got that back to front.'

'You sure?' I asked.

'Yep'.

'B....ger', I muttered. 'You got any more useful advice?'

'No, that's it for now.'

And so he left again. My self-esteem in tatters but his intervention saved us from the tricky dilemma of having to travel the remaining 800 km of our journey in reverse.

In Gannay we caught up with Sue, a single-handed narrowboater who we met last year. My last memory of her was hacking away at a piece of plywood with an ancient saw while trying to make a box for her batteries. Well, she'd managed that and now joined us for a meal - she is good company. Gannay's only other jog to my memory was the nasty little statue I found there. It was of a chap who had apparently had a major disagreement with the sculptor – he had such a miserable look on his face it was as if someone had just kicked him in a sensitive area and stolen his dog. Good job the chap wasn't around to see it, unless of course it really is a true representation.

In the company of Bill and Rosemary we head off towards Decize, a town built on an Island on the River Loire. Our two boats are a combined 33 metres so ideal for sharing the 40-metre locks and we both seem happy to progress at a 'stately' speed. If we travel 2 hours a day it's considered overdoing it a bit and our frequent halts are tailored to finding a butcher to buy meat for our daily barbys. Jan has concocted a sauce which is fantastic – it was her first attempt and just hits the spot. As I write I can almost taste a thick pork chop smothered in that sauce and cremated by yours truly.

Spurred on by our somewhat fortuitous success, the saga of Bills barby is worthy of note. He started with a small gas one attached to the rear rail but decided that he wanted a more 'authentic' char-grilled effect – so he bought an electric one! This new implement was a fraction larger but not only used a great deal of electricity it also took about three-quarters on an hour to cook a burger. When he wasn't plugged into shore power Bill had to run his engine to create electricity from the dynamo on his engine. He hadn't got the set-up quite right which meant having to run his motor at a minimum of 1400 revs to create enough power to run the electric grill. It really wasn't very conducive to a relaxed dining experience due to the fearful noise of the engine and resultant exhaust fumes. So... using a variety of tools he dismantled the electric grill, removed the cooking element and filled the void with charcoal! What all this means is that while travelling he's got every base covered. With a little on-the-spot adaptation (dependent on the power supply available), he's ended up with a choice of gas, electric or charcoal on which to cook meals for one (or two small people) at very slow speed. Hereafter Bill became Director of Operations (non-operational) and head

Vintner – twin roles that suited him just fine.

Decize is where the Canal lateral a La Loire, the Loire River itself and the Canal du Nivernais meet. It's also where we meet what must be one of the most impressive and expensive barges I've seen – you can just tell, it oozes class and charm and the Swiss guy who owned it generously allowed us to help him moor. Never leaving his floating palace he quietly issued instruction to us workers. He was actually rather a 'remote' chap who probably dashed out in the dead of night to wash his ropes after we plebs had handled them. But the boat was nice.

We also met a Bahamian couple on a hire boat with their 'so bored' daughter. He was a gregarious bloke who had a quick wit and was up for an adventure. He was white-skinned but suntanned and was probably loaded – they owned a marina in the Bahamas. His wife however didn't seem suited to roughing it on the canal. It's not easy to be chic when carrying your cassette toilet to the sluice, it's a bit of a social leveller, so one-upmanship doesn't carry much weight. I'm afraid (very unusually) I took an instant dislike to her. Rather than asking the usual questions about how to empty the bog, her opening gambit was, 'I'm just exHAUSTED with all the travel recently. I'm a professional palaeontologist actually'.

I asked her how many palaeonts she'd dug up recently and after that the conversation petered out somewhat!

We bumped into them again over the next few days and both adults had mobile phones glued to their ears remotely resolving some crisis or other. I'm not sure in retrospect that they should have chosen a holiday on a fibreglass tub in the middle of nowhere.

It's approaching Bastille Day so we have to find somewhere to hole up for 3 days while France grinds to a halt and eats dead fauna.

Nevers is a large town built on the banks of the Loire and is capital of the Nivernais region. Nevers is pronounced with the accent on the 'vers' with a silent 's'. 'Vers' (loosely) translates as glass – and that about sums up the holiday weekend! That's 'vers' WITH an 's'.

We are here at a special time as its Rosemary and Bill's Golden Wedding anniversary. I know full well that no one could put up with me for 50 years so I have great admiration for anyone reaching this milestone. At the beginning of the weekend we share reminiscences of their travels and travails, remembering countless adventures on their boat Makita 11 (that's two not eleven). By the end of the weekend we can remember very little about anything.

The Port de Plaisance is adjacent to an abandoned water park, whose disused pools and slides silently echo to holiday-makers past, now sadly full of frogs. There is a very helpful 'Capitain du Port', a young lad who shows us to a mooring (more suited to a boat half our size) that necessitates some sideways shuffling down an avenue of moored boats; a manoeuvre that would have filled us with dread had we not had at least some experience. As much by luck than judgement we kept our no-claims bonus intact and I received a pat on the back from the skipper, the first I'd had since I'd tried my hand a milking a cow in my youth. We settle in to use the free WIFI to realize that it is probably free because it doesn't work. Not free exactly, it's included in the 30 Euro mooring fee.

We stay here for 3 days and nights which comprise one 'Golden Wedding day' sandwiched between two comprehensive piss-ups. Not that the Golden day was without indulgence, no, it was rather a sustained effort than the sprint of the evening barbys.

Actually, the group thrown together this weekend may have been considered a (fairly) typical representation of inland boaters. Apart from the four main protagonists, Jan, me, Rosemary and Bill, we had the two wealthy Bahamians with their now 'really bored' daughter. When he wasn't on the phone solving problems in the Caribbean he was a good laugh. Also moored was a fun Aussie couple, Ian and Sue, who owned a half-share of a lovely barge (Wobbe). Ian had 'shrewdly' purchased a 'solid silver' candelabra from an 'antique' shop for 5 Euros. Convinced that the provenance of this priceless heirloom originated with one of the French Louis', he took it from the ship's vault and allowed it to be the centre piece of our concrete BBQ table. I can honestly say that it really did alter the whole tone of our gathering. Such was the weight and design of the piece it could easily have passed for Australian. Ian and Sue had guests, namely Mick and Teresa who had just bought a share in the same boat and who were on their inaugural familiarization trip. Quite what they thought of Ian and Sue's furnishings (candelabra) and the company they kept (us) was never clear. Safe to say that Mick and Teresa were either too stunned to say much or were naturally 'reserved' (or well-behaved!). Actually, they are really nice people.

Also present were another English couple with their lovely daughter (early 20's) who was also finding life in the middle of nowhere in a hire-tub a touch 'uninspiring'. They all joined in, having been dragged kicking and screaming to the party, and enjoyed it, or so they said.

Resident in the port are two further boats (steel cruisers). The first owned by a really friendly English couple, he Roger and she, whose name, shamefully escapes me, who remind us very much of another couple (whose identities I won't reveal in case they don't agree). Not a great deal of information here but they kindly took us shopping in their car and joined heartily in the festivities. The second Nevers live-aboards are French-speaking Belgians (he was called Wills) who are rooted on their boat in the Port for the summer. You know the sort, very tanned, always park their deck chairs under the same tree, can answer any questions at length (so much so that by the time he's finished his protracted monologue the boulangerie is shut) and don't join in much.

Bill and Rosemary asked Jan and I to share their big day with them. We were very touched and I still can't really understand why they chose to spend the occasion with a short, fat chap and his wife rather than dining at the top of the Eiffel Tower. But ask us they did and we had a great day. We cooked a special breakfast for them (including smoked salmon, scrambled eggs and black pudding) which they politely ate, accompanied by a distant-relative of Champagne and fresh orange juice. The centrepiece of our dining table was the 'solid silver, antique candelabra' (which looked even worse in daylight) loaned to us for the morning by the Australian gentleman for a very reasonable 5 Euros.

Shortly after breakfast we had drinky-poos on the grass in the shade of the plane trees. Rosemary had squirrelled away a few bottles of a rather closer relative of Champagne and nibbles were provided. Bill has taken an alarming liking to smoked sausage so there was plenty of that, jambon-persil (jellied ham with parsley), crisps etc. etc. Gradually people came out of the woodwork and a dozen or so of us had a very civilised shindig that dribbled on into the afternoon. Certain people are in their element during a weekend such as this because, due to the determined, if steady, intake of alcohol the same stories can be related over and over again without anyone realising.

But, hang on a moment; I don't want to give the impression that it was all pure indulgence, oh no, not at all. We were able to witness the town of Nevers shut up tighter than a goose's backside for the holiday, and marvel at the wonderful wildlife. Seagulls pooping on the picnic tables and rats gaily swimming about the port, not to mention the fishing match across the harbour where nothing larger than an anchovy was caught during the 8-hour marathon. There was even one chap washing his works van – the wonders of rural France just went on and on.

The day was rounded off as Rosemary cooked a lovely meal for the four of us (roast beef) enjoyed on a warm summer evening on their rear deck. The fairy lights that Bill had installed twinkled and we'd all dressed for dinner. Which was probably a good job because (with respect) we are all beyond the point where sitting around with nothing on would enhance an occasion. I know it was really not the point but Jan and I thoroughly enjoyed the whole day! Bill and Rosemary are still a 'young' couple and long may it remain so.

The only other thing of note was the 'Bastille Day' firework display that would have been spectacular if we'd been about 3 miles closer.

Leaving Nevers we had the first of two encounters with a particular hotel boat. For those that don't know, automatic locks are set in operation in different ways. One is a 'magic eye' where the passing of your boat breaks a beam roughly 300 metres from the lock. Technology a bit like 'Cyclops' making automatic line calls at Wimbledon, without the beep or bad language. Another method is where a flexible hose, previously mentioned, which dangles about 5 metres into the waterway. You turn the hose through 45 degrees and the red / green lights next to the lock ahead begin their sequence.

The aforementioned hotel boat was moored with its rear about 5 metres from the pull cord making it near impossible for a boat to reach it and start the lock. I realise these guys have to make a living and finding a mooring for a 38-metre boat can be difficult (depth restrictions) but this was a touch inconsiderate.

Anyhow we escaped Nevers and motored to a small place called Herry whose little general store appeared in to be in it's death throes. Neither item on the shelves appealed to the skipper so we decided to have our monthly treat and eat at the local restaurant. No joy there either as, despite sounds of jollity emanating from within, we were locked out. It wasn't just us either, the Irish family we met suffered the same frustration. By now we'd accepted the vagaries of the French food-supply system, shops and restaurants that open when, and if, they want, well-stocked or not. The Irish family took defeat in their stride and had a singsong. It was great to hear their boat throbbing to drum and fiddle as they wailed away the night.

We were moored about 30-metres below the lock and the following morning our friends the hotel barge came by at full throttle and ripped out our mooring lines. Our poor old boat bounced and scraped off a ledge and ended up in the middle of the canal. I realize these guys have to make a living but.........

Not in the rudest state of mind I marched up to the shop to buy a baguette. It was closed so I was even more rude when I set off along the canal on my bike on search of basic food. This turned out to be a shop some seven and a half kilometres distant, that was also shut, for 'the holidays'! Fortunately, the little bar next door was open and had a sack-full of baguettes for sale. A surrogate bread shop like this is called a 'Depot du pain'. The elderly lady proprietress was a treasure and had the largest bosom I have ever encountered. I say encountered because wherever you were in the tiny bar you had to navigate with some circumspection. You could have parked a family saloon on her frontispiece and so flustered was I that on leaving I bid her, 'au revoir Monsieur'.

The towpath was quiet (I encountered one single fisherman in my 15 km round trip) so I saw red squirrels playing on the asphalt and black kites swooping overhead. My photographs don't do them justice, the squirrels look like little dark pebbles and the kites like insects. At least I have my memories. Note: need zoom lens.

Because the library here was open only on Wednesday, between 5 and 7 in the evening, I had to seek alternative amusement so once again turned to my bike. The River Loire has a cycle-path so I set off along there. The peace and tranquillity was stunning and the beautiful river my companion. It is a large river even this far from the sea but nowadays too shallow for navigation except by all but the shallowest drafted, flat-bottom craft. You see the odd pleasure boat or fishing dinghy but the river is largely left in peace. The water meanders ponderously, treacle-slow, around sandbanks where water birds abound and gentle currents and eddies swirl in the sunlight. I sit on a bench to rest and take it all in. Sadly, there is a huge bush right in front of my seat so all I can spot of note is an empty Gauloises packet stuck in the branches. There's either a foliage-maintenance issue here or a bench installer with a sense of humour.

Further on, superfluous flesh poking out of my lycra shorts, I encounter a proper athlete. He's a 67-year-old man in the process of running 369 kilometres alongside the Loire accompanied by his wife on a bicycle. She is his support vehicle and the bike is bedecked with spare clothes, tent, water-bottles etc. etc. They are taking a fortnight over their trip travelling roughly 25 kilometres a day in the most wonderful setting.

The main streets of some rural towns and villages are generally pretty tidy. It's when you walk the back streets that you see the decay and neglect suffered by these dying places. The average age of the inhabitants is perhaps 50 and there are few children. Soporific canines doze in the shade escaping the heat of the day, opening a lazy eye as a foreigner walks by. What rural industry there was seems to have gone and the agricultural workers are in a similar condition to their aged, rattling machinery. Canal trade during the summer cruising season is insufficient to sustain local shops as are increasingly are dwindling populations. There really is not much to encourage youngsters and many villages are too remote to be dormitories for larger towns. It's difficult to see beyond a slow death for these places. The ones that thrive have something going for them, a wine-growing hub for example but I think that these, although prosperous, are merely self-sustaining and unlikely to expand much further. Hence the upwardly mobile younger mortgage-payers and their offspring move to the outskirts of larger towns and cities leaving the elder generation to exhale rural villages' final breaths. It seems that when the elder generation passes on, village properties are left to children who can neither afford to sustain them nor rent or sell them because no one wants to live in a dead space. Maybe that's a gloomy assessment but our inability to find a shop is perhaps testament to something rather more fundamental.

One place definitely not in the dead zone is Sancerre. Perched on a hill surrounded by hectare upon hectare of vineyards, the town is thriving; continued success is due to its famous wine. Unless you are fit or broke you take mechanised transport up to the town. We took a taxi both up and down. The return trip, in a vehicle driven by the first chap's wife, cost 5 Euros more than the upward journey. This we felt was a touch exploitative. Sancerre is internationally renowned for its wine (particularly white and rose) but the bottle we had to accompany a modest meal was expensive and palatable only because we'd paid for it. 'Reserve' it said on the bottle. Reserved for tourists no doubt. Even Bill screwed is face up, and he'll drink anything.

The views from Sancerre are incredible, particularly towards the Loire valley, made more spectacular by alternating thunderstorms and bright sunshine. The town is centred on a square dotted with cafés and Caves where visitors are able to spend a fortune if sufficiently endowed. Before we returned to our boats with total purchases of a corkscrew (Bill) and a tube of toothpaste (me), I met an Australian couple, both eighty years old, who had cycled up the hill - which is not for the faint-hearted even in one's prime. They had taken three weeks over it mind.

So, leaving our cash behind with the natives, we motored on towards a nuclear power station. Some distance short of this huge power plant, which is sited at Belleville, the canal-side villages looked to have been born in another world. Flower-bedecked Capitaineries, pristine moorings and clean facilities are testament to an input of cash from somewhere. That somewhere is the Power Station who pays the local department a substantial annual sum, for the 'inconvenience' of having to put up with one of France's Nuclear Power Stations and its inherent dangers.

As I write, Fukashima is battling to avoid a disaster of biblical proportions.

Bill and I went to visitors centre. We were assured that the plant is absolutely safe (emitting far less radiation than naturally occurring background radiation). We approached past large reactor buildings that were themselves dwarfed by enormous cooling towers venting enough steam to literally create the plant's own weather system as white clouds drifted away on the light breeze in an otherwise clear blue sky.

The lady who ran the visitors centre had a real glow about her with sparkling eyes and a 'zappy' hairdo. Despite this she was politeness personified and showed us a scale model of the plant's reactor buildings, associated cooling apparatus and miles of pipework. TV monitors ran loops of 'the construction of a power station' and 'how safe nuclear power is'. It wasn't easy to concentrate however, turning your back on the fizzing, bubbling goings-on a couple of hundred metres away.

It's difficult not to be awed by the enormous power of the place and nigh impossible to ignore the terrifying nuclear reaction taking place within the reactor buildings. Bill and I produced almost as much energy cycling up a gentle incline back to the boats.

As we returned to the canal, about a kilometre away, I try (not) to imagine the potential consequences posed by an idiot with an aeroplane and a bomb. However, despite the enormous amount of electricity being produced nearby, we were unable to connect our boat to the shore supply because it was the Capitainerie-manager's day off!

Fire in Bill's Hole

Chatillon is notable for two reasons. Firstly, I set fire to my charcoal bag on the rear deck while tipping fuel onto the barby. Not the charcoal, just the bag. Went up quite well really and by the time I'd dropped it in panic and stamped out the flames, the deck was littered with bag-less charcoal. An interested native stood and watched ready to leap into action and steal my sausages if I'd been rushed to A & E, but he and his slavering dog were denied.

Secondly, at 7.15 the following morning a plumber in a Transit van drew up across the canal. A tradesman intent on doing a bit of fishing, ensuring he was late for his first appointment of the day. He unpacked box after box of equipment, fishing stuff you understand, not tools of his advertised trade, and methodically prepared his four rods which he gently cast upon the water as each in turn was readied. Then he went for a pee in a nearby bush, returned, packed up all his tackle and left. Equipment: conservative estimate 1,000 Euros, time spent: 50 minutes, fish caught: nil. I hope he's better at plumbing.

The wonderful River Loire has been our constant companion for about 200 kilometres but we part company at Briare where the river passes below us as we cross the Pont Canal de Briare. It is a spectacular aqueduct, completed in 1896 and a wonderful testament to the skills of the 19th Century engineers who built it. The Loire flows away to the west where it enters the Atlantic at Saint Nazaire while we continue north towards Paris. 'The Loire Valley' has a magical ring to it. A place of dreams and wealth and beauty. We feel privileged to have been wrapped in its charm.

Stretches of the Canal de Briare are very rural. I can't recall the exact spot, it was certainly a long way from any town or village, but we happened across a chap in his garden. He was notable because all he was wearing was a leather condom. It was held in place by a piece of string tied round his waist above his sunburned buttocks! We weren't sure whether he was getting ready to fornicate with a passing animal or protect his manhood from the blazing sun. He gave us an enthusiastic wave while tending his vegetables in his garden. His own 'two veg' were exposed to the elements and in real danger of resembling a couple of walnuts one sees scattered on the canal bank in the autumn.

We're still travelling with Bill and Rosemary and at Chatillon-Coligny poor Bill had the first of two mishaps. We are to share an order of diesel to be delivered by tanker. The nozzle on the end of the tanker's hose was too large for the small filler hole on Bill's boat so he borrowed a large funnel from us. Due to a language mix-up the tanker driver, rather than turning the flow down, turned his valve on to maximum and the fuel shot back out of the funnel covering both Bill and Rosemary and their boat. Bill got a face-full and was immediately in agony. His eyes were stinging and the normally laconic Bill was in real discomfort. He washed and washed his face with fresh water but he was in real trouble. Rosemary raided their medicine cabinet and gave Bill some ointment to help. It didn't, the eye salve dated back to 1984 (approximately 27 years out of date!!). It was three days before his eyes stopped smarting and his vision cleared properly. Fortunately, his wine-drinking appendages were unaffected so he could continue to enjoy the delights of Château Marne. When he could find his glass.

It was also here that a fellow on a hire-boat came to ask me where he should pay for his night's mooring. A conscientious English chap desperate to part with his money. I pointed out that, because there's no one around to collect, you'll probably get a free night. He told me he was on his honeymoon so I congratulated him asked if he and his good lady would like to join us for a BBQ later on. Error! His new wife was not only three-parts pickled but was poorly trained in the use of the 'F'-word. Now I'm no prude but she went on and on………. 'Whose effin idea was all veese effin locks? Makes it such effin hard bleedin' work. Can't wait to get back to effin Larndun. Effin France'. Bill and Rosemary are gentle, well-mannered folk who could barely believe their ears. The only time she stopped swearing was when she had a mouth full of pork chop or her face buried in a wine glass. He was a nice-enough chap (a journalist I believe, who now had some material for a forthcoming article) and was a tad embarrassed. Where he found this one goodness only knows, possibly the re-cycle bin.

We two boats communicate between ourselves via VHF radio on one of the open channels. We'd not long left Chatillon and had just come out of a lock when our companions had their second mishap. Rosemary came on the radio and said, quite calmly, that they were going to pull over as smoke was coming out of their dashboard. At this point on the canal they were too deep-drafted to pull into the side so we moored up on the bank and they came against us. Bill lifted the floorboards in his wheelhouse and smoke poured out of the engine room – in the gloom he saw a battery lead sparking and fizzing so immediately turned off all his electrics and sprayed a full extinguisher of CO_2 into the engine bay, and then another. The smoke subsided for a short time then started again. This is pretty serious because their boat is all wood, that's hull, topsides, the lot. It was dark down there so we rigged up a work-light from our boat but it was impossible to identify the source of the smoke. He had no electrics so no lights or water pump so we ran a hose from a connection on our tank and Bill went down below to see what he could see. He couldn't find anything obvious but squirted water around before having to retreat because of the thick smoke, which if anything was getting worse. So I went down before I too was beaten back by the smoke.

Jan meanwhile had retreated to the bank under the trees fearing an explosion.

Bill and I were at it for half an hour before we noticed that the galley wall, that adjoins the engine room, was hot. We hacked the tiles off behind the sink and a wisp of smoke came through a gap in the wallboards. We finally found the source of the smoke as the insulation between the galley and engine-room bulkhead. The only way to reach the source of the problem was from within the engine room, but it was in a really tricky place, accessed by squeezing past the engine (that was still hot) and reaching behind the generator. Bill's a bigger chap than me so couldn't get in easily, or more importantly, get out in case of a real problem. I hacked off the wood while constantly spraying water. Finally burning insulation, glowing red, fell into the flooded bilge. At last we damped it down and made it safe. It was a bit dangerous and very mucky work.

What was puzzling was that there were no wires or obvious source of fire in the area it had started. The fizzing battery lead initially indicated an electrical fault but the shorting cable was nowhere the fire itself. It was very strange and they were lucky (in a number of ways) that they didn't lose their boat. It has been their home for 35 years. Had they been on their own they would have had no auxiliary power, no water and been unable to moor up. Bill is approaching 70 and pretty fit but I'm not sure he could have managed on his own, indeed me either had the roles been reversed. Anyhow, after a clean-up and a bit of re-wiring, we set off again.

There are numerous relics along the Canal de Briare, some, like me, piloting boats. (Even) more impressive though is the disused 7-lock staircase at conveniently named Rogny-Les-Sept-Ecluses. Though no longer in use the locks have been left as another testament to the enormous undertaking of building four canals linking The River Seine to The River Saone, thus completing a north / south inland waterway through France.

Montargis is a beautiful town known as the Venice of the Gâtinais due to it's many bridges and 'petit' canals. Not only is it the home of pralines (almond based confectionery), the town is also garlanded in beautiful flowers which adorn the canal bridges and shopping areas. Ancient, gnarled plane trees shade the canal and an early evening walk round this lovely town is a joy.

The port itself is large but not that cheap. Fees were collected by two chaps who seemed to have negotiated a good working contract. They would drive slowly past the moored boats in their brand new car shouting instructions for people go to their brand new hut and part with their hard-earned cash. As is fairly typical of French bureaucracy paying our dues was a two-stage operation. First we encountered the 'port-fee' man (Captain, harbour dues) who carefully filled in a receipt book with boat name, boat length, registration number, our name and duration of our stay. He handed us a carbon copy in exchange for 15 Euros. Then we proceeded to the adjacent desk where his steely-eyed subordinate (First Mate, tax division) would carefully fill out another receipt for (tourist) tax, replicating all our details – in exchange for a further 40 cents! People in the queue were getting a tad agitated at the protracted nature of this arrangement as it was eating into V.D.T. (Valuable Drinking Time).

It was here too we met a very amusing Australian chap. He spoke loudly with a slooow, deliberate drawl and when he eventually got to the end of a story he had us in stitches. He also had the most amazing facial hair. A hairy, grey caterpillar came out of one nostril, down past his mouth, back along his jawline before heading north and disappearing into an ear. It re-appeared from the other ear whence it mirrored its outward journey and shot up the other nostril. As the breeze ruffled the facial beast it looked to slither around in an endless progression.

During one of the daily (protracted) lunch breaks we saw Natrix Natrix – yep, that's right, our first grass snake! Not being venomous, the snake's only defence is to produce a garlic-smelling fluid from the anal glands, much the same as some members of the 'Homo Sapiens race after a good Rodent Josh. It was probably a female as it was over a metre long and despite there being three boats rafted out together, she swam by quite happily. It's a bit unusual to see anything moving during a French lunchtime but she was probably on the hunt for a dozing frog.

The Briare is a truly delightful canal, in fact there is much to recommend all four on this route. Many of the lock cottages are inhabited and the owners take huge pride in the presentation of their locks. Some are ringed by gorgeous displays of flowers where others have sculptures. Many sell produce such as honey, jams, vegetables or wine and occasionally you come across a little café or tea room. You also frequently see various livestock such as chickens, ducks or goats so eggs and cheese are on offer too. Sometimes there's an honesty box where you take a few veggies from a basket and leave behind an appropriate offering. Not to put too finer point on it but there are locations I've visited where the baskets would have been nicked, never mind the sprouts!

St Mammes is the junction of the Canal de Loing and the Seine and as such you'd have thought it would be a major port – none of it. There are a series of small pontoons designed for small boats; nothing to suit us. As we leave the canal we're now on a tributary of the Seine. Big water where sleeping commercial boats are moored, probably at rest during the summer holidays. We find a nasty place to pull in on a sloping wall, difficult access and right next to a cocky, noisy Parisian woman. She's only had her boat for a few weeks but is suddenly THE authority an all things boaty. Bill and Rosemary have lived on theirs for 35 years so know a thing or two so just agreed politely with the woman's ramblings. We're not far from the French capital here so maybe a more aggressive approach is the norm – anyway we'll steer clear.

OK, anyone know what a tingle is? A boat-related tingle that is, as opposed to that creepy feeling you get when you receive a utility bill? If you know, skip the rest of this paragraph, if you don't, it's a thin sheet of metal you pin onto a wooden boat (sometimes with a sheet of heated tar paper underneath it) with which you can effect a temporary repair, or to prevent a problem from getting worse. Just around the waterline, particularly right at the front which always gets the full force of water when you're moving, the wood can become damaged over time and can develop into a leak if not protected. Anyhow Bill decided he needed a tingle. They are usually copper sheet, held on with copper nails. There was only one shop nearby and the boulangerie had run out of copper sheet so he needed an alternative. He spotted a tin box in our lounge. It was a presentation box for a bottle of Benedictine (my favourite liqueur). Three sides were full of holes but the back was solid – so out came the tin snips and into the water went Bill. Job done. OK, the tin wouldn't last for ever but it was certainly good enough to get him back over the channel and home to Sandwich in Kent.

The weather's turned as we head out onto the Seine, it's horrid in fact, and it's rather a shame that we see this magnificent river in such dire conditions. We're back among the large commercial boats, one of which was a pusher-tug pushing four, fifty-metre dumb barges (engine-less boxes in effect). The whole ensemble was about 250-metres long and to drive this lot would have taken some degree of skill, particularly in a strong wind.

As we near Paris we see many awesome river-side properties, homes for the seriously wealthy, some with towers and castellations, many with extensive lawns extending down towards the river. There is also a ribbon of houseboats along the bank – good sized boats and a great way to live close to the city without the massive price-tag.

We've been lucky enough to visit Paris a couple of times in the past on the train so we have no real desire (or budget) to moor in the centre. Instead, we look out for the imposing Chinagora Hotel and restaurant (Chinese) on the junction of the Seine and the River Marne where we'll turn east. It's rained constantly for the past three days and although the Seine is not flowing quickly we are rather alarmed when approaching the junction because a 40-metre peniche shot out of the Marne onto the Seine like a bullet from a gun. It was really travelling. When we make the turn we find out why - the river is in flood. We learn later that not only has the recent rain increased the flow, but a barrage (weir) has been opened in error up stream allowing a real old deluge to come down. With the water comes mountains of weed and logs. We can only make about three kilometres an hour against this flow (indeed struggle to get through the bridges at all where the flow is squeezed) and we have to slalom round all the debris coming towards us – it's really quite alarming. It takes us an age to get to the first lock through which we pass without difficulty. It's at the second where our problems are compounded. The sluices in the gates are clogged with weed so the lock is closed. We have to moor on a high steel wall which means reaching up with a boat pole to hook over a bollard nearly 3 metres above the water. Fortunately, we are out of the flow here in the lock entrance but it's not nice. The only way off the boat is by jumping from our wheelhouse roof to the shore. A gap of 4 feet or so and a drop of 3 metres. Not really recommended for a chap whose athletic heyday was not long after 'One giant leap for mankind', and whose record long-jump was only four and a half feet!

When I go and investigate it transpires that the sluices in the top gates are clogged with weed so cannot close fully. This means water is constantly flowing into the lock chamber. The sluices on the bottom gates are also clogged so the water can't flow out fast enough. In other words the water was entering as fast as it was exiting. It's a status quo and despite the lock being 7/8 empty, they are unable to open the bottom gates due to the pressure of water within. The bottom gates open inwards. The only way to allow water to flow is to clear (or at least partially clear) the bottom sluices. There are two workmen way down in the lock in a small boat physically hoiking weed out of the sluices with pitchforks and the only way they can empty their little boat of weed is by filling the lock so they can dump the rubbish on the lock-side. These guys really are working beyond the call of duty and it is three hours before they have cleared enough weed to resume operations.

While we waited a small boat inched up the river behind us. It looks like a converted former hire boat and it's outboard engine barely coping. Decorated in multi-coloured swirls and whorls it looks like a floating sperm bank. Struggling to manoeuvre in the strong current it is nearly wiped out by a laden sand-barge that's powering past. It is easy to see how people can get caught out when conditions change quickly or their boat is not up to the task.

The river is canalised, in other words has locks with adjoining barrages (weirs) which can be raised or lowered to control water flow. There are 18 locks in 178 Km between Paris and Épernay which is the extent of the navigable river. The flow had eased a little the following day but there is plenty of 'fresh' water about flowing over the weirs so it's still a bit of a struggle. But the sun has come out and the river is wide and beautiful; still weedy, but lovely.

That evening we have to bribe the commodore of a boat club to moor on his knackered old pontoon. He strides across the grass with some purpose in his official cap and I have to pull the old 'engine overheating' ploy – 10 Euros and a bottle of beer later he's placated, in fact a really nice guy.

Sadly, that evening, tragedy befalls the club when one of their members dies in a boating accident and it's sobering to see their clubhouse illuminated by the eerie blue glow of the emergency vehicles' flashing lights.

The city of Meaux is twinned with Basildon, England. A fact that is probably only of real interest to the respective civic employees who doubtless enjoy 'complimentary' exchange visits. In France, Basildon councillors can savour the delights of Brie de Meaux, a delicious, world famous cheese sampled in a café on the delightful river frontage. Meanwhile on their return trip to Essex, Meaux councillors can experience a comedy musical performer delightfully named Kunt and the Gang – I kid you not, go on, Google it!

Mooring proves a bit of a trauma here as the large finger pontoons are perpendicular to the river (actually slightly offset downstream) and we crunch into the upstream side while Bill crunches into us. Bill is pinned to us and we are jammed against the pontoon by the current so getting off the mooring might be a bit tricky. We were spat at by a moron on a bridge who ran off when I took his photo. Perhaps there was a civic exchange visit in progress.

Meaux has a delightful aspect on the river and is home to the Musée de la Grand Guerre du Pays de Meaux, purportedly the biggest World War I Museum in the world.

We are pushing on a bit because Bill and Rosemary have to get past Berry-au-Bac (further north) before a lock closes for repairs. We don't have to stick with them of course, but Rosemary can sniff out a good sausage. We often exchange meals on our respective boats and in La Fuerte-sous-Jarre we moored against a high wall. I took a 5-litre box of wine round to share between us (fully expecting to bring the majority home again later). Well, I forgot it. I left it overnight on their rear deck. Bill's bow was close to our stern so the following morning he shoved his boat hook through the plastic handle on the top of the box to pass it over the gap. Unfortunately, overnight dew had weakened the box. The bladder, with most of the wine still in it I might add, broke through the soggy bottom and the important bit plopped into the river. It wouldn't have been so bad if another boat upstream hadn't emptied his bilges leaving a diesel slick on the water. Passers-by, of whom there were numerous, were surprised by our antics as we tried to fish what could have been a bloated, dead animal out of the river with a net. Luckily the wine was considerably improved by the addition of diesel and we were able to to enjoy a nip with our breakfast croissant (kidding).

We are getting up towards Épernay (Champagne Capital) and acre upon acre of vineyards line the gentle slopes by the river. It's not just the major centres that reap the rewards, small towns and villages too are home to independent wine growers, bottlers and distributors – so many people in the region rely on the age-old vines for their livelihood.

Épernay is famous for being an 'entrepot' (formerly trading post, now literally warehouse) for an estimated 250 – 300 million of bottles of Champagne per year.

The region is particular about the use of the term Champagne, in fact so particular that no-one else (within the EU) can use the name. One of the four methods of sparkling wine production is called Methode Champagnoise but only in the Champagne region. Anywhere else in the EU it is known as the Methode Traditionelle, or the local language equivalent. In Germany for example its called "klassische flaschengärung", which doesn't have quite the same ring to it.

We didn't help much with overall consumption figures but I'm sure the efforts of the good folk of Champagne Ardenne region are appreciated by the boaters of Henley and the posh-frock brigades at weddings. A decent ale and a meat pie was standard fare in our territory up north. Traders along the Leeds Liverpool canal had benefited from our 'weakness' a few years previously.

It's not easy to pin down exact numbers but I believe that Moët & Chandon produces more than 13% of all négociant-manipulant Champagne (2 million cases in annual production, 200,000 of which is Dom Pérignon, twice as much as its nearest rival, Veuve Cliquot.) In all there are 261 houses selling Champagne under 1,316 different brand names. Anyhow, that's enough of that. Hic**! Zzzzzzzzzzzzzzzz

So, after two months and a number of 'incidents' we say cheerio to Bill and Rosemary. They are off for a sandwich in Sandwich while we head for a bottle in Burgundy. I know where I'd rather go.

We are now on the Canal Lateral a La Marne and got tangled up in a fishing match. It's Sunday morning and it appeared that half of northern France had missed mass. The line of competitors went on for well over a kilometre. They are basically a surly bunch who seem to derive little pleasure from their craft. Maybe there aren't enough fish to go round or perhaps it's our craft blanketing their tackle in diesel fumes, who knows?

In Vitry-le-François I had a stroke of luck. The doctor oversubscribed antibiotics three-fold when he treated me for a throat infection. I offloaded the spare tablets to a youth on his way to a rave and the profit went on a couple of oil filters. It seems the norm is to oversubscribe; the drug companies must love the GPs.

As we were stuck for a few days I befriended our neighbour who was fettling his Perkins engines. Mighty proud he was of them too. ('A pair of Perkins' aptly describes the French couple we were to encounter within a few days – of which more anon). Our new friend had know-how. He also the ability to let us know that he had know-how. He explained his engine maintenance programme in detail and my throat was fully healed by the time he was due to test his engines. Now the problem with showing off a bit is you'd better get it right. Well, actually he did, and number one turned over a few times and exploded into life with a roar and thick a cloud of smoke.

Simultaneously a huge dead fish wallowed up from underneath the rear of his boat.

'Blimey', said I.

'Carp', said our friend.

'Yep, that about sums it up'.

Jan and I were looking away tittering as number two engine exploded.

I told him our internal combustion device has developed an insatiable thirst. He told us not to travel as far. Good job I didn't offer to pay him for THAT advice. But he did tell us about his dog and how it used to nip the back of his legs, like a sheep dog herding a flock. I asked him what he did about it. 'Put a bit of strong English mustard on my trouser legs'.

'So'? I asked.

'I ended up with a dog partial to mustard and holes in my trousers'.

'Stick to engines', I told him.

I asked him where he was off to now his engines were sorted.

'Just over there', pointing to a boatyard 20 metres across the canal, 'I'm leaving it on the hard-standing for the winter'.

'Oh'. I gave him a card. 'Here', I said, 'just in case you have a problem en route'.

A few kilometres down the way we rounded a bend, three-hundred metres before a lock. There was already a small boat waiting. We could see the lock starting to empty so we twisted the overhead chord on the hangman's scaffold and motored slowly up. By now the cruiser had entered the lock. We were creeping along and were less than 10 metres before the lock when the woman shouted and waved her arms about - and the lock gates began to close. I jammed our boat into reverse and we stopped virtually touching the gates.

The lock is 40-metres long. We are 19, they are 12 so there's comfortably enough room for both of us you would have thought. Anyway, we had to reverse 300-metres back to twist the pole again and re-set the lock.

We finally got through and less than a kilometre later came across a stranded boat. And not just any boat! They had pulled into the site of a former commercial quay. The canal had widened to around 60 metres and they had tried to go in and moor against the bank but were stuck fast. They gesticulated, so I gesticulated back. Despite their moronic behaviour at the lock, Jan persuaded me to stop and help. We reversed as close as we dared and threw them a rope which the lady tied to their bow. We were pulling at an angle and very nearly managed to pull them right over on their side before they scraped free. We left them, probably feeling a bit sheepish, and we never saw them again.

We moor in a lovely little place called Chamorilley and are set upon by an enthusiastic native called Bernard. He is an absolute delight and immensely proud of his village, particularly the work they have done to improve the facilities for visiting boats – and rightly so, it is one of the most pleasant spots we've ever stayed. And what a difference a cheery welcome makes. Just over a grass bank a young river Marne meanders gently through the trees. It's progress is slowed to almost nothing as it backs up behind a small, rocky weir. The water oozes along the consistency of honey. The sandy riverbed is mottled as the bright sun filters through overhanging trees. Shoals of fish dance and play in the crystal-clear water in the shallows. It's just one of those moments.

A different moment arrives when the fan-belt snaps and we have to take emergency sanctuary in the loading dock of a disused factory. As usual I get covered in muck and grease and Jan prepares the antiseptic cream and plasters knowing full well that I'll emerge with some injury or other. To be honest it's a good job I've learned how to do these basic repairs because some stretches of canal are very isolated and having to call out a repair team would be very expensive. There's also a degree of luck involved because if your head 'whatnot' goes, or your injection 'thingy' gives up on a river, you need to able to find safe haven. We were fortunate to be very close to an ideal spot. Note to self – repair anchor winch!

By now we're into September, it's almost eerily quiet, but sunny and warm. Jan returns from a promenade having spotted something swimming across the canal, that she reckons is either a snake or a rat – which narrows it down a bit. Then she proudly reported that she'd managed to hold a conversation with a French man, 'who spoke good English'. He was one of the crew of a theatre ship, a large peniche called Cristal Canal that travels the waterways staging plays and musicals to audiences of around 50 (I think) in it's converted hold. We later saw them 'rehearsing'. The play was centered on a group of people enjoying a long, raucous lunch on the deck of their boat, and I must say they were jolly good actors. After that it went quiet for a few hours. 'Resting' I think is the actor's term.

Unexpectedly we pass a sign that says, 'Welcome to Patton's US Army Club'. Now I think this is part of the Musée de Blindes at Saumur. There is a small tank on the forecourt and I believe the museum houses tanks (and photographs of tanks) from the US, Germany, France and Italy and even includes Soviet machines. Patton competed in the Olympics in modern pentathlon and learned some of his fencing skills at the fencing and cavalry school here, hence the connection. Nonetheless it was rather a surprise to come across this museum here after days seeing almost no one.

Advertising signs is one thing the French are truly good at. They are everywhere, a bewildering array of irrelevance. They adorn buildings, fence posts, billboards, bridges, lamp posts………. unfortunately, very few of them refer to anything relevant to modern day life. In actual fact what they are is a historical timeline of events and businesses that entertained and served in days gone by. Some of the tin ones attached to the sides of buildings, promoting vehicles or tyre manufacturers for example would fetch a pretty penny on Bargain Hunt. The boulangerie promoted in paint on the side of a house is a reminder of when a particular village actually had commerce, the travelling circus probably went straight from it's last performance to join Noah on his ark. Roadside 'A' Frames are usually pretty current. They advertise Vide Greniers (literally 'empty attic' or car boot sales to you and me) or local Lottos raising funds for community projects.

So, we return to St. Jean for another winter for another round of frivolity and frozen appendages among our transient friends.

Winter in St. Jean de Losne. (Part 2)

We're having a chilly snap. If it warms up a degree or two and the snow turns to rain we'll be able to witness the rain bouncing off the cabin roof before cascading over the side to merge with the retreating ice sheet.

The weather, discussing it, sheltering from it, wrapping up against it, drowning in it or merely accepting it is a big feature of our lives in a Burgundian winter. One Aussie lady (Di) recently slipped on their icy deck and fractured her wrist. With the true grit of a mid-European winter boater she was soon back chopping logs one-handed while her husband held the umbrella to prevent her plaster cast getting wet. Holding an umbrella in a force 5 in a deluge is after all a two-handed job.

There are perhaps gentler places to over-winter where it stays warm and the worst you can really expect is a stiff breeze or damp. Southern Spain for example, or the Antipodes. Here in mid France you do away with the 'warm' and add all sorts of other nasty adjectives. If it gets brighter over here it's generally because someone's turned a light on. We regularly inspect the long-range weather forecast for signs of an 'easing', longing to be able to put the woolly socks in the store cupboard (or plastic bag if, like me, you haven't got round to building a cupboard yet).

True, we are a bit short of cupboard space but boy have we got lots of shelves. My wife is a shelf addict. Whenever a small patch of wall appears (often due to something that's dropped off because I've not fixed if properly) she wants another shelf. In fact, I've had to build some shelves to put the spare shelves on. And yes, DIY is something we can tackle over the winter.

As is the case the world over these 'little projects' are performed with varying degrees of proficiency, usually by the male of the household whose skills are over-estimated. If we can get the car out of its igloo we slither round to the local Bricomarche (self-build store) where the manager rubs his hands with glee as another boater approaches. We males have that self-assured gait as we walk into such a store. It's a look of casual efficiency designed to make everyone else in the shop appear second-rate. Not true in my case as I'm often returning something I've previously bought which is quite unsuitable for it's intended purpose. Even wearing dirty overalls with a pencil behind my ear I can't quite disguise my shortcomings. I also have the unenviable reputation of being able to rearrange a perfectly respectable collection of raw materials into something unrecognisable. Hence the boat is a jumble of part-finished projects lying in the rubble of my over-optimism. The only advantage of working inside is that no-one else can see your work. Inadequacies are only exposed when you have someone round to dinner where the man has to sit on a part-finished indoor dog kennel while his wife perches on an unstable tower of boxed power-tools.

One thing new to our winter social scene is Tai Chi (T'ai Chi Chu'an). It's run by Helen whose patience and flexibility know no bounds. It is described as 'an internal Chinese martial art practised for its defensive training and health benefits which can allegedly promote longevity. It is performed in a manner that most people categorize as 'slow movement'. Mmm.... I found that some body parts simply weren't meant to go where we were instructed and the only indicator that life had been prolonged was an entire body ache. During the session you make an exaggerated noise while breathing. Unfortunately, my dear wife found herself next to a lady who rather over-exaggerated this aspect of the regime. Jan described her co-masochist's 'death rattle' as sounding like Darth Vader of Star Wars fame, where-after Jan descended into a fit of giggles. She subsequently gave up, never to return, reasoning that 10.30 in the morning was too early for vigorous exercise. I pointed out that there was a second session at 2.30 on Wednesday afternoons. 'Still too early.' She said.

Helping each other through is partly what it's all about. We have a friend Peter who is a retired London cab driver. One couple (Aussies unless I'm mistaken) needed a lift to the local rail station, 4 kilometres from where they were moored in St. Symphorien. They were told by a third party that Peter would probably help them out. Without any form of introduction whatsoever, the stranger said to Peter, 'We'll be ready to be picked up at 7.00 am tomorrow morning'.

'Oh!' replied Peter, absolutely clueless as to who these people were. 'It's a van', he added, 'with only 2 seats'.

'It's ok,' the bloke replied, 'the wife will manage in the back'.

Well, in the true spirit of the boating community he did give them a lift. He got up at 6.30 am, defrosted his van, re-arranged assorted building materials so 'the wife' could clamber in and then ran them to the station. He was given the princely sum of 2 onions for his trouble, one of which he ate with his breakfast, three hours earlier than usual.

One of the joys of being in a new place is seeing ancient ruins – and there are plenty of them here! Most of us are of a 'certain age', or older. When people start to venture outside after hibernation there is the distinctive aroma of Ralgex and liniment in the air. It is however a chosen lifestyle that keeps you active. Many boaters are retirees, indeed one couple, with a combined age of 175, although not live-aboards, they visited regularly until recently. She was taken to hospital in the medevac helicopter when her replacement hip popped out to be told by the doctors here that the original operation had been poorly done and would need re-doing – at a cost of 17,000 Euros. She chose to take advantage of her free health care in the UK (despite being entitled to claim much of the cost back through a Europe-wide reciprocal health-care agreement) so was back on her boat (by road ambulance) the same night. The following day she set off for the UK driven by her 89-year-old boyfriend! This included an overnight stop en route, a ferry journey and a long drive in England with all the clambering in and out of the car that that entailed – all with a hip strapped tight! How they managed it, goodness only knows but their 'have-a-go' spirit enabled them to visit their boat at an age when others would be tucked up under a rug watching daytime TV.

WINTER IN ST. JEAN DE LOSNE. (PART 2)

Christmas Day is a week past and it seems like yesterday, particularly to my wife who sleeps a lot. A distant memory. One of our (fairly) senior citizens (somewhere north of 60) played Father Christmas, dressed in a moth-eaten old suit, a massive effort just so he could have the local bar-owner come and sit on his knee. Sadly Natalie (an attractive, splendid female) wasn't on duty so he had to put up with Giles (pronounced Jeel), her male business partner and chef. Our senior member has just about recovered but Giles, who appeared to rather enjoy the experience, is considering a full-time switch!

And suddenly......a new dog!

He's a terrier / poodle cross, a mix which apparently is fairly common. We got him from the rescue centre in Dijon, known as the S.P.A. (Société Protectrice Animaux – society for the protection of animals). We wanted a portable model – my memory of carrying our previous dog, Bonny, a total of half a kilometre down a steel jetty for a poo was still fresh. There were numerous dogs in the right weight category and they all barked furiously as we walked past the line of cages – except one. One little fellow just came to the bars and cried. That was it for Jan, this poor lad was at the end of his tether, and we took him home. Medically he was sound (all dogs leaving the SPA have been fully checked and all injections are up to date and they are electronically tagged) but his coat was long and matted and his eyes were dull and horribly sad.

We cut and washed him and he emerged as a terrier. Not much sign of poodle except that his hair doesn't drop – which is a massive bonus. We're glad terrier emerged from the thicket, after all we didn't really relish him looking like one of those fatuous fashion accessories you see defecating on the streets of Paris. Less of a bonus was his behaviour. He has more issues than an unsuccessful magazine salesman and is real handful. He hates men in work boots (perhaps he had been kicked) and he had a little nip at a drunk who we passed. He lunges on the lead and barks whenever we pass another dog and we begin to wonder if he'll ever mix with other dogs. We took him to a dog trainer who owned a fenced-in field on a hill-top above the town of Dole. We let him loose with the dog trainer's dog and after a few introductory growls they played together for a good half hour without the demise of either dog. This was considered a bit of a breakthrough and gave us hope. It was wonderful to see our previously incarcerated hound having some fun. Overall, it can't be that easy for him, he's had to learn to speak English after all.

He's called Tache (Tash). They'd called him Moustache at the rescue centre because they didn't know his name when someone dumped him. I shortened it to one syllable to 'assist' with his training. They said he came from the north. Whether that was the north of Dijon or north of France no one could tell us. He's insecure and chews things in his anxiety. After one month we have incurred incidental costs of more than 200 Euros. This includes a coat (one of ours, not his), 2 leads, a pair of shoes, his doggy-bed and a car seat belt.

We'll come back to Tache.

The boating community has been immortalised on film. France 3, a national TV station one up from the Shopping Channel, did a documentary about life in St. Jean de Losne during the winter. They focussed mainly on three couples, one French, one Swiss and one English, who allowed intimate details of their lives to be arrested and released on strict parole throughout France. The documentary creator, cameraman, director and editor (Jean-Paul, a one-man band of prodigious talent) poked his equipment into the darkest recesses of the community. Exciting scenes, such as the English people filling up their water tanks, was further enhanced by moody music and French commentary. They did miss some quintessential aspects of French life though, like dogs crapping on the towpath and natives eating horses but it was a nice snapshot of our alternative way of life. The film was shown at prime time – 3.00 pm on Saturday afternoon – and pirate copies have been zipping round northern Europe chased by Inspector Clouseau of the fraud squad. I guess one thing that comes across is that boat-dwellers are all aware what living in a house is all about but house-dwellers are not necessarily aware that there is an alternative way.

Another winter activity is 'Franglais'. This is where French and English-speaking people get together and hold very limited conversations. It is a pleasant way to integrate with the natives and can provide respective nationalities with a few words of anothers language. One session was filmed for the above documentary and my dear wife has been immortalised on celluloid (or the modern equivalent). Asked, in French, by a French lady how long our boat was, she replied, 'vingt kilometres (20 kilometres)'! OK, you may snigger, but from knowing no French at all a couple of years ago, she has responded to a question in another language – only two words maybe, and one of them is the same in English, and she got it wrong, but she had a go, and good on her.

The circus has been to town! We know because not only is there a smell of dung in the air but also a 10-foot plastic elephant is towed round the streets behind a rusty van. The van blasts out 'ice-cream-van' music and an unintelligible commentary yelled by a chap who sounds like he has a mouth full of snails. It's basically an animal circus. There are many such touring France and the debate about animals for show is for another place. The fact is they turned up here and parked their wagons on a patch of waste ground near the Gare D'eau where we moor. They knock wooden stakes into the ground and tether the beasts to them where they munch away on fresh grass. Not lions or tigers you understand but donkeys, camels, buffalo, horses and goats. Now this is my dog-walking route. In the time since we 'rescued' him we've just begun to reel in his 'boisterous' instincts while walking on a lead. That morning however we were confronted with a whole new set of problems! In actual fact all the circus animals were calm (and to my untrained eye looked really healthy) and our beast took it all in his stride. Confront him with a large black dog and he goes nuts. Walk him past a camel and there's not a peep. Perhaps he's never been persecuted by a camel?

Apparently there are up to 200 circuses operating in France (not all feature animals) and although numbers are declining, it is still a significant number.

For a country known for it's gastronomical prowess, France has a surprising affiliation to junk food. Here in St. Jean there are four restaurants, a couple of cafés that do food and five fast-food joints. Also, a couple of days a week a mobile pizza van appears. To be honest the restaurant food is 'middle of the road' (not roadkill, more mediocre) and the fast food outlets re-shape various off-cuts into kebabs and burgers which don't half smell good.

Now is a period of transition when boaters start to prepare for the coming cruising season. In fact, 3 boats went south down the river Rhone in mid-February. Not for the faint-hearted usually at this time of year but we had a settled spell of cold, but dry, weather. The river calmed down and despite being very cold (and 5 out of the 6 boaters getting bronchitis en route) they made it to the Mediterranean in a couple of weeks. One couple Murray and Cate are on a mammoth trek on their Bavaria yacht heading from Britain (last year) back to New Zealand (in the future). Cate gave me an exercise programme to help with a dicky back which is why I'm writing this on the saloon floor at an odd angle (me not the floor).

So as winter slowly unravels people venture outside and there are a few surprises, some pleasant, some less so. Trees and shrubs have a hint of colour, a magical regeneration considering the ravages of winter. Beautiful, pink cherry blossom is the first to appear – or because of its beauty you notice it first. If it lingers a while we're lucky. If the blossom is blowing horizontally it's windy and if it's brown and shrivelled, like much of my cooking, we've had a severe frost. But while it lasts it's a delight.

The summer crowd start to arrive – fair weather boaters. People who haven't the constitution to battle out the winter here, or have more sense. You can spot them a mile off, firstly they don't look like tramps and secondly they drive late-model cars, usually German or Scandinavian, not the rusty, dented things that have slithered around here all winter. On arrival they remove full-body protection from their boats, huge tarpaulins that would protect a small French town through times of crisis or shelter the herd of horses destined for high-quality burgers.

Ambrose Pierce said: 'Painting is the art of covering flat surfaces from the weather, then exposing them to the critic'. Yes, now is the time to retrieve rock-hard paint brushes from the nether regions of the bilge where they have been festering for 6 months and touch up all those bits that weren't done properly last time. Here again you can tell the professional over the amateur. The well-seasoned painter prepares with a light sanding and a wipe-down with a 'tack-cloth' whereas I, and other amateurs, hack away with a rusty paint scraper before wiping down with half a gallon of white spirit and a pair of old underpants. The application of paint can be a joy to behold. Done well, the paint settles beautifully into a smooth, glossy finish whereas the method I employ does afford some protection but is short on aesthetic wonder, often 'blooming' or settling in nasty dribbles. I doubtless provide canon-fodder for the critic but have the satisfaction of knowing that I've cocked it up all on my own. One word of warning. Neutral, traditional colours are a conservative, but wise, choice; particularly if your boat is new to you and you are likely to make a mess of early attempts at boat-handling. A case in point is the Antipodean boater who painted his boat in 'the colours of his homeland' so it stood out like a beacon, then made a hash of a mooring manoeuvre. Had the boat 'blended in' he might have got away with it, were it not for the frantic revving of the engine and sickening steel-on-steel grinding noises.

So, as we await the arrival of the rest of our friends, who have wintered in centrally-heated isolation, I hope you appreciate the efforts we've gone to in preparing Burgundy for your visit. We've cut the grass, slowed the river down and re-awoken trees and flowers. We've also burned the effigies we made of you when you went home. When things got desperate here we'd stick pins in your mini-icons, testament to the envy with which we view your cosseted 'winter' existence.

However, we'll welcome you back with open arms, particularly if you bring the sun with you.

Spring is when open-air events begin again. We hold a port BBQ on a Sunday in either late March or early April, depending on the weather. Up to fifty people turn up, goodness knows from where, but we all enjoy an assortment of charred objects accompanied by a glass or two of something refreshing. In fact with enough wine you can manage to forget what you've eaten. I'm being unfair, we have a number of pretty accomplished cooks who do us proud. This is thanks largely to the 20 or so 'experts' who don't actually make any effort but feel qualified to offer invaluable advice.

People have been known to overdo it a bit at these BBQs. One Kiwi, who shall remain nameless (probably because he's forgotten), had a bit too much vin rouge and slumped off his chair against the shop window. He dislodged an orange life-ring mid-slither, which ended up round his comatose Antipodean shoulders. When he finally got mobile again (a couple of hours later) he staggered home. He was so unsure about 'making' the gap between the shore and his boat that he slept on the grass verge. Turns out he'd lost his boat keys anyway somewhere between sobriety and oblivion.

Vide Greniers (basically car-boot sales) are another spring 'wonder' where people with nothing better to do can get rid of the stuff they acquired the previous year. You can pick up bargains though. Jan pick up Dennis for a couple of Euros. Dennis is a donkey, a small, stuffed toy with bug eyes and a silly grin. He is our new dog's best friend. A tolerant toy, whose smile is ever-present despite being growled at and chucked around the lounge as Tache practices his rat-catching skills.

Dennis is for indoors but while on a lead he needs 'healthy' distractions to avoid him pestering fellow walkers. We seem to be having some success a little water pistol that grabs his attention at the appropriate moment or with toys that make a noise – of particular note is the squeaking carrot. (Think we'll avoid the squeaking pea!).

I have been training the dog to walk and stand close to me when on his lead (mark 3, as he's now destroyed the previous two), particularly when there are distractions about when he gets a bit 'excited'. One evening we had a bit of a crisis as were simultaneously approached by another dog, a cyclist and a group walkers. He came to sit close to me as bidden. All went pretty well considering, but as I was watched all the approaching distractions he peed on my foot!!!!!!!!!!!

We'd taken him to a quiz night and tied his lead (number 2) round my chair leg. He was quiet as a mouse throughout but towards the end of the evening we were surprised to see him walking down the room in search of refreshment. He'd just silently nibbled through his lead and without any fuss whatsoever, left his mooring!

Before we set off again there are a few things to tackle.

One of these involves modifying our tiller-arm. Our boat is steered by a big wheel in the wheelhouse attached to chains and a steel cable which in turn are connected to the rudder. Before this system was added (in the days of sail for example) it was steered direct from the rear deck by a tiller arm attached to the top of the rudder. The rudder itself hangs on large pins off the back of the boat. When the previous owner had added the steering-wheel the tiller arm was left in situ and it extended out over the rear deck by about a metre. The problem now is that when the rudder is operated from the wheelhouse the tiller-arm sweeps across the rear deck – so anyone sitting there is liable to be swept off into the water. The plan was to chop the tiller-arm in half and fold it back on itself out of the way. This still enabled it's use in an emergency by merely folding it down again.

We had a wooden carving of an eagle's head on the back of our tiller. A nasty, mean-looking bird that I've always disliked. I had to remove it to make my modifications but 'accidentally' dropped it in the water - I was not displeased. I smiled as it floated away until Jan shouted, 'you can pick that up too!' Foiled, I had to re-mount it on top of our nameplate on the cabin roof right in front of the wheel-house window. I was thus taunted by having to glare at the eagle's rear end whenever I looked forward.

The tiller modifications went well and not having the bird perched there is far more inviting for anyone having to give us a push start. Basically, the bird move went OK, but yesterday the poor bird finally succumbed to wood rot and fell off it's perch. Aware of Jan's liking for our eagle I felt duty-bound to try and fix it. I caused some confusion in the local DIY store when I asked for some 'eagle repair compound'. The bloke behind me (who was just trying to purchase a small tin of paint and get out of the shop) obviously didn't realize the serious nature of my dilemma - and had a sense of humour failure. He was built like a second row forward with teeth like a knackered fence so I left hurriedly without any bird-patching tackle. We cremated our eagle on the wood-burner. R.I.P. (Rot In Peace).

Beaten by The Weather

I remember watching the impressive Jubilee pageant, an occasion the Brits proved they can stage without equal, celebrating the queen's longevity on our throne. Partnered unfailingly by a loyal, yet foot-in-mouth, consort and an unpredictable melange of bit-players who range (and have ranged) from the sublime to the fatuous, she's endured a 60-year reign. Eating rich food in France also offers the potential to spend considerable time on the throne but the Queen's effort is dedication of the highest order.

Our lives differ somewhat. Hers a busy, yet pampered, existence made possible by (our) riches galore while we are hampered by lack of cash. She Fortnums we Lidl, palaces and country piles to our little boat that needs a paint job and an engine refurb. We have to take our own photographs, perching the camera on a nearby wall hoping that a hoodlum doesn't spring from the undergrowth and pinch it while she has her own band of colour sergeants. Let's face it, the only royal news of real interest is when 'Philip the Unruly' opens his mouth or the delightful Kate's summer frock rides in the wind – no one gives a hoot about our photos.

The Queen allegedly wept when Britannia was decommissioned, we also wept when our dear old engine failed to start on our morning of departure. A complicated technical problem that was resolved by re-connecting the starter battery. The date is 3.6.12 which has a pleasant symmetry.

Close to both the longest day and the wettest early summer in living memory, we were off.

We pulled into a boatyard to have the aforementioned starter battery checked. A pretty crucial piece of kit that it took them a number of chargeable hours (including a 2-hour lunch) to pronounce healthy. Lighter of both wallet and heart we set off in search of perfect moorings with free electricity, water and wifi, somewhere where we could frolic and BBQ and follow others misfortunes on the internet. Also, where we could teach our new dog at least some tricks. The first night we spent at Abergement-La-Ronce (where the only facility available was something to tie on to) where the dog training didn't get off to the best start. He leapt out of the wheelhouse, dashed down the pontoon and attacked a fisherman's rod. It wasn't a prolonged mauling, more a quick chomp. He returned with a 'well, he wasn't catching anything anyway' look on his face and settled down to growl at anything worthy in his new world.

We're heading north-east on the River Doubs and Canal de Rhone au Rhin which flows from the River Saone at St. Symphorien (4 kilometres up river from St. Jean de Losne where we had wintered) all the way up to the River Rhine a place called Niffer (pron. knee-fair).

This waterway is alternate canal and river (Doubs) and we arrive in Dole (Twinned with Northwich, Cheshire, UK) after a one kilometre stretch of river, which is flowing reasonably quickly after heavy rain. While moored in Dole it continues to rain and rain...so much so that they close the waterway completely further up stream – so we're marooned; moored on a sloping wall. The port is overlooked by the town itself, dominated by a large church, which like many we come across, looks better at night when illuminated. Home to Louis Pasteur, thanks to whom your bout of gastric difficulty is probably not due to infested milk, Dole is a lovely, medieval town constructed round small tributary waterways at lower levels and narrow, hilly streets that climb the hillside in higgledy piggledy fashion. Streets that are largely cobbled, likely to ensure that the personal injury claims department continues to prosper.

Our sloping wall is opposite a hire-boat base and we're amused (but sympathetic) to the hire-boaters trying to reverse their boats onto finger pontoons at right-angles to a river current. By the time they get lined up they've invariably drifted a few slots down river which is now occupied by the boat that originally tried to get into the slot the current boat was aiming at! One boat set off, 6 people all late sixties or seventies, with 'rudimentary' training. So rudimentary they went 200 meters downstream towards the lock (which has a weir right next to it), got frightened and came back. Therefore, after an hour, in something that would have cost something over 2000 Euros for the week, they have travelled about 400 metres and had a collective change of incontinence pants. Because it's now after 6 pm the hire-boat base is deserted one of the ladies on the boat called to me to see if I would help. I agreed to follow them down the riverbank and 'talk them' into the lock. However, they were still not happy so they persuaded me to get on the boat with them. I ended up driving the boat into the lock then explain about how to set the lock in motion and how to tie up safely (the ropes were all on the floor in a tangle under the plastic dining table). I got off the boat and watched them descend until the gates opened. However, by now it's 6.55 pm and they are heading out onto a short stretch of river, with a considerable flow on it, and they have to negotiate a lock an approximate kilometre away to get back on a canal section. The locks close at 7.00 pm so they faced a night moored on a 'waiting' pontoon the river, not for the faint-hearted for people who had an idea what they were doing, but for this lot, downright dangerous. Fortunately, I managed to persuade a lady VNF (Voies Navigables Francais, the body that manages the French inland waterways) employee to go and make sure the lock down the river was kept open long enough for them to at least get into the relative safety of the canal. Now OK, perhaps these people shouldn't have been hiring a boat in the first place but having done so, someone should have ensured they were at least competent to do something with it.

While marooned I decided to catch up on some BIY (bodge it yourself) so went to the local store to pick up supplies. I've patronized many such stores during my attempts to ruin the interiors of both houses and boats and had chosen my irritatingly expensive bits and pieces before joining a 12-deep queue. There were 3 check-outs available but only one was operating. The operator appeared to be a numerically dyslexic trainee so things weren't progressing very fast. Meanwhile nearby 3 BIY-shirt-clad employees were standing at the 'Customer Services' counter discussing lunch. Noticing the ever-increasing queue at the till, one of them sprung into action. He dashed through a door and re-emerged with two paper cups asking if anyone would like a cup of coffee while we waited. A number of queuers pointed out that he might be more gainfully employed by opening up one of the two remaining tills – which he didn't.

Because our existing hosepipe had deteriorated to 'revolting' level, a new one was purchased at the same store. I asked for assistance, specifically requesting hose of drinking-water quality. I returned to the boat with 50m of pretty green / yellow hose which I connected to the tap and tested for taste before putting it into our tank. Good job I tested it because the revolting mixture that came out of the end tasted like liquid plastic - despite running it for half-an-hour to try and clear it. I returned to the store with 50m of hose draped round my shoulders. While dribbling noxious water on the floor in front of the Customer Services counter I had increasingly intense discussions with increasingly senior (and ratty) staff before they agreed that what I had purchased was not fit for purpose. They did replace the hose (which is now fine) but was not offered coffee this time.

We meet many lovely folk on our travels. For example, a Dutch man and his good lady who we had invited to our boat the previous night. He called round mid-afternoon to repay our hospitality. 'Wine at 5.30 at our place', he said before dashing off in search of an internet café. We duly arrived at the appointed hour. While I continued on a while to give the dog a quick walk, Jan climbed onto our friend's boat and sat down on the back deck. The lady of the house said, 'Oh, hello. Have you've come for a drink then? I'll just put my soup on hold.' The chap had invited us without telling his wife so she was a bit surprised when Jan just plonked herself down on their boat! We could have managed quite ably on our own actually as we were prepared. It appears to be the (Dutch?) tradition to bring your own supplies. When they visited us they brought with them wine, glasses, nibbles, a spare cushion and an ash tray – so we reciprocated, with the addition of a soft drink for Jan and a dog's bowl, dog's blanket – and a dog! We'd only come 50-metres round the port but it looked like we'd come for a week, and we were only half invited.

Soup is one of the few things the Dutch do well, another preparation of note is meatballs, but in our experience (admittedly in provincial Holland) their cuisine is very limited and basic. They have ovens but rarely use them, preferring seemingly the one-pot simmer on the hob top. We could buy chicken (kip) but only breasts, the skipper had to negotiate with the local chicken supplier to buy a full bird for us to roast, something greeted with amazement by the locals. In fact, her penance for a whole chicken was allowing the vendor to sing her the British National Anthem each time she shopped there – which in effect drew attention to the fact that she had peculiar shopping habits.

Here, on a final shopping trip, I spotted a man in a supermarket obviously struggling to see the price of a small portable radio. He had very limited vision and his face was literally inches away from the shelf. When I asked him if I could help he told me he wanted a cheap radio, the cheapest in fact, but it must have a headphone socket. I pointed out what I believed to be the best model for him. He picked it up and held it, a tad suspiciously, right in front of his eyes. He thanked me profusely – and told me he wanted to listen to the radio while riding his bike!!

Right, the river level has dropped to a mere torrent so we set off up the river.

The next evening we're back in Dole! A combination of reasons really, firstly the weirs on the river spooked us a bit. When going upstream you exit various locks and 'deviations' (lock-cuts leading to or from locks that bypass stretches of river) and emerge to face weirs, some 2 or 3 hundred metres in length, on your starboard side. They begin at 'point zero' at the lock and run away from you at an angle of perhaps 15 degrees. Although the flow has now decreased significantly you are still pulled towards the weir as you head away from the lock up-stream. That's not too bad but it's the thought of coming back downstream that gives us the willies towards a narrow lock entrance alongside the weirs in an ever-decreasing waterway. By the time you actually enter the lock (or deviation) the weir is no more than 10 metres away on your left. We do go upstream for a day but find that moorings are few and far between – in fact at 6.00 pm we are forced to double up to an 'accommodating' boat that itself is not on a secure mooring and staked to the canal bank. We are actually blocking the waterway near a bridge. We took our neighbours for a thank you beer at the nearby café and asked another boat to honk their horn if a boat arrived and wanted to pass. Thankfully nothing came by but already we had had enough of this waterway – at least for now. The weather is still unpredictable so any more substantial rain would see us marooned waiting for the river to drop again. So next morning we turned round and implemented plan B. That's B of F - where F is getting a camper van.

On our return leg we did have trouble at one of the weirs. 'Give way to downstream traffic' is the (unofficial?) regulation. This presumably is because a boat going against the flow has far more control than one which is being swept down a river with the current. It's a rule near-meaningless after a prolonged dry spell when the river is barely moving (we saw one boat once that didn't even bother tying up for lunch, just drifted a few hundred metres downstream over the course of a half-hour's association with pate and chablis) but when you encounter a thousand tonne commercial barge on a river flowing at 4 or 5 knots, its best to keep your wits about you and get out of its way. The burk that we encountered didn't bother with the regs. It was a British-flagged cruiser (of a mere 12 metres) that was obviously not going to cede and just as we were on final approach to a lock cut we had to do an emergency stop. You lose speed, you lose way (direction) so as we came to a halt we were drifting towards a man-made waterfall. Actually, waterfall is overdoing it a bit, it's a drop of a few feet down a gentle slope, but you still don't want to get stuck on the weir. Using the 'foul language manoeuvre' (with the help of the bow-thruster) we managed to avoid disaster and shuffle out of the way. Passing said cruiser with a few well-chosen words of appreciation we soldiered on.

We made (relative) haste back to point of origin (St. Jean de Losne) before setting off for pastures new – namely the Canal du Nivernais.

Moored on the main quay at St. Jean we decided to avail ourselves of the shore-based electricity point. This is a slightly unusual system where one has to buy 'jetons' (tokens) from either a local bar or the nearby fuel pontoon. My conversation with the young man on the pontoon, conducted in French, went like this:

Me: Is this the place to buy tokens for the electricity on the quay?
Him: Yes
Can I buy one please?
No, it's all broken
Oh, does that mean I can't have any electricity?
Yes
Is that, yes, I can't have electricity?
No
I can have electricity then – it's not broken then?
Yes
Yes what?
Yes it's broken but you can have electricity
Oh
It's the token machine that's all broken, not the electricity!
Oh I see. So, I can just plug into the electricity on the quay
Yes, OF COURSE! This is what I tell you!
Thank you. I'd better end this conversation before my batteries go flat.
Do you need water?
Not at the moment thank you.
OK good – because that is not working as well.
Oh, right. We'll perhaps talk about that on another occasion.
Yes, Au revoir
Au revoir

So, back at the point of origin after about three weeks, we'd had what you could call a 'Tom' Cruise – short but action-packed.

We are sorely tempted to stay a while when we see a poster advertising the delightfully named singer 'Dick Rivers', but we resist, and it's off to pastures new.

To get to the Canal du Nivernais (that people tell us is stunning) we have to cover old ground, namely the trip down the Saone to Chalon and up the Canal du Centre as far as Decize. We have never liked repeating experiences, they are never as good second time round – but we don't have a choice, unless we get craned out on to a lorry. However, we weren't fooled into thinking that this short hop would be incident free, nothing is incident free on an old boat, especially with a psychologically challenged captain.

Things were going well, had been for a couple of weeks to be fair. I'd even stopped travelling in my work overalls when...

TWANG!!

The tiller cable snapped! This is the thing that connects the big wheel in the wheelhouse to the rudder at that the back, without which steering is a bit hit and miss.

At least I've avoided having to make the tricky decision as to when to replace it.

Actually, it was twang, rumble, thump, roar. A thick 2-metre chain connects to the rear of the steering wheel via a reducing gear running over a sprocket. The chain in turn connects to 10mm Bowden (steel) cables that run to the rudder over a series of pulleys. The twang was the Bowden cable snapping, the rumble was the chain running off the sprocket and landing in the bottom of the boat behind a diesel tank, the thump was the rudder swinging sideways and banging against it's 'stop' and the roar was the engine in full reverse - engaged thus to stop us careering into the bank. In reverse the boat quickly skewed off line and it was only thanks to the bow-thruster that I was able to stop the boat crunching into the steel pilings.

Fortunately, we were on a straight stretch of pretty wide canal with no other boats nearby and there were two perfectly placed trees to which to tie when we finally hauled the boat into the bank. Unfortunately, we were in the middle of nowhere on the off side (the side away from the tow-path).

The skipper was a doldrum of calm in an ocean of angst. At the height of the crisis as we were stranded at 45 degrees across the canal, rudderless and there was some smoke about as it's rare (rarer that rare actually) that we push the throttle to the stops and the dear old engine showed her displeasure. As I was in a state of some discomfort Jan said, 'it's OK, let's be calm and just tackle one thing at a time'.

'Right', I said, taking a deep breath, 'what first?'

'No idea', she replied.

Well, we got tied up and having had a quick look at the situation I realized that it would be a mucky and tricky repair, one that I wasn't sure I could do at all. At the very least we would need some new cable and there were no steel cable merchants in the adjoining meadows. So we decided, after due consideration, to try and use the emergency tiller and travel the 7 kilometres to Gannay (where there was a port with a small boat-yard, electricity and water). This would involve me standing on the back deck with the tiller and Jan operating the throttle and bow-thruster as required from the wheelhouse, four metres away. Standing right at the back operating the manual tiller, I had to look forward through the wheelhouse and not having my hand on the throttle was very unnerving. In a way steering like this was like narrowboat days but with an obstructed view, a bigger heavier boat and without control of the power. We tested our 'walkie-talkies' but over the engine noise it came out as a series of squawks and mutters so we decided to rely on shouting. There was a 20 kph crosswind blowing which was going to make things tricky especially as we had a lock (down) to negotiate.

The previous day we'd seen 3 boats in total, in fact there had only been perhaps a dozen in the last week. We set off slowly and a touch nervously but had to have some 'way' as the wind was blowing us sideways towards the bank. Just as we approached the lock we saw two boats half-way up it and a hire boat came up behind us. This meant having to hover and wait. The canal in general has many trees offering some degree of shelter from the wind but near the locks the lock keepers have de-forested to create their vegetable plots and we're exposed to the wind proper. Hanging around in a wind is tricky enough when you've got full control, indeed entering a lock with a stiff breeze is not easy but with a lot of shouting from me and calm, deft touches of throttle and bow-thruster from Jan we managed to wait for the two boats to exit and waggle ourselves into the lock.

From the top of the lock (to our delight!) we could see four further boats hovering below the lock awaiting their turn to come up. So, with an additional hire boat that arrived behind us as we started to descend, that made a total of eight boats in 15 minutes – two thirds of a full week's worth!! We got out of the lock and managed to pass the waiting boats only to pass another hire-boat finishing lunch around the next bend. That's 9. This new one set off in pursuit soon after we passed it and shaped up to overtake us a little further on as we were not going 'full throttle hire-boat pace'. My actual language would have made the devil blush, but paraphrasing here for your sensitive dispositions, I asked them to have a little patience and please hang back as we were in a bit of trouble. We would be mooring (hopefully) in a couple of kilometres anyway.

Well, we made it to the port of Gannay - which was full. Thankfully a very pleasant English barge allowed us to come alongside but, because of our 'Heath Robinson' approach to navigation, he and his wife were a bit nervous as we approached. Anyhow we managed. Within a few minutes a boat left the public moorings and we moved there and tied up within 3 metres of electricity and water points. What we had also forgotten from our last time here is that there is also a small boatyard, Entente Marine, who were very considerate. Although I managed to effect the repair myself it was reassuring to have them nearby and judging by the testaments of two people who had recently had work done by them, they would have done a good job. In effect we had been incredibly lucky. Entente Marine didn't have any steel cable and I would have had to wait up to a week if they ordered some so they suggested that a nearby agricultural merchant may have some. They did indeed and I bought 6 metres of steel cable for 24 Euros - and that was the total cost of the repair – the details of which I won't bore you with.

But it could have been so much worse. Had this problem occurred a few weeks earlier on the Rhone au Rhin canal (Doubs) approaching a weir we could have been in real trouble. So, what lessons? Firstly, have an emergency tiller. Secondly, have a plan and know how to operate the boat with it. I'd actually had a very brief test run with ours in Holland, but on a big mere with no other boats about. Thirdly, carry spares, in this case cable. Lastly, have a super-calm wife who can not only operate the propulsion system but also calm down a panic-stricken skipper.

The episode was later described as a classic case of Dutch Helm Disease.

Back at Beaulon, where we cavorted for a week on our previous visit, there is a very different scenario. One third of the 200 metre mooring has been taken over by a contingent of Dutch boaters for the summer. They are very protective of their personal haven and have even roped off their patch with red / white 'crime-scene' tape. Apparently they have had permission from the local Mairie but to occupy foreign soil (indeed one of the juiciest bits of mooring on the whole canal) for a whole summer seems rather 'inconsiderate'. We were moored just outside Little Holland when a big chap on another Dutch boat pulled in behind us. He was also moored outside the 'restricted zone' but was having none of it. Ranting that his fellow countrymen were simply not allowed to rope off part of a public mooring, he stomped off and ripped out the temporary fence – much to the displeasure of the occupying force. The insurgents rallied and a delegation of three approached our lone warrior. A fierce skirmish ensued (in Dutch) which lasted a good twenty minutes, two men rumbling and pointing and a woman shrieking. Our hero bravely stood his ground and survived the Battle of Baulon. He later explained that he was accused by his fellow countrymen as 'not being a true Dutchman'. 'Hollanders should stick together,' they had told him, 'look at how the English behave!' I'm still not exactly sure what this meant. Theirs was a distractive rather than constructive argument aimed at deflecting criticism from their narcissistic behaviour. OK, we Brits are occasionally hyper-stimulated by the fruit of the vine and our BBQ sing songs more chamber-pot than chamber, but we generally afford foreigners a meaty welcome. And we don't build fortresses on foreign soil – except at organised rallies where the 'elite' of our barging community occupy part of a port for a few days – certainly not for a whole summer.

The upshot of all this was a new friendship with one Dutchman and a healthy disrespect for another bunch.

Wonderful Canal du Nivernais

The Canal Du Nivernais (Nivernais Canal – see we're getting the hang of the language already) is renowned for it's low bridges. It's not so much the height at the centre, rather the sides, due to their arched profile. Any boat with an air-draft (height above water-level) in excess of 3 metres needs to plan carefully. In effect, the wider the boat at it's high point, the more chance you have of destroying part of your expensive wheel-house on a bridge or clacking your head on a coping stone. We should be OK but I still take precautions, such as removing the search-light, horn (large bugle-shaped thing) and TV aerial pole. This takes a while as they are all 'hard-wired' through the wheelhouse roof and I need to block up the resultant holes – just in case it rains you understand.

Confident that our boat's proportions are suitable, we turn right at Decize, traverse a short stretch of the Loire and enter the canal – and promptly run aground! Yep, it's not only low, it's also not very deep. We are as shallow drafted as almost any boat (80 cms) so I can only put this set-back down to a navigational cock-up, for which I naturally blame Jan.

'I think you got a bit close to the edge,' she pointed out helpfully, as nasty scraping noises accompany our attempts to get free.

I respectfully suggest that the art of successful navigation is based on preemptive information. After all there's little point telling me that we've already collided with a lighthouse.

She replies, 'I've just checked the barge-handling guide and unfortunately there is no reference in to overcoming the abject stupidity of a pilot.'

So we settle in for another period of 'contemplative reflection'.

Fortunately, tiffs are few and far between. In fact, the last one was about six years ago on the narrowboat. I was steering up top when Jan popped her head up from the cabin to ask if I would like some cornflakes, to which I enthusiastically agreed. Not five minutes later, as I'm battling away with my cereal, she arrives munching on a delicious-looking ham sandwich. I was rather taken aback and suggested that, had she offered me the choice, I may just have preferred the 'juicy honey-roast ham on buttered brown with a smear of mustard' alternative. Thankfully it ruined her snack as she couldn't eat for giggling.

Just before we'd left the Canal Lateral a La Loire (about an hour previously) we'd 'done a shop'. People had told us that getting supplies on the Nivernais was a bit hit and miss because of the rural nature of the canal, so we'd taken on stores in bulk, this entailed lugging heavy stuff like milk and tins of beans / fish etc. half a mile from the supermarket. Through a housing estate, across a busy road and up the canal bank with cycle panniers straining along with limbs. Now barely 500 metres up the canal we pass two supermarkets barely seven strides from a very respectable mooring! A further example of poor advance planning – for which I spitefully blamed Jan again. This time she pointed out that if I hadn't borrowed someone's beer-stained waterway guide and bought a map actually printed this century, it may have shown the location of the new supermarkets. I had to concede this one – purely in the interests of re-opening channels of communication you understand.

I had built two gates, one for each wheelhouse door, to allow ingress of fresh air and prevent egress of a particular dog. When Jan opened one the dog, in a bid for freedom, promptly fell in the canal. We think he just lost concentration for a moment. He's not a natural swimmer, the Eric the Eel of the canine world, but manages to stay afloat long enough for us to grab him. Most doggy-paddlers are graceful and hushed because most of the serious action takes place below water-level. Dear old Tache slaps the water with a panicky, attention-seeking whirl of his front limbs. On the one hand his natural aversion to water is a good thing, it will hopefully prevent him from diving in after a duck or rat, on the other it would be nice to encourage him to have a paddle to cool him off in hot, dusty times. We'll try and strike a balance but it won't be easy.

Cercy is a little town with an idyllic mooring on the junction of the rivers Aron, Awl and Cane and the Nivernais Canal. It's late July and the water barely moves, an early morning mirror in which one can see reflected the statue of Notre Dame du Nivernais standing sentinel above the town. Pristine white and dressed in a shawl and full-length robe, she is suspended in a sapphire sky. The sculpture replaces a concrete one that collapsed, which in turn replaced a limestone tower that was filched by locals, stone by stone, to build their houses.

I engage in conversation with a Dutchman with whom I'm eager to share my knowledge of Dutch fishing boats. It's a brief and disjointed association because he grumbles at length about why he paid too much for his flag. I had as little interest in flags as he had in Dutch boats so I was glad when our friends, Dave and Hazel, arrived unexpectedly. We had something in common here, Dave and I talked toilets (as many boaters do) while the ladies discussed French hairdressing (as many men also do!). The charcoal was long dead and airborne pests becoming a nuisance as they tottered off to their campsite.

At Pennecot, a small rectangular 'port' off the main line, I made a complete rickets of re-varnishing a hatch. Something went wrong. Perhaps the old and new varnishes were incompatible, I'm not sure. What is clear is that I'll have to get the Work-Mate out again and have another hack at it at a later date. It has gone on the ever-lengthening list of re-hacks. It's eerily quiet here and we wonder if the little settlement has been abandoned until a very posh lady in a frock marches up and demands 8 Euros for the night (that's mooring dues you understand!). Was she an official rent-collector? Who knows, she had a receipt pad but she could have been anybody. Probably how she pays for her frocks. The thriftier boater moors outside the port against the bank in the nettles, but we've either contributed in a small way to the upkeep of this wonderful waterway or bought someone a new dress.

Just round the corner is a beautifully presented lock. A small, blue-shuttered cottage is home to a proud man. Rightly so, the lock over which he presides is a joy. It is ablaze with colourful flowers and shrubs. There are historical artefacts including wine barrels, painted cans and an assortment of blue-painted machinery. There are also two life-size figures of a man and a woman, dressed 'of a period'. He stands before an antique grinding wheel, sporting a fine moustache wearing a black felt hat and carrying a scythe. She dressed to promenade in a simple, white dress and bonnet with a baby in a pram. We buy some jam, thankfully made with fruit unsullied by our noxious engine fumes. Due to our passing, next year's crop may not be vintage.

At Chatillon, a port approximately 250 metres long by 50 wide, we moor at the far end on the low stone quay, well away from the bustling hire-boat base. There's nothing in front of us and nothing behind, in fact, apart from us, there's only one boat in this half of the port. Inexplicably we are accosted by an irate French chap who tells us that they can normally moor three boats on the bit we are on. I explain that there's nobody else here but that if he is prepared to wait, I'll go and try and find another boat, or hang around perhaps till ours gives birth. To this day we don't know what we did wrong despite prolonged discussions over a glass of Merlot and a BBQ.

Past an impressive canal-side Château and a few kilometres up the canal we moor in an isolated spot where the river Aron flows by just over a grass bank. A gently sloping sandy shore is perfect doggy paddle territory. It's hot and a tug of war ensues as Jan drags a reluctant hound towards the cooling waters. The contest is probably a draw as the dog is hauled to teet level before the danger of strangulation brings the exercise to a premature conclusion. He's still learning and when we leave him to visit a nearby café, to sample the coming and going of the village (singular, note, as we only see one person moving in half an hour), he learns a new trick, how to remove a wheelhouse curtain from it's pole and chew it to shreds. He's not starving, nor has he developed a penchant for linen, no, this we are told is 'separation anxiety'. There's no such problem when we let him off the lead for a romp as he separates rather rapidly in search of prey – a rat, or a fisherman perhaps.

Despite being midsummer, it is incredibly quiet, two or three boats a day is all we encounter. You can go hours without social interaction, particularly when we've had an internal discussion about something or other. OK, I jest about Jan's navigation but she retaliates by having a go at our new fly-curtain. Purchased at very little expense from a little quincaillerie (hard-ware shop) it is, I admit, not the deluxe model I was too tight to pay for. It was over-long you see so I chopped it down with Jan's best needlework scissors. When I screwed it to the roof the plastic tentacles began to curl up. They curled up so much in fact that the dog could walk straight underneath. He was followed by a swarm of flies and a few wasps. The brightly coloured strips gently dancing in the breeze were like a magnet attracting all things airborne. Jan wasn't impressed.

'We're just short of a buzzard now for a full-house', she said, waving her arms about like a whirling dervish to keep the flies off her tuna sandwiches.

To distract Jan from her fly problems I was playing Supertramp on the wheelhouse stereo. We'd just entered a lock and 'Take the Long Way Home' was blasting out when we were approached by the young lock keeper waving his arms around. He was gesturing for me to turn the volume down, which I did. I thought it was a safety-related thing whereby it would be difficult for us to hear his issued instructions in case of a problem. When the lock had filled and we were bobbing around he began a series of horizontal arm flaps. It was obvious that I was to turn the music off altogether. I was a bit mystified but, in the interests of Anglo-Franco relations, I concurred. The young lad (sporting a relative of the Australian bush-hat) then took a seat under a parasol and began to play a Vielle. A rudimentary instrument popular in the Medieval period, the Vielle, is a cousin of the Hurdy Gurdy. Shaped loosely like a violin it is played by turning a small handle at the blunt end (which sets up a resonating whine from four strings) and fingering a rudimentary 'keyboard' situated over the fret board. It makes an assortment of noises (not dissimilar to our engine) which range from a whine to a to a drone. Some of the sounds are vaguely musical and judging by the grin on the musician's face, at least one of us was enjoying it. I dropped a few Euros in his tip jar until he eventually released us. I'm not being fair of course, he was a music student earning a few extra Euros in the holidays and he told me he also plays in re-enactments of medieval banquets where noblemen and women get drunk and throw gnawed bones around a vaulted hall.

The hamlet of Baye marks the summit of the canal where a 25-acre lake supplies water to the canal. The lake and canal are separated by a long dam wall. We moor next to an Irish couple (Michael and Rosemary) and erroneously I try to match their legendary Irish hospitality. This results in both men ending up in a bit of a mess and suffering a number of 'ailments' the following day. There's a 'mega-store' in Baye, at least compared to the previous 50 km where there's virtually nothing at all. The 'shop' is in fact a small room in a guest house and conveniently has a healthy stock of non-essentials. In other words, after you've pre-ordered your bread the night before, you can accompany it with either anchovies or carpet cleaner. There's a campsite nearby, but quite what a camper needs with carpet cleaner is anybody's guess. There are fishermen galore and a yacht club, in fact the whole place has a holiday feel about it – in fact it's far too busy.

On leaving Baye you encounter a 3-kilometre, single-file section governed by traffic lights. Much of it is a steep-sided valley where the sun rarely reaches and it's all rather primeval, damp and gloomy with bracken, ferns and stunted trees. Ground cover reaches right to the water's edge and there is a slight chill in the air. It is also narrow, made to feel increasingly so by the steep sides. The channel itself is ill defined and you must make sure to keep central to avoid scraping boulders that lurk below the surface. Jan drives this bit (with the odd 'left-a-bit, right-a-bit' from me) and does a fine job.

This valley precedes a flight of 16 down-hill locks set in beautiful woodland. We roar past a café halfway down - because we're short of cash. Well, not roar exactly as that implies speed. As a friend pointed out recently, 'despite all the technical wizardry, big engine and fearful noise, you don't half go slowly'.

I questioned the technical wizardry but was forced to concur with the rest. I think he was just peeved because I referred to the Asian meal he'd cooked as 'a cow pat on a pile of driftwood.'

'Seaweed,' he corrected me.

'What about that thing on top?'

'It's beef'.

I peered at it. 'Was it actually attached to the animal at time of slaughter?

He ignored me.

'Or perhaps it could set a new culinary standard as something that's passed through two different species within a week'.

'Look, just shut up and eat it. I don't get paid for this'.

'Really'?

'Besides, it was on offer'.

'What is it?'

'Not sure, but it's my interpretation of a 'surf and turf'.'

'Slurry and curry more like'.

Something's happened here - 'dish' and 'interpretation' are definitely new to his vocabulary.

'Look, you have to develop your cooking. Learn from the experts on telly. I've been studying flavour and texture. Do you really want to stay in the stone age, kill yourself with an offal-factory-produced donner kebab?

I looked at him.

'Don't answer.' he said, as he opened a bottle of Shiraz, all the way from the Co-op, Rochdale, England.

Food is a big thing in France. Actually, it's a bit risky saying 'big thing', because they eat just about anything. A big thing could well be a 'defining' ingredient in a regional delicacy. Food is a religion. No, actually it's more important than that. But there's one item here that will need more than a dose of missionary zeal to convert me – The Andouillette!

It's the 'Marmite Syndrome' – love it or hate it.

We're in Chitry les Mines 'taking lunch' with our Irish friends in the marquee of a small café in the port. While I order something sensible (with chips!), a man just along the way sharing our trestle table, has ordered andouillette. Dear dear! They are basically a coarse sausage made from intestines (chitterlings) mixed and seasoned with pepper, wine and onion. I'm not offal-averse (indeed love kidney, liver etc.) but had the partaking of these things stopped with flavour, I might have managed – it's the smell. It's as if someone has bottled the odour from a decaying horse's autopsy and released it into the atmosphere. So unpleasant is the pong that we have to move further down the table. Now andouillettes are popular but I'm not alone in finding the smell revolting. Someone dragging their fingernails down a blackboard doesn't bother me, not the sight of blood, or spiders, but the toxic andoulliette makes me gip. Incidentally, I believe that if they are made from the colon rather than the small intestine, the smell is even more pungent. No need to guess where this bloke's sausage came from – or indeed where they are going for that matter!

Actually, lunch got worse. The café is quite busy and the tables and chairs tightly packed, so when a wasp alighted in my lap I pushed my chair back in a panic to escape. Unfortunately, I collided with the lady behind and her bosom landed in her lunch. Not best please she turned and gave me a right old mouthful (language, not lunch). I apologised profusely, using my command of her native language, thankfully stopping short of wiping stew off her frontispiece. However, when she realised I spoke her language and had explained about the wasp, she calmed down and became friendly. Had I not been able to explain my behaviour in her native tongue I may well have had to pay a visit to A & E to have a regional sausage removed from an orifice.

Communication with the outside world is not easy here. There's no mobile phone signal or internet connection. We needed supplies and the nearest shop was in Corbigny, some five kilometres distant – and it's hilly, so the bike was not an option. The only way I could hail a taxi was by visiting the office of the local deity, namely the Marie. I was lucky to find it open as he or she is a part-time deity, but they allowed me to use their recently installed, newfangled, telecommunications equipment and hail a taxi – and would not accept payment. I shared the taxi with Michael and we returned a couple of hours later with a collection of supplies very different to the collection had the 'girls' gone instead – despite detailed shopping lists. In front of me in the check-out queue was a man stocking up on essentials. He had twelve rolls of loo paper, thirty-six cans of beer and six family-size packets of crisps – yep, he was a fisherman preparing to settle in for a protracted session.

En route to the delightful town of Clamecy we overnighted at a sparsely habited 'halt' next to a wood-yard. I was fascinated as a long truck pulled up close to our boat to unload huge tree-trunks using a mechanical grab attached to the lorry. Goodness knows what these things weighed but as he hoisted them up onto a large stockpile, they often swung out alarmingly close to our boat. One slip could have sunk us.

We moored below the old town walls in Clamecy. The Olympics were on telly and I enjoyed our success with a glass of wine from the pressure-cooker atmosphere of my armchair. However, the cycling coach would have been dismayed by my performance. I fell off my bike while carrying a couple of portions of chips back from the take-away, ending up in an untidy heap in a car park. I lodged an appeal but was informed that 'lack of coordination' was no excuse. The french fries were in some disarray, and, according to the skipper, was far more serious than the nasty graze on my knee.

Later the same evening while having a drink on a friend's boat we had a bit of drama. Near the lock in the town there is a small port, perhaps 50 metres by 15, with room for a dozen or so smaller boats moored around this small basin in a 'U' shape. As we chatted with our friends, a camping car pulled up across the port. It was about eight in the evening and they wanted some water. A French lady on a boat next to the water point objected and told them to clear off. The camper-vanners were a young family with a small child and needed about 40-litres of water to see them through, but the lady was having none of it. Because she had paid for her mooring she didn't think anyone else was entitled to help themselves to 'her' water. A shouting match ensued. Reinforcements arrived in the shape of two men from nearby boats who got into an increasingly rowdy exchange with the young camper man. Then there was a fight which got really nasty, we couldn't see all of it as it took place behind the feisty French lady's boat but you could tell by the sounds that serious blows were being exchanged. It got considerably worse however when the bloke from the camping car reached the end of his tether and attacked the two male boaters (one German, one Danish) with some sort of dual-headed hand-axe!! There was some hysterical screaming before the camper van sped away – without water. The Danish guy was bleeding quite badly from a defensive wound to his forearm but he had the presence of mind to smear blood onto the rear of the van before it left. We were 15m away from them across the small port so not involved but I did go round immediately the camper had fled and bandaged what were really horrible wounds on the two guys arms. The police and ambulance were called. We never saw the police as they probably set off straight after the camper having been given a description of the van by a local. The Danish guy was worst affected, his skin peeled back to the bone down his arm and both he and the German guy were in mild shock. No-one else seemed to have much of a clue so it was me who patched the guys up with cling-film and bandage before the ambulance arrived. The Dane had numerous stitches and had to stay around for a week to have repeated follow-up treatments but they were both lucky not to have been more seriously hurt.

I could see the French lady's point, but I think I would have given the guy a few litres of water, particularly at that time of the evening.

We'd been there for a few days when the 'rent-collector' came by. He looked in the wheelhouse but carried on. I called after him that we hadn't paid anything but he told me, it's OK, it's good for tourists to see nice boats in the port. I suspected the guy had been taking illicit substances. Our boat may be old but it's a bit frayed round the edges. This sure isn't the normal reaction and without doubt the first time we've been deemed a tourist attraction! I gave him a 33-cent bottle of beer for his kindness.

The yin and yang of Clamecy.

The town itself spreads up the hillside overlooking the canal and River Yonne, which had become our companion after the canal summit. Ancient, twisty streets are home to a classic French market and it's a lovely wander round. Though not that cheap, you don't half get some tasty treats at the specialist food stalls. We've visited plenty of French markets and they are without doubt one of the defining aspects of the way of life here. They not only stock wonderful and varied produce but are a way for locals re-affirm bonds and friendships in the bars and cafés around market squares. Even in winter the hearts of small towns and villages beat to an age-old drum. I remember visiting one in The Lot in February where one old lady had set up a small table offering four dozen free-range eggs for sale. Profit was not the motive, more a chance to meet friends and gossip. Another old chap, whose craggy face below a French beret, told of a tough life in the country. He wore an old tweed jacket tied with string and mole-skin trousers above hob-nail boots. He had an equally ancient Citroen van, the 'stretch' version of the classic 2CV, and sold 'country wine' from a modified plastic dustbin to locals with plastic water-bottles at a Euro a litre. He was probably the only person in Northern Europe with teeth worse than mine but his smile, when exchanging a story with a punter, lit up a winter's day. We've (temporarily) left behind the obsessive sterility of our previous life and the French markets have re-awakened dormant senses.

Our plans to leave the following morning are thwarted by a group of lunatics who have taken over the canal. It's a water-borne festival where locals parade up the lock from the river in an astonishing assortment of home-made craft wholly unsuited to support human life. 'Kids', age range five to eighty, float by on rafts decorated with flowers and flags, competing to win the prize for the daftest ensemble – and there are plenty of candidates. It's another way for the locals to massage their community spirit. Bankers in pink tutus act out a secret fantasy as a taffeta dancing group compete with kids as clowns selling fake ice cream from a boat the shape of a giant mousetrap. Everyone gets wet and everyone laughs. As a naked, blow-up doll (with extraordinary boobs) floats by two tattooed men in life-jackets swim over to our boat and offer me a glass of a locally brewed aperitif from a demijohn. It's rather tasty and probably lethal enough of offset the potential danger of leptospirosis.

So ends an eventful sojourn in Clamecy and we're waved off by the injured Dane. A fearsome sight, he's sporting a cow-horn helmet and brandishing a hunting horn. Our warrior, bandaged arm in a blue sling, salutes us on our way.

We're soon back to rural ways, getting caught up in another monster fishing match (that's a lot of people catching small fish as opposed to a few hopefuls catching big ones). They are lined up like a guard of honour in the shade of the trees below limestone cliffs that have been scooped and gouged into improbable shapes by the elements. It is a lovely stretch that gives way to fields shaved to stubble and rolls of straw bronzed by the sun. We pass Mailly le Château perched up on the hillside to the south. It's imposing castle is visible from miles around and it commands views of the canal surrounding landscape. Sister town Mailly La Ville nestles on a section of the Yonne River a few kilometres further on. It is an ideal mooring during the sweltering weather as we can have a dip in the clean river water. Guarding the lock is a statue hewn form local stone by sculptor Yves Varanguin, a native of the town. The virginal white statue is a naked lady perched on a pile of rocks holding a duck.

'You do manage to throttle the romance out of things', says Jan, who goes on to tell me she's a lovely young girl at repose for eternity on her plinth of local stone. 'AND', she adds, 'it's not a duck, it's a dove of peace'.

She's probably right of course. Whether it's a dove or not, I didn't have my glasses on.

Vermenton is known as the 'Cite de flottage du bois' (City of floating wood). Timber from the Morvan National Park was collected in Vermenton before being lashed together into huge rafts (known as 'trains') before being floated down the rivers Yonne and Seine to Paris. Each train would be guided by just three or four men, two at the front and one / two at the rear. Around 75-metres long and 4.5 metres wide, the trains would be steered using long poles jammed into the riverbed. The practice effectively died out in the 1880's when river barges and the railways took over but in its heyday an average of 600 'trains' of timber per year would be man-handled to Paris.

It's one example of the waterways being responsible for the prosperity of what are in effect, quite isolated towns. Nowadays we, as part of a largely leisure-based industry, have taken over. You see the odd timber-laden barge but it appears to be mainly transported by road now.

Stuck in The Loo

In the UK many travellers, including me, are partial to a pint of fine ale. I have to be honest, you don't always get a fine ale, some of it is less than fine, but nevertheless, while planning routes on our narrowboat, we were guided by the scientific maxim: 'the shortest distance between two pints'.

Here in Burgundy 'wine-posts' guide us towards purveyors of the fermented grape. Les Caves (cellars) at Bailly Lapierre is a fine example. And a very large one, which specialises in Cremant or Mousseux which is non-Champagne sparkling wine. Ok, bear with me...from the 12th Century limestone was extracted from here to create some of the great French buildings, the Cathedrals of Chartres and Notre Dame in Paris and the Pantheon for example. Originally stone was taken from open quarries but in the 15th Century (the end of the medieval period and the start of the Renaissance) extraction moved underground. By the end of the 20th Century 10 acres (4 hectares) of tunnels had been excavated – by hand. The temperature below ground is a constant 12 degrees and there is a high level of moisture – perfect (thought some bright spark in 1927) for growing mushrooms.

Now this is all well and good for the discerning fungiculturalist, but in 1972 an even brighter spark realized that conditions were ideal for the maturing and storage of Cremant and wine. So the subterranean galleries became home to one of the regions most appealing exports. Every year around 3.5 million bottles of Cremant are produced from grapes supplied by 430 winegrowers and there is a permanent stock of 5 million bottles. Dotted around the galleries there are wonderful scenes carved into the limestone depicting life below ground and out on the river.

As you would expect there is a large 'sales area'. I came out with 2 bottles of Cremant each costing the equivalent of the usual rubbish I buy by the 5-litre in supermarket boxes. It's a classy operation though. In fact, the carrier bag they gave me was better quality than my rucksack and to this day is proudly languishing somewhere behind the washing machine. No doubt we'll dig it out sometime and 'parade' haughtily through the streets of Rochdale – till we get mugged.

In Auxerre we moor one lock above the town adjacent a park where families gather, students lounge and dogs do what dogs do. One dog that's just done is savagely attacked by ours. The fact that the other one was about 11 times the size of ours didn't deter Tache one bit, he just leapt off the boat and started nibbling the other one's kneecaps (if a dog has kneecaps).

It's a bit expensive for us down of the official moorings. Who wants to pay 17 Euros a night for a safe haven which is fully serviced? Plus, a full range of shops within easy walking distance. All with a fabulous view of the city across the river including stunning Auxerre Cathedral perched on the skyline. Put it this way, if we'd stayed 2 nights there that's 20 litres of wine! If I drink even one litre I'd soon forget that we're a bit tight (for cash).

OK, so it's a very attractive place that's got everything going for it, including us not being there, but I do find a chink in its near-perfect persona, it's twinned with Worms in Germany, a wonderful city on The Rhine with a daft name. See, they don't get everything right!

As we descended the lock and headed down river towards the town Jan took a wonderful photograph, described by her as her finest fluke. It shows the limestone cathedral lit by a ray of sun against a slate-grey, stormy sky. In the foreground is an ancient seven-arched, stone bridge through which we pass. We 'cock a snoot' at the rich people moored in the port to our right and head off into the hinterland towards Migennes and the start of the Canal du Bourgogne.

En route we stoop at Gurgy. It's a beautiful mooring where we share facilities with around thirty camper vans strung out along the riverbank. The sharing of facilities is quite common on the waterways. It means the local communities only have to run one set of services to accommodate two sets of adventurers. And the natives have the bonus of watching pitched battles between boaters and motor-homers over the last remaining power points. I got a muted round of applause from one group of campers, awoken from their comas by the throb and stench of our engine, when I managed to moor in a tree. It would have taken too long to explain that the only available mooring bollards were subtly placed either side of said tree so I accepted their acclaim with good grace and gave the engine a final revving belch before shutting it down – which brought the applause to an abrupt halt. When the smoke had cleared I went for a chat with some camper-vanners. This place is free, as one can ascertain by its popularity, but staying on official sites is not always that cheap for campers, often twenty plus Euros per night. Most people have a story to tell though and I like chatting. Many of the vans are French. There are a few German, Dutch and Swiss and all are pretty smart and well equipped. There is one English one parked at the end in the nettles. It's a knackered old Transit van that looks to have been converted by an optimist rather than an engineer. Actually, I'm being unkind because in our experience, on the boating side of things anyway, it doesn't matter how big your boat is or how well appointed, all you need is the desire to have a good time and mix. In fact, some folks on the larger boats can be a bit aloof.

When we leave in the morning it's 'one of them'. There's a dark blue sky and not a breath of wind. The river is wide, tree-lined and barely moving so once again we shatter the mirror as we creep north.

We have another tree moment at Migennes where we have to ascend a deep lock into the canal basin. This time due to the over-eager lock keeper rushing off for an early lunch. I'd made the mistake of papping the horn. The lock closes officially at midday for lunch for an hour. It's about 11.45am and we'd already been hovering about for a few minutes like a piece of rusty flotsam. I gave a quick 'parp' to alert the lockie to our presence. Another few minutes later a silhouette arrived on the skyline, pointed to his watch and stomped off. Had he arrived when we did we would have got through quite comfortably before lunch but he obviously had some livestock bubbling away on the cooker and was not to be distracted from it. Hence the tree. More of a big bush really which left us covered in foliage as we forced our way in. We could have gone out and pottered up and down the river for an hour but the hound was showing signs of urgency so we had to moor up I scrambled up the bank with him.

I like Migennes. It's a bustling stop with plenty of boats buzzing about and locals promenading around the basin. We stayed a few days and each evening the starlings would come to roost by the canal. They would perform their aerial dance, fluid clouds of a thousand birds or more creating intricate patterns before funnelling down into the trees. Occasionally you can hear their chatter. Sadly, many of the more intricate birdsongs are drowned out because what is probably the busiest railway line in Europe runs parallel to the port. Twenty-four hours a day freight and passenger trains thunder by as animal, vegetable and mineral hurtle through France.

It's in Migennes that Jan had a disconcerting coming-together with modern technology.

She'd been to the local market, centred on an impressive market hall. She was all but finished shopping, with a bag full of veg, when she needed the loo. The boat was perhaps 500 metres away but she spotted a queue at the front of which was a 'WC' sign. It was all buttons, single occupancy and the instructions were in French. So as not to make a fool of herself by being unable to open the door she slipped in as the previous lady was exiting. Whereon the door closed behind her, the lights went out and the self-cleaning operation began. Firstly, the loo set off with a whoosh, then water cascaded from the ceiling, then more water shot out of the walls before finally, a deluge fired out at floor level. Now Jan was in the dark and rather alarmed. She and her vegetables were wet through and she couldn't find the button that opened the door because it was dark. Shortly after the deluge finished she finally managed to get out, drenched from head to foot carrying a soggy bag, to be faced with a group of bemused natives. She still hadn't been to the loo of course so had to explain to the next lady in line that she wasn't done. 'I've not been yet', she told the lady, while performing a mime that involved a series of semi-squatting motions and some pointing, 'I've not been yet'.

So, she turned and went back in, at the orthodox stage of this fully automated lavatory.

Finally, mission accomplished, she could return to the boat. But couldn't find her bicycle. She was sure she'd left it locked up just outside the door to the market hall but there was no sign of it. She did two full tours of the hall before realising that a man selling baskets had arrived and erected a six-foot high display of baskets right in front of her bike. By the time she'd extricated it the man's display was in some disarray so needed re-building but at least she was free at last.

She returned to the boat in a state of some agitation looking like she'd been caught in a thunderstorm. 'You're not going to believe what's happened', she said, 'look at this I'm shaking'. She held her hands out palms down to show me and she was indeed a bit of a wreck.

The next morning she went to 'Attack' supermarket, just across the road, to finish the previous day's curtailed shopping. 'Be careful', I told her.

She went on her bike again but was back in less than ten minutes. 'You're not going to believe this', she said, 'look at this I'm shaking'.

And she was.

This time she'd been propositioned! Ten O clock on a Thursday morning wearing baggy shorts, a blouse and Jesus sandals, she'd had a coming together with a lecherous local. It all started off OK as she arrived at the supermarket when this bloke told her she was beautiful. 'Mursee', said Jan in her best French. Then the chap made a grab for her boob and tried to kiss her. He backed off and, with the help of some suggestive hand-signals, asked whether she wanted sex. Needless to say Jan just fled and the bloke was marched away by a security guard.

So that was twenty-four hours in Migennes.

One vaguely amusing story, the other certainly not.

It was also here that we encountered a solo Australian. A man who did everything by halves because he hadn't the money to do everything by fulls. An insurance pay-out following a dispute with his employer had been sunk into his large barge and he was now tight for cash. He faced the possibility of staying on his boat in Migennes for the winter. He didn't speak French nor did he know anybody local it was a lonely prospect so we persuaded him to navigate the full length of the Canal du Bourgogne to over-winter in St. Jean de Losne. There he would at least have people around who speak the same language (nearly – he's Australian after all) who could help him if necessary. His problem was that any boat over 20 metres needs at least one extra crew member, and he knew no-one.

There was a French chap on his ex-hire boat moored behind our Aussie, so, speculatively, I asked him. Sure, he said, he was up for an adventure, providing he could bring his lady friend with him. He was prepared to travel halfway along the canal – that would take perhaps two or three weeks travelling dependant on how much they pushed.

Bit of a strange arrangement the French guy had in all honesty. He paid a lady friend to be his 'companion' for the six months of summer. She had a young son back in Poland and, despite being a teacher, it was more profitable for her to be paid by our new friend than to stay at home and work. He was a normal guy really in most respects. His small boat here was one of three he owned. This one used during the summer, another was being repaired and the third was permanently moored in Paris. He also owned a house part-way along the Bourgogne canal. And, talk about our Aussie mate landing on his feet, his new crew insisted, with complete agreement from the boat's owner that, while travelling, they stop every day for a proper restaurant lunch – at his expense! Le Monsieur was a decent guy and his friend a lovely lady – but it was all a bit peculiar.

A 'Vide Grenier' (literally; 'Empty Attic') set up on the car park right outside the boat. They are a popular pastime for those with nothing better to do and are, in effect, flea markets or car-boot sale equivalents. Much of the stuff looked suspiciously like other stuff offered for sale at the far end of the canal, in St. Jean de Losne, nearly 250 kilometres south. We were 'conservatively enthusiastic' when we visited a sale there four months ago and things hadn't improved much now. It seemed that stallholders had bought a job lot in St. Jean and taken it to the next town along the canal where it had been bought by another 'investor' who would take it to the next place...and so on.

Many of the artefacts could be described as priceless purely because they would fail to register any economic worth. Hence boxes-full of things had leap-frogged (can I say that in France?) all the way to Migennes. The canal ends here so the logical next step is to chuck all the unsold stuff straight into the River Yonne beyond the lock gate – unless someone has the gall to turn round and attempt the return trip. And, almost without exception at these Vide Grenier's, there's always a stall selling brand new beds and mattresses (either that or second-hand ones re-wrapped in polythene). Now why someone would want to sell beds among the mountain of tat is a bit of a mystery. You would have thought that people who haggle over the price of a bent bicycle wheel are unlikely to shell out for an expensive bed. It's a vagary over which you can mull while munching on a waffle. I suspect the waffle stall and coffee hut are the only two traders to come out with a decent profit.

I'm painting a pretty vivid picture eh? In fact, it's hard to believe that this whole experience could get better, but it did. A singer was laid on. Visitor and trader alike were whipped into a fever pitch of excitement by a lady whose voice was as lusty as her proportions. She warbled folky tunes through an inadequate microphone / speaker combo singing songs written by people nobody had ever heard of about things that induced a collective torpor among her public. She was sited under the trees by the coffee hut and her camouflaged blouse made her almost invisible in the dappled shade. She emerged from hiding after half-an-hour to a smattering of tolerant applause and with international anonymity still intact, headed for the waffle stall. A note of realism augmented her camouflage in the shape of a couple of dollops of bird poo on her top.

The only footnote worthy of mention is that Jan's bike was filched off the back of the boat during the following night. Fortunately, in the cold light of morning, whoever stole realised it failed to reach the minimum standard required for it to be offered for sale so we found it dumped behind a pile of collapsed trestle tables the next morning.

So, our experience of Migennes is consigned to the note-book and a few photos and we head south. We soon get tangled up with weeds, thick, cloying stuff that gets in our filters and even clogs the propeller. A theme that will frustratingly continue all the way home. Our boat used to ply her trade in the deep, clean waters of Holland. I won't go into technical detail, save to say that I have to stop the engine and clean out our water filters regularly, on some particularly bad stretches, at every lock.

We catch up with our Aussie friend and his companions at St. Florentin. Or rather their boat. It's lunchtime and they are off sampling the delights of some local eatery. The town is named after a Saint of the same name who was martyred in 406 AD along with his disciple with the extraordinary name of Hilaire by Crocus, King of The Vandals! We moor opposite the main port with a magnificent view of the distant church that dominates the skyline. We bump into old friends Toby and Jan and have an aperitif. Plagued by mosquitoes we are forced to light the BBQ to smoke them out. Then we are forced to drink sufficient red wine to forget the taste of the food. So, another evening developed, inevitably, into a bit of a heap.

We're now in Hotel Boat territory. The luxury behemoths that rumble up and down the canal during the summer months. At over 50,000 Euros for a six-berth boat for a week they need to be luxurious. Their guests we encounter are largely American (largely American – can I say that?), living the classic dream of boating in Burgundy. I can't say I blame them, some of it is truly delightful. We generally get on fine with the hotel boats and their crews – in fact it's fair to say that without them there would be less incentive for the authorities to maintain the smaller waterways, which includes this one. They have designated mooring spots at various towns and pleasure boaters generally respect that. These boats travel very slowly so sometimes we see guests cycling along the towpath to try and shift some of the gourmet food before the next onslaught. To be frank, some of them are better suited to eating than cycling but it doesn't deter them. They are invariably enthusiastic and chatty but cycle at a conservative pace – even by my standards. So, when I pass a line of them on my bike they often call an individual greeting along the lines of: 'Gooood mornin', splutter, 'ya have a good one now', wheeze, 'gee, it's a fiiine day', hack/splutter......and so on.

At Flogny (pron. flon yee) there's a fine butcher a kilometre up the hill from the 'halte nautique'. We're on our own and the mooring is eerily quiet, at least it was for a while. There is a substantial parking area where the local youth gather in their souped-up bangers and throw coke cans in the vague direction of a rubbish bin. Music blares out of one of the cars so I tend my sausages to what sounded like a Swiss accordion – which was rather out of kilter to the tough-young-man image the tin-throwing mob portrayed. This after all is rural France and this gathering was probably their equivalent of a rave. They were no trouble though and left about 10.00 pm – off home for a glass of warm milk no doubt.

One of the attractions of a canal trip in this area are the Châteaux. These are partly what the hotel boat guests pay the big bucks for. The first we come across is at Tanlay where I also have a rare altercation with a hotel boat. It's more accurately perhaps to say I had a bit of a do with one of it's representatives who'd been sent on ahead to 'smooth the waters'. The mooring is perhaps a hundred and fifty metres long. Right in the middle is a fifty-metre slot reserved for hotel boats – and a notice stating which days they would be over-nighting. When we'd arrived the port was pretty full so we moored on the designated hotel boat slot but moved off immediately another became available. Moving is a bit of a palaver – untying the ropes, firing up the engine, retying etc. etc., but move we did. We were now right at the end of the mooring, well out of anyone's way. Then a fat young lady with a finishing-school accent arrived and said in clipped, snooty tones, 'you're going to have to move, there's a hotel boat arriving within the hour.'

'Oh really?' I replied.

'Yes really,' she pouted, 'this place is reserved for hotel boats, you'll have to go somewhere else'.

'Oh. So, what about that bit down there with the 'Reserved for hotel boats' sign in front of it?'

'We don't use that.'

'And why not?'

'Our electricity lead won't reach.'

'I beg your pardon?'

'We plug into our electricity point there', she vaguely waving a chubby hand, 'and our cable isn't long enough'.

'Well, might I respectfully suggest that you buy a longer cable. Besides, I've just moved from there,' (waving my equally chubby hand) 'specifically so you could moor in your allocated slot.'

'You'll still have to move.'

'Will I really'

'Indeed. If we have to moor back there we'll have to run our generator all night and you will be smoked out.'

'Might I respectfully suggest that while you're purchasing your new electricity cable, you get your generator seen to at the same time'.

I was getting proper irate by now I can tell you, and Tache wasn't best pleased either. He made a whiny, growly noise and it was all I could manage not to laugh. We did move again of course but someone else, faced with that haughty attitude, may not have. A friend who had witnessed the exchange, and described the young woman as having *'a face that sunk a thousand chips'*, agreed that she was totally out of order.

Contrast that with another occasion when another hotel boat politely asked us to move and we went to double up with another boat – no problem then. That skipper bought us a couple of bottles of 'house wine' as a thank you. Gawd knows what the decent stuff tasted like because this was delicious. Mind you, anything is after the bilge I drink.

Perhaps the main reason the hotels stop here at Tanlay is the magnificent Château. Built in the 16th and 17th Centuries (on partly older foundations) it is said to be one of the finest examples of Renaissance architecture in Burgundy – it is a real treasure. As you pass through the arch in the gatehouse you emerge in a world of fantasy where the Château, moat and parkland immerse you in a bygone age of peace and opulence. Much is written about it so there's no need to repeat what more knowledgeable folk than I have already said. Just take it from me, it is worth a visit.

Tanlay thrives probably because of the Château. Many small towns this size without a 'draw' are merely dormitories without shops or even a heart. One fabulous 'gentleman's' shop here is the quincaillerie (hardware / ironmongery). It's got everything – and what it hasn't got, it will get. Wooden drawers and cubbyholes hold an astonishing array of, well, just about anything. It even has that old-fashioned smell as musty ghosts from times past check on the present proprietors, encouraging them to maintain a standard rarely experienced today.

Just ten kilometres away is another fine château, this one at Ancy-le-Franc. It's striking in its symmetry and simplicity of design – basically square, with a square turret at each corner. Although built at a similar time to the Château at Tanlay it is very different in appearance. It is, according to the blurb, 'an Italian creation that also pays homage to French tradition'. But it the interior that is really breathtaking featuring wonderful 16th and 17th century painted murals, some of the finest in France. Again, don't take my word for it, if you get the chance, go and have a look.

The port is around a kilometre from the Château which borders the town. It's here that I give my home-made bicycle trailer a proper road test. I'd built it from a pair of wheelchair wheels and a pile of odds and ends from the boat-yard scrap heap back in St. Jean. Not a great success initially if I'm honest. It developed a wobble, like a caravan without a stabilizer behind a car, but even slower and less attractive. Jan nearly fell off laughing while following me up the road as my bottom waggled east and west. I added a bit of aluminium as a stabilizer and the thing was much improved - until it developed a squeak from somewhere underneath. It drew unwarranted attention in the same way a noisy bow-thruster highlights a poor boating manoeuvre, or a broken exhaust in a high street. Liberal spraying of WD40 cured that too, but made the baguette taste rather peculiar. Overall, a relative success I feel.

If there had been an Academy Award for mucking up a repair job I would, at the very least, have received a nomination. I tried help a passing cyclist, a French chap. His machine was laden with gear for what was obviously a prolonged trip, and he noticed me battling with modifications to my tailor and recognized a skilled engineer when he saw one. Consequently, he enlisted my help. His rear tyre was only half inflated and asked if I could pop some air in so he could get to a shop to buy a new pump. It was a valve-type that I hadn't encountered previously but nevertheless I had a go. Ten minutes later his tyre was completely flat.

'Is there no beginning to your talents?' asked my friend, as the frowning Frenchman pushed his steed away.

Then the Aussie arrived, completely ignored us and went for lunch. Oh, the fickle nature of friendship.

I was telling you about the weed. Just before a place called Ravieres we were forced to stop for lunch and part way through the allotted lunch hour I went to examine the adjacent lock. Even when the locks are inactive the lock keepers leave paddles partly open on both front on rear gates to maintain a gentle flow of water down the canal. What it means is that the water is constantly fresh, clean and oxygenated; in fact, a perfect breeding ground for the plague of rats that copulate and frolic in the secure, harmonious environment. Anyway, due to this flow, the weed builds up against the top gate – and here it was a real mess. I was looking pointedly at the island of weed when the lock keeper emerged from his cottage to contemplate the afternoon shift. He stood by me and we looked together.

'Do you have a pitch-fork?', I enquired, hoping it would spur him to shift some weed.

'Oui' he replied. We continued to stare for a full minute.

'Does it work?' I asked him.

After a few moments he glanced at me and strolled off in the direction of a shed. He returned a few minutes later with a fork. It was very smart too, brand new in fact, completely unsullied by any work whatsoever. It had a pristine ash-wood handle and two shiny, red tines. He passed it to me and disappeared back into his cottage. I have to say though it's gratifying to see my cruising license fee being spent on such high quality equipment.

Canal du Bourgogne

The canal is generally clean. OK, weed is a problem for us, but the water is healthy and clear. Then all of a sudden we come across a huge lump of misshapen metal in the canal – which turns out to be a weed-clearing machine. It's close to the bank and leaning at a peculiar angle. It's a very strange shape, with a big lop-sided mandible at the front (or what I presume is the front), a large blue plastic bucket at the other end and a paddle wheel on the side. On top is a windowed cabin suitable for a single occupant – which is abandoned. It's also going a bit rusty. All in all it looks to have given up the struggle, realizing that the man with the posh pitch-fork is unrivalled in the weed-clearing business, or would be if he could tear himself away from lunch.

The scenery is wonderful. We're now into September, the sun hot by day but the nights are cooling. I go for an early cycle ride as the morning mists shroud the valleys and drift slowly across the water. A silvery shroud of bejewelled spider's webs cling to grass and flowers along the tow path. They are unmasked by the morning sun refracting off the dew. Ghostly skeins woven among the stems. Just for a time we are allow a brief glimpse of one of nature's wonders.

Most towns and villages have a walled cemetery. The one I pass is cloaked in wisps of mist as the spirits rise to meet a new day. And in the distance smoke curls up and away as distant village folk light an early autumn fire. It's a lovely time of year.

Immediately after Veneray we'll start the 55 locks in forty kilometres to reach the canal summit. The lady lock keeper here is a pleasant lass. Not long out of hospital following a pretty severe head operation she's chatty and all smiles. We're here for a couple of days so each morning I go and help her with her lock while taking Tache for a drag. She thanked me by giving me a dozen fresh bantam eggs which I would have eaten with bacon if we could have found find any. In fact, if I'd have been into eating carp I'd have been OK as a chap and his young son caught a 17 kg one next to our boat.

Pouilly en Auxois is the town at the summit. It's a sizeable port (perhaps 250 x 80 metres) on one side of which is a cereal (grain) depot. A constant stream of tractors and trailers arrive from the surrounding countryside bringing grain - thousands of tonnes of it. It's bone dry and there is a constant mist of fine dust from the open-backed tailors. Formerly the grain would have been transported on by boat, but now, here at least, it's trucks. This depot is one of around 40 (I believe) in Burgundy, collectively known as Dijon Cereals. It's basically a cooperative created by and for farmers to manage their production of grain, oilseed and vegetables. As we travel we're constantly amazed by the sheer scale of the agriculture, mile upon mile of farmland - and this cooperative offers the farmers not only collective bargaining power to sell their produce but also technical and marketing support. Farmers are a powerful body here; and by gum, do they have some expensive tackle.

Across the port is the quay. The Aussie is here and we've managed to organise another victim to help him down the other side to St. Jean de Losne. His previous crew (and benefactor and meal-ticket) has left him. He's having a breather after a fortnight of large lunches and midday wine – poor lamb. We've persuaded his new crew member (single white male) to let The Aussie do all the cooking – no going out!

There are a few boats here drawing breath before heading north or south. We have a mini boules tournament followed by a gourmet soiree. Actually it's a few (largely) overweight foreigners chucking lumps of steel around (with limited success) followed by sitting at a 'community picnic bench' ploughing through an assortment of multi-shaped sacrifices of mythic origin. The wine was OK though. We had our photograph taken by a 'freelance' who travels Burgundy 'in search of interesting objects', as he put it. Quite why we were involved is a bit of a mystery but the photo did appear in 'Bien Public' a few days later. Bien Pubic is a regional paper that has local supplements produced for differing communes. It's like many provincial publications that have a newsworthy front page but after that it features things like 'Granny drops handbag in puddle'. Presumably our photographer got his commission. Where's my agent when I need him?

Between the quay and the flight of locks that begin our trip south, there is a tunnel. Quite a long one, 3.333 kilometres, according to my map book. Said book is a fickle publication drifting between the exact (in this case) and the unhelpful (as in where to buy wine and diesel). The dimensions of the tunnel preclude some boats from passage and our Aussie is pretty near the height / width limit. He's been mollycoddled so far but he'll earn his spurs from here on. There is also a trip boat that runs (almost) daily through the tunnel and back. A glass-covered affair that takes about 50 or so passengers. The glass top is useful so you can peer at the tunnel roof in the dark or get fried when the sun's blaring while out in the open.

We have friends, also Aussies, who had a bit of a run in with the tourist boat. The antipodeans were 'taking a cautious approach' and going too slowly - in the eyes of the trip-boat skipper anyway who had his schedule to maintain, and he got proper irate. The trip-boat hooted his horn and flashed his tunnel-light in an effort to spur the Aussies to greater endeavour, getting so close at one point to the rear of our friend's boat that he could have pinched a fender or two. Actually, when you are in a long tunnel it can be quite claustrophobic, particularly when it's your first passage. You do have to concentrate to keep the boat in the centre. It's not as easy as it sounds because the handling characteristics change somewhat due to the enclosed space and the narrow channel. Plus, the reflections of the tunnel lights (if they are working) are a little off-putting. They can cause weird reflections and a strange sense of perspective. In addition, you are piloting a very expensive bit of equipment (in some instances!) that is also your home – I don't blame the Aussie in any shape or form for being conservative. Anyhow, a few pleasantries were exchanged when the two boats moored up (about 2 weeks later!) and the trip-boat skipper flounced off to tend his lunch. This incidentally is the same Aussie who gamely held the umbrella for his wife when so she could chop logs with her plaster-cast on.

We watched the other Aussie set off for the tunnel the following morning. He was a bit nervous due to his boat's dimensions and it wouldn't have done his confidence much good when he demolished his VHF antenna while entering the tunnel. There was the nasty sound or rending metal as he disappeared but, after that, he told us later, he 'sailed through' – which, after all, is about the only way you can get through. The authorities do take it seriously though. There is a traffic light system because you don't want to meet someone coming the other way, and you are given a radio in case you get into difficulty. When we went through the main tunnel lights were only working in stretches which made it more difficult than if they'd been either all in or all out. When we did tunnels in our narrowboat in the UK, our spotlight was right at the front of the boat and we used to point it sharply down towards the water. The reflection lit up a defined semi-circle of tunnel-roof in front which made it easier to steer down the centre. I'm not keen on tunnels.

Down eight locks we arrive at Vandernesse en Auxois which is another place bustling with very little – a bar / restaurant and a 'tearoom'. But the little port does afford a magnificent view of the castle on the hill, namely Chateaneuf, one of the stop-offs for the hotel boats who ply their trade on this, southern, section of the canal.

We're doing OK, the skipper and I are in full communication mode and we haven't had a row with anybody recently. Mind you, apart from the friends we shared a day or two with in Pouilly, we haven't seen many boats. Even the dog's behaving himself.

Pont d'Ouche is where we make friends with Briony, the lady who runs the café / shop. She's a well-known character on the canal and has a good little summer business. It's also where our friends David and Pamela (who also moor at our home port, St. Jean) have holed up for the whole summer to 'rest' and paint their boat. One of the highlights of David's summer was bumping into a celebrity – the one who created that infernal lump, Mr Blobby! David gave Mr Edmonds and his wife directions. So, they are probably still driving around the maze of country lanes! To be truthful (unfairly?) I'm a bit Blobby averse. One Christmas a number of years ago Jan asked me what she could buy me. I requested a CD featuring Peter Cook. He and Dudley Moore were popular in my youth. Come Christmas morning I settled down for a laugh with a glass of port and lump of mild Lancashire cheese (a traditional treat to myself). What did I get? Mr Blobby!!! If I ever find the joker who slipped that CD in there........... I did go and exchange Blobby for Cook and wished I hadn't – the comedian, on this occasion, was not at his best.

Our mates had their car with them so they took us to visit Chateauneuf en Auxois. It really is a delightful medieval village. It is one of the last remaining examples of 14th century Burgundian military architecture. During the Hundred Years War, towers and curtain walls were built to defend the village and the Auxois plains. The views are quite stunning. Quite why I ended up with so many photographs of a bee in a flower is a bit of a mystery. My macro side coming out perhaps.

As we got back to the port word must have got out that we'd been to a shop because we were pounced upon by two couples in search of supplication. We had met them before, they weren't just passing strangers you understand, but they treated my beer with such reckless abandon that I had to go shopping again - with the kindly assistance of our friends in their car. Bligny-sur-Ouche, seven kilometres up a hill, is a pretty, little market town. Once again there is the titillating choice of assorted fauna and flora. Some of the former is obscure. In fact, probably obscure enough to close a restaurant on health and safety grounds in a sanitised city environment. We've largely lost the excitement and gamble of eating something different. 'Twas ever thus I suppose in a bygone era but customers these days demand bulked-up, pre-packed cuts that have been verified by consumer watchdog. (Actually, 'consumer watchdog' is also an unfortunate phrase for somewhere that eats most things). I suppose that just about anything is available anywhere – it's just that here the unusual is more prevalent.

We moor up at La Forge and get caught up in a vicious little storm. A very localised and violent twister that brought chimneys off roofs in the nearby village and felled an oak tree onto a caravan (thankfully unoccupied). I've seen caravans and cars that have been caught in summer hailstorms. It's like they've been pitted with machine-gun fire and reports tell of hailstones like golf-balls (or larger if the story has been embellished with Merlot). We didn't have hailstones but the wind for a few minutes was really ferocious. We were moored very close to some poplar trees, forty-footers that were whipped to and fro like grass. Within minutes the boat was covered in debris but thankfully none of the trees actually toppled. It was quite extraordinary how the storm had scythed a path through the woodland. When I later cycled along the canal bank there was a definite line about two-hundred meters away where the storm damage suddenly ended. For a stretch it was chaos as branches and leaves covered the canal and towpath, then within the turn of a wheel, complete normality.

We're nearing Dijon. The closer we get the more the real world unravels before us. Take-away cartons fight for space with snappily dressed joggers. Roller-bladers zip along weaving between dog-walkers and promenading families. We look at these folk and they look back, Both of no doubt wondering why the other chooses their particular life. Hereto we have always chosen to live quietly and periodically go in search of bustle and noise. Doubtless there are times when the hassle of daily life in a city gets on top of some people and they crave a spell of peace and quiet on the water – indeed there are times when we'd just love to pop round the corner and buy a good sausage without having to cycle ten kilometres over an escarpment.

Dijon is a great city. The port is perhaps a kilometre from the ancient centre and a short ride away on the new tram system. Typically, locals and tourists alike are drawn to the water so the port is usually pretty busy. Some people even stop and chat – a phenomenon not common in cities as people always seem to have a destination and need to get there promptly. It appears that the larger and busier a place, the less eye contact you have with passing strangers. People either walk eyes down or fixed rigidly forward on a point in the middle distance.

We've been here a couple of times now and one lady has made eye contact from the first time we saw her. It's difficult to tell, she is probably in her early forties, but terribly disabled. She's hunched in her wheelchair as if her limbs and back are being pulled inward towards her core. She moves by pulling herself along with one leg. Out in front is her little dog. Straining it's leash, it helps to tug the lady along the tow-path. They have a special bond and despite her difficulties, it may be that friendship which allows her the luxury of a laboured smile and a croaky bonjour in response to my greeting. What on earth are we doing complaining that the bakery shuts for lunch?

We had a special treat - a meal out. Our monthly foray into the world of fine cuisine (if the budget holds up). Actually, fine cuisine is beyond us but you can find good food for reasonable prices. We just have to avoid places with cloth napkins and too many numbers on the pricelist. We arrived at a lovely little square surrounded by restaurants of all types. It's called Place Emile Zola (who I thought was a footballer till I looked it up). He's actually a writer, an important contributor to the development of theatrical naturalism. Mmmmm! Wicker chairs and tables spread out into Emile's cobbled square lit by multi-coloured lanterns. The air was rich with tempting aromas. Sadly, just as we arrived there was a major power cut. We hadn't even chosen a place to eat when all the lights went out and the air was thick with flowery, Gallic language. Mutters and grumbles rumbled around the square. Fortunately, the restaurants across the street were unaffected so we dashed to the nearest establishment before anyone else got the same idea and treated ourselves to French pizza.

Opposite the wonderful indoor market, that houses classy purveyors of fine food appropriate for the poodle-pouting chic of the city, there is a 'Golden Arch' restaurant – which has free wifi. This is a university city and I am in the company of the next generation of bright sparks who'll take us onward and upward. As they talk many of them operate little hand-held communications devices. Their fingers skip around these modern (and probably very expensive) machines in a blur. The variety of ringtones sounds like you've landed in a Pink Floyd album. They are slightly smug but tolerant of a portly 50-something who hauls his old lap top out of a scruffy rucksack. My machine is the approximate size and weight of a paving slab and just as much use as a means of communication until a youth explains that I have to actually buy something to receive a code, which I must then input, to encourage it into life. I feel quite safe leaving the slab in the protective custody of my new friends while I go and get a coffee. I thought I might as well take advantage of the fact that I'd had to queue so decide to indulge in another gastronomic delight of La Belle France. Conservatively, with health and well-being firmly in mind, I decide on a Big Muck and large fries. The slab is safe and I begin my feast. Pointing to my machine I tell my friends that I've 'gone large' – which brings a titter or two. I have to say that, as with many places we've been, the young do seem very well mannered.

Because the quay is low it affords the perfect opportunity to paint the side of the boat – which I don't. Instead, we prefer the 'just collided' look rather than prim and proper. When I say we, I actually mean I, the skipper is the glistening type. Besides, if we leave it tatty enough people are less likely to pinch stuff – partly through the fear of contracting some nasty disease picked up in the wilderness of Burgundy. It's not reason enough for a period of 'communicative isolation' but enough to encourage her to persuade me it's time to set off and get back home where she can find solace among her friends. I really can't blame her, a few months cooped up in a box with me would test anyone.

It's half an hour by car to St. Jean - or two days by boat - about thirty kilometres. The canal is very straight but has 20 locks. The road is twisty with fewer locks. We descend the lock under the tram tracks and sail alongside railway tracks into open country again. There is one amazing stretch, particularly at this time of year (late September), where for well over a kilometre the canal is bordered exclusively by walnut trees. Although we eat very few of them ourselves, we enjoy foraging. Many natives scavenge and are a bit frustrated when we give the upper branches a battering with our boat pole bringing down a cascade, thereby availing ourselves of fruit out of their grasp. They can be eaten straight away but are better left for a month or two to dry out so our windowsills are stuffed with nuts. We barter them with our nutless friends for goodies from the homelands – such as proper tea bags and suet.

The autumn colours are magnificent as we return and by means of appalling planning we've arrived back a month early for our winter mooring. Even now the temperatures can reach the mid-twenties so we can still BBQ and, most inconveniently, it's perfect painting weather. We moor on the quay on the river and while the skipper reacquaints herself with her mates I get out the sandpaper, old underpants and white spirit to prepare an onslaught on all the dented bits.

As an old friend of mine used to say. 'Well, that's another one they can't take off us'.

About the Author

'Aren't you lucky,' people say to us when they hear we're mucking about on a boat. We have loved it, still do, but it's not for everyone. We've lived on two narrowboats and our current old barge. I'm sure there are many who would swap places in an instant. However......nearly twenty years ago, Jan was told by her oncologist that she probably wouldn't see the new millennium.

Against the odds she's still here. She carries the scars but we're still sharing our dream. What her diagnosis and prognosis did was to re-focus us. For the most recent ten of those years we've been boating. Even prior to that we had a fresh start, moved county and renovated a house together in Shropshire. It gave us a new direction and most importantly, something to aim at, look forward to. I'm sure that starting afresh has played a large part in her recovery. Ironically, without Jan's desperate battle, a lot of strength on her part and some luck, our life together would have been very different.

If we could do it again, would I change things? Of course I would. I wouldn't wish Jan's troubles on anyone. Would I change the way she, and we as a couple, tackled things – no.

A Barge at Large 11 awaits............ À bientôt, Jo

Jo lives in Lancashire with wife Jan and dog Tache.

He began writing monthly articles for a canal magazine in 2007. Following an 'editorial misunderstanding', after which they parted company, Jo began to properly chronicle their travels.

They commissioned a bare shell and started fitting out their own narrowboat back in 2003. They did a second almost immediately because, as Jo says, the first one was a bit basic! They cruised many of the UK waterways on their second boat called 'M' after Jo's Godmother who died during the build.

They decided to expand their adventures so bought an old Dutch Barge in Holland and spent eight years on the continent cruising in Holland, Belgium and France.

Jo describes the memories chronicled in the 3 'At Large' books as being a huge warm memory on which they can draw during long winter evenings.

You can connect with me on:

🌐 https://jomay.uk

📘 https://www.facebook.com/JoMayWriter/?ref=bookmarks

Also by Jo May

A Narrowboat At Large

Revised January 2021.

Jo and Jan May take the crazy, wonderful, potty, life-changing decision to live on a narrowboat. This first volume of the 'At Large' series spans four years as they begin a new life on the canals and rivers of the UK. The First question is why in the world would anyone want to do that? Well, here's Jo answer:

"Back in 1995, Jan was told by her oncologist that she probably wouldn't see the new millennium. Ever since those brutal words, time has been the most precious factor in her life. So together we set out to create a new normal. But why choose a life on the water? Jan can't swim, the dog hates it and I prefer beer. Financially we were afloat and we lived in a perfectly decent house until Jan came up with the zany idea of living on a boat.

We knew nothing about how narrowboats work or waterways lore, nor how we would cope being cooped up together – particularly when it's minus five and the nearest shop is miles away. We had a mountain to climb. You can only do that by using locks, and we'd never done a lock. A more accurate analogy is shooting the rapids, because our venture took on a life of it's own and we were washed down stream on a tide of enthusiasm and ignorance. We had to make it work or the people who had laughed and scoffed would be proved right – that we really were loopy. Well, make it work we did; we boated for twelve years. It was exciting, scary and marvellous and it quite possibly saved Jan's life."

A Barge at Large II

A Barge at Large II is the third book in the 'At Large' series as we follow Jo and Jan May's European boating adventure. There has been much fun in addition to some daft and amazing moments. Jan says, 'I'm lucky to be here at all but we've had some wonderful times, memories we'll look back on and say; boy, did all that really happen?'

There is a new chapter in this edition covering the final three days of our 12-year adventure. The River Yser in winter was flowing fast so the start of the trip was exciting yet scary. Ultimately though it was poignant as we said goodbye to our beloved boat. She'd kept us safe for eight wonderful years in three countries.

Incorporating further boating tales, a short road trip and a shambolic introduction to camper vans this volume sees them expand their horizons and begin an uncoordinated search for a life after boating.

Jo says.......

'I have always believed that you only get the chance to do something special for the first time once. Don't bother what is round the next bend, that will come soon enough, try and make the most of now because once you've turned the corner it's too late. All we have to look back on is today, so make it count.

Did we make the most of it? Very nearly.

Would we do it all again? No, it would never be the same. Instead we'll park it all there like a huge, warm dream that we can draw on during cold winter nights.'

Operation Vegetable - a novel

Deep in the English countryside live a group of unlikely characters on their narrowboats.

Life at Watergrove Marina is carefree until a local landowner decides he wants to build luxury houses on the resident's vegetable plot. In an unaccustomed act of decisiveness, the boaters decide to form a committee to fight this scourge. Step forward Judy, a lady of physical substance, fierce determination and jocular disposition, who selflessly elects herself chairwoman.

H.Q. is the local pub and it's here that our ageing boaters raise a creaking battalion. Judy leads our disparate band into battle, implementing a plan code-named Operation Vegetable, a hare-brained scheme of doubtful focus. The boaters find help from an ageing rock star and a TV Gardening programme. Skirmish follows skirmish until one of the boaters is severely injured and the stakes are raised. Has the despotic landowner, a man of few morals, driven by power and greed, finally met his match? Will the boaters look like toothless turnips or can they cajole wobbly bodies, ideally suited to tea-drinking, to mount the barricades?

Or....have the boaters simply lost the plot?

Operation Vegetable was formerly published The Marina. The manuscript has been altered and updated.

A Bike at Large

A Bike at Large is the fourth book in Jo's *'At Large'* series.

When he was overtaken by a jogger on a borrowed mountain bike, Jo knew it was time for drastic action. Welcome to the world of a man in his 60s and his new e-bike.

His first injury occurred within one foot! Setting off for his first practice ride round a car park, he misjudged the width of the handlebars and scraped his hand on the cycle shop's stone wall.

'You'll go places you'll never have dreamed of,' said the shop owner. Prophetic words indeed. Eighteen hours later Jo was embedded in his neighbours hedge due to a clothing malfunction. Fortunately, before setting out he'd put his ego and self-esteem in the top drawer in the kitchen.

With the emergency ambulance on speed-dial, Jo climbs a steep learning curve on a series of mini adventures throughout the north of England, mercifully with a diminishing distance to injury ratio.

By calling his e-bike a 'Lifestyle Investment', it took his wife's mind off the cost. At the time she needed some new slippers, so it was a sensitive issue. Asked whether he was searching for eternal youth? 'Not really,' he said, 'more trying to keep out of my eternal hole in the ground.'

Fuelled by red wine and optimism, off he goes.........